ON
CHAMPAGNE

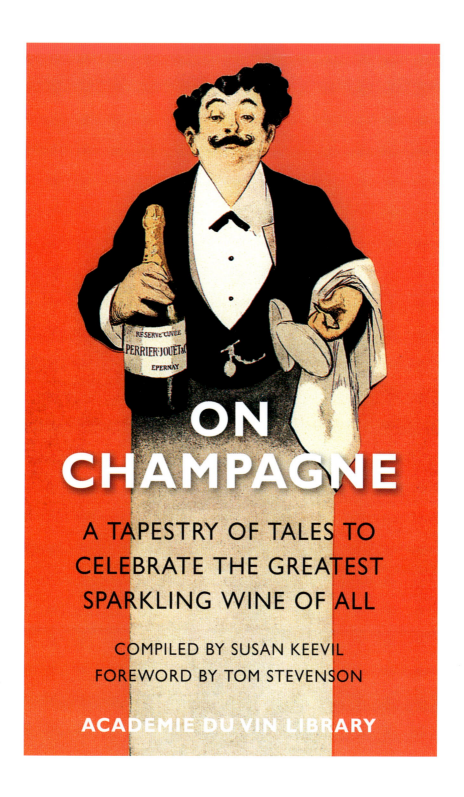

ON CHAMPAGNE

A TAPESTRY OF TALES TO CELEBRATE THE GREATEST SPARKLING WINE OF ALL

COMPILED BY SUSAN KEEVIL
FOREWORD BY TOM STEVENSON

ACADEMIE DU VIN LIBRARY

Published 2022 by Académie du Vin Library Ltd
academieduvinlibrary.com
Founders: Steven Spurrier and Simon McMurtrie

Publishers: Simon McMurtrie and Hermione Ireland
Editor: Susan Keevil
Art Director: Tim Foster
Design: Roger Walton Studio
Index: Hilary Bird
Text © 2022
ISBN: 978-1-913141-35-6
Printed and bound in the EU
© 2022 Académie du Vin Library Ltd
All rights reserved. No parts of this publication may be reproduced, stored in a retrieval system or transmitted, in any form or by any means, electronic, mechanical, photocopying, recording or otherwise, without the prior permission of the publishers.

CONTENTS

FOREWORD — 9
PREFACE — 13
INTRODUCING CHAMPAGNE
CHALK ABOUT CHAMPAGNE Margaret Rand — 14
THE MÉTHODE CHAMPENOISE — 18

1 ON YOUR MARQUES — 21
FIZZING FORWARDS Adam Lechmere — 22
JEWEL IN THE CROWN Fiona Morrison MW — 27
HOMAGE TO THE WIDOW Elin McCoy — 30
KING OF CHAMPAGNES Tyson Stelzer — 39
BOLLY AND POL Jay McInerney — 46
FOR THE GODS ONLY… Tim Triptree MW — 50

2 BEAUTY OF ITS OWN — 55
THE RISE AND RISE OF ROSÉ Victoria Moore — 56
SUGAR RUSH Jane MacQuitty — 60
TRILOGY OF CHALK LOVERS Essi Avellan MW — 66
VINTAGE GLAMOUR Serena Sutcliffe MW — 72

3 CHAMPAGNE'S STRANGE WITCHERY — 77
THE COLD, SINGING FIRE Andrew Jefford — 78
DEATH TO THE FLUTE! Robert Walters — 80
THE MAGNUM EFFECT Tom Stevenson — 84

BEYOND THE ICE-BUCKET Natasha Hughes MW   88
LITTLE BOMBS EVERYWHERE... Kelli White   93

4 ELEVEN ERAS OF CHAMPAGNE   99

1 THE ENGLISH INVENT IT... Stephen Skelton MW   100
2 FRANCE PERFECTS IT... Hugh Johnson   106
3 CHAMPAGNE'S ARTISTIC DEBUT Tom Stevenson   117
4 THE BIRTH OF MOËT Henry Vizetelly   121
5 MOËT GETS INDUSTRIAL Henry Vizetelly   125
6 GOOD TIMES IN THE BELLE EPOQUE Serena Sutcliffe MW 134
7 WAR, RAGE AND THE 'ROARING TWENTIES' Tom Stevenson 139
8 ESCAPE FROM THE WEINFÜHRERS Don and Petie Kladstrup 143
9 FIZZ, BUBBLY, POP IN THE SWINGING SIXTIES Evelyn Waugh 156
10 CHAMPAGNE, OUR SOCIAL SIGNIFIER Joe Fattorini 160
11 THE PLATINUM ERA Robert Walters   167

5 TANGOING WITH TERROIR   171

SMALL STEPS BACK TO BURGUNDY William Kelley   172
THESE CHARISTMATIC HILLS Peter Liem   182
MAP: THE SEVEN REGIONS OF CHAMPAGNE   183
GET SET, GO! Robert Walters   193
THE GREENING OF CHAMPAGNE Tyson Stelzer   199
BUBBLE, BUBBLE, TOIL AND TROUBLE Tyson Stelzer   207

6 BLAME IT ON THE FIZZICS Gérard Liger-Belair   215

7 BETTER, BRIGHTER, BUBBLIER... 225
THE 'O' WORD Margaret Rand 226
MARRIAGE OF AGE AND YOUTH Anne Krebiehl MW 234
QUALITY TIME Tom Stevenson 244
THE UNDERCOVER MAVERICKS Margaret Rand 248
CELLAR IN THE SEA Essi Avellan MW 255

8 CHAMPAGNE ON THE MOVE... 261
CHAMPAGNE'S BENEFICIAL PILGRIMAGE Henry Vizetelly 262
BETTER THAN ARMY TEA Peter Carrington 264
CHAMPAGNE AT 30,000 FEET Hugh Johnson and Oz Clarke 266
JOURNEY INTO SPACE Giles Fallowfield 268

ON CHAMPAGNE, THE AUTHORS & EXPERTS 270

INDEX 273

ACKNOWLEDGEMENTS 279

FOREWORD
Tom Stevenson

Champagne is the most seductive of wines and yet, in a very real sense, it is the least natural. Unlike other wines, it could never have manifested itself from a few grapes that had fallen into a depression in a rock long before humanity's ancestors were even able to stand upright. Arguably, other wines could.

Anyone with an inkling of the conditions required and processes involved will realize that a consistently sparkling champagne was never going to be an accident. It had to be invented. It is also had to be honed, refined and enhanced over 300 years to become the world-famous wine it is today. So famous, in fact, that its name is instantly recognized by almost everyone in the developed world.

When I started exploring Champagne almost 45 years ago, even the most experienced members of the wine trade would have struggled to name more than a dozen different brands and they would all be *grandes marques*. Virtually no one had heard of co-operative champagnes, let alone grower champagnes.

The *grandes marques* formed in 1964 with 25 members, but the wine trade press would often state there were only 12. This inaccurate habit began when first writing about the Champagne Academy, which formed in 1956 and had just 12 members, each of whom also happened to be listed as a *grande marque* some eight years later. From these beginnings the error propagated until it reached such a point that Claude Taittinger threatened to take legal action if anyone published that there were only 12 *grandes marques* or only members of the Champagne Academy could be described as *grandes marques*. Champagne Taittinger was a *grande marque*, but not a member of the Champagne Academy. Until 1987, when it became one of four new members, and that little spat evaporated.

In those early years, there was no talk about ancient grape varieties, autolysis, yeast-complexed fruit, Maillard Reaction, pre- or post-disgorgement aromas. No thought about glassware beyond flute over coupe. And the term 'magnum effect' had not even been coined. In short, no one was digging around over there. No one was asking questions. So I had the time of my life.

Initially, I found that even in the region itself, champagne, was regarded as little more than a wine of celebration. Crack open a bottle and raise a glass in salutation, but God forbid you let it near the table to accompany the food.

From my very first day in Champagne I found a lifelong friend by the name of Philippe Le Tixerant, director of communications for the *Comité Interprofessionnel du Vin de Champagne* (CIVC). Strange things happened from the very first moment we met. It was in Le Chapon Fin over an espresso that he asked me whether I had a favourite champagne producer. I said: 'Yes, Pol Roger.' This was true at the time and for a number of years after. In the future I would taste Pol Roger 1892, the oldest and greatest champagne I have ever come across. Over the last four decades I have tasted much older vintages, but they were all, to one degree or another, brown, oxidized and without bubbles. Pol Roger 1892 remains the only 19th-century champagne I have experienced that still had some bubbles. It had a remarkable, pale gold colour and fruit with no undue oxidation.

However, I have digressed. Philippe asked me what was (in 1980) the best Pol Roger I had tasted. 'Without a doubt, 1953, the Coronation year.'

'Have you tasted any older vintage of Pol Roger?'

'No. My father used to drink Pol Roger 1928, Winston Churchill's favourite vintage, but unlike the great man, my father drank his in 1938, whereas Churchill liked to drink a more mature champagne and kept his Pol Roger 1928 until well after the war.' At that precise moment, the shopkeeper's doorbell rang and in walked a diminutive figure with one of those faces that always smiles. Philippe looked over and he too smiled. 'Well, isn't that a coincidence? Monsieur Christian de Billy of Champagne Pol Roger!'

In typically French fashion, Monsieur de Billy shook the hand of the manager, then the receptionist and then the waiter. In what seemed like a well-rehearsed performance, he wrote a cheque, handed it over to the receptionist, who duly noted the amount and counted out a number of French Franc notes, handed them to Monsieur de Billy, who thanked her, tipped his hat to her and bade them all farewell. 'You might meet him on Thursday,' Philippe said.

That Thursday turned out to be quite surreal. I did meet Christian de Billy, but my time was with Christian Pol-Roger and we ended up at La Grillade for lunch. There were just two other tables occupied and after 10 minutes, the lone occupant of one of them came over to me and enquired: 'Tom Stevenson?' I was astounded. No one had heard of me at that juncture and I was sat with Champagne history personified in the form of Christian Pol-Roger. He introduced himself as Hubrecht Duijker and explained that he had heard that I was in the region on the longest visit made by any foreign journalist. I introduced him to Christian Pol-Roger, at which point one of the two occupants of the other table got up and introduced himself in an American accent: 'Monsieur Pol-Roger, my name is Sheldon Wasserman. My wife and I are touring France to research a book on sparkling wine. Next week we move on to Italy, but I want you to know that we are so impressed by the quality of champagne that we are stopping in your region for a full three days.' Three champagne authors at three tables!

A Champenois by birth, Philippe knew a lot of champagne producers, but I was visiting so many he had never met that he asked if he could tag along. I was delighted to have his company and thus we learned a lot about the more obscure parts of Champagne together. One belief we found in common was that even in the region itself, the full potential of champagne was not being exploited.

When entertained by champagne producers, they would almost apologetically ask whether it would be acceptable to continue into the fish course with the champagne that had been served as an apéritif. There were very few gastronomic pairings and as soon as any hint of meat hit the table, out would come the red wine, even if champagne might have been a superior partner.

Perversely, the red wine that was served would invariably be Bordeaux. Why not burgundy? Surely Pinot Noir would form a natural flow? But, no. History was too well ingrained in the Champenois. Woe betide anyone who brings their centuries-old arch enemy to the table. Champagne and Burgundy fought for royal patronage centuries ago. Forget the fact that the French monarchy has long since gone and the champagne in question was a pale rosé or *vin gris* with not a bubble in sight, the aftershock from those bitter wine wars still echoed around Champagne's corridors of power in the early 1980s.

As for marketing, champagne had always been sold on celebration, with no mention of it being a fine wine. Even the CIVC was complicit in ignoring the intricacy of its provenance and flexibility of usage. When Philippe was barely a year into his position, he was asked to give his opinion to one of the CIVC's committees on how champagne should be marketed in the future. He had hardly managed to get out a couple of sentences about how it should be promoted as a fine wine that deserved its place at the table, when he was told to sit down and given a lecture on champagne being a dream that should be sold as a dream. He must learn to stay on message!

It has been the reversal of this attitude, not by champagne producers, but forced on them by successive generations of their consumers, that has been the most important change in Champagne I have witnessed. Regular champagne drinkers still use it for toasting and celebrating, but regard it primarily as a food wine, deserving its place at the table, and having more flexibility when partnering dishes than any other wine.

When I embarked upon researching a book on champagne, in 1980, it was not to carve out a career as a specialist; it was simply because there had been no English-language book on the subject for 20 years and no truly definitive study of the wine since Henry Vizetelly's in 1882. At this time, the two most ubiquitous vintages were 1973 and 1975, the latter being a glamorous one from the start, while the former was underrated, unfairly as it turned out. The 1973 vintage took a beating by the trade press due to its unprecedentedly large volume, which not only exceeded the legal maximum, but also outstripped the region's storage capacity, requiring the temporary use of swimming pools for the overspill.

Tasting these champagnes and my first-ever *vins clairs* in the near arctic conditions of January 1980 (it was -14°C) was an interesting experience. At Louis Roederer, which even then was known as the most cash-rich house in Champagne, I was taken past a row of desks, where everyone sat in their hats and coats, to the office of Jean-Claude Rouzaud. I found the man himself, wrapped up in a padded coat, two scarves and bearing a red nose. After being introduced, I immediately said: 'Well, that's my first question answered!' 'What's that?' asked Rouzaud between sneezes. 'I wondered how you became the most cash-rich house in Champagne, but it's almost Dickensian in here. You obviously don't spend money on heating, even in your own office.' He laughed and coughed at the same time.

This was just the beginning of my career, but as I slow down into semi-retirement, I am happier about the world of champagne than I have ever been. I am delighted that it now has the respect it deserves, as a wine and at the table. And I am so impressed by the enthusiasm of the consumers who have driven that respect. It was fun being a pioneer and easy to get work when there was little competition, but I am contented to see so many talented colleagues now specializing in champagne. It tells me I was right; it was worth pursuing.

Champagne's story is not so much about Nature, but about how men and women with a shared vision have put their own signature on her gifts, a tapestry of tales that weaves its way through the pages of *On Champagne*. With contributions from Hugh Johnson, the greatest living wine writer; Essi Avellan MW, probably the best informed of today's champagne specialists; and Henry Vizetelly, the incomparable 19th-century champagne author; and with other famous and exceptional writers providing their own insights, *On Champagne* promises much and delivers more. Good reading!

PREFACE

Susan Keevil

Champagne is as celebratory as ever. As ready to dignify our ice buckets and sparkle at our special occasions as it was in the heady days of the Belle Epoque. But how to capture its more serious side? The easiest way would be to ask an expert, a writer with the skill to observe the sky, land and cellar and gather this wine's story into a book. But that would be just one person's version of events.

How much more thrilling to learn about a wine through a multitude of voices and opinions? They might conflict, contrast, tell the same story from a subtly (or strangely) different perspective, but brought together in one volume they can, as here, provide a deeper and richer knowledge. It seems appropriate, really. The coming together of a team of authors to bring the story of champagne to life is a little like the blending of the wine itself. Many parts make a beguiling whole.

No one gets more excited about champagne than the authors in this book. From scholarly historians and highbrow novelists, to inquisitive journalists, passionate champagne specialists and a professor of chemical physics, they all get a buzz from fizz, and handle their investigations into its character in their own unique ways. The questions they raise focus on everything, including how champagne came to exist in the first place; how to uncork it safely; how it survived world wars; and what is so special about those little bubbles anyway…

The answer to Robert Walters' query, 'Is the flute really dead?', can be seen on the front cover of this book. It's a glass you may not expect. Not a flute or a coupe – those are the champagne glasses of yore. This one has a tulip shape, narrowing towards its rim to capture the precious bubbles and unravelling aromas within its sphere. If these look like the contours of a glass from which you'd taste any other fine wine, you'd be right. For champagne's cognoscenti, the tulip-shaped 'swirling glass' is the one in which this wine can be its true self.

Dip into this book to discover the champagnes that interest you. Or enjoy it in chapter order and watch this wine's story unfold. Margaret Rand's introduction conjures up the beauty of the place (pages 14–17); then the magic of *méthode champenoise* (the way champagne gets its fizz), revealed on pages 18–20, explains all you need to know to venture into the heart of this wine.

CHALK ABOUT CHAMPAGNE

Margaret Rand introduces this place – this wine…

Champagne vignettes: a deep, damp, cold chalk cellar in February with rain seeping through the roof, dark because the water has fused the lights. A celebration of rosé at Veuve Clicquot with pink and yellow balloons, pink and yellow flowers, pink and yellow paper lanterns, and monogrammed yellow wellies for walking in the vineyards. A scientist scattering metal bottle-tops on a table: this kind of lining allows in a tiny amount of oxygen during lees-ageing, this kind more, this kind none. A promotional video of celebrity models, all flowing hair and fabulousness. A grower apologetically brushing mud and dog's hair off the seat of his car.

There are many champagnes. Sometimes they seem barely compatible. Growers might dismiss the big houses, the *grandes marques*, as producers of safe, industrial wine; a *grande marque* might comment acidly that the growers are all millionaires now. There is tourist imagery – cellars dug into the chalk by the Romans and happy growers picking succulent grapes. There is myth – lifestyle, parties, celebrity. And there is reality: computer-controlled winemaking, intense research and, in places, a return to pre-industrial methods. This is the main tension – between industrial and artisan champagne.

The big négociant houses – Veuve Clicquot, Pol Roger, Louis Roederer, Moët & Chandon – have spread the taste for champagne globally with marketing skills and non-vintage cuvées blended for year-to-year consistency. To the world at large, these wines are what champagne is.

The world should be pleased. To achieve the level of quality of Veuve Clicquot or Roederer or Krug, on such a scale, year in, year out, is only possible because they are extraordinarily good viticulturists and winemakers. It's just that they don't talk about it.

Making a blend that tastes the same year after year isn't easy. Any of the *chefs de caves* (the winemakers of champagne) will say their flagship non-vintage is the most challenging and rewarding wine to blend. There may be adjustments to flavour over time – dosage may be reduced, or the use of oak introduced or removed – but consumers aren't meant to notice. Consistency is what matters. This is where terroir comes in. Every year is different: the Chardonnay may be

Champagne's famous chalky soils mirror the clouds on a cool, sunny day. Chalk's fragile, porous structure makes it an ideal reservoir from which the vines can tap moisture in even the driest summers. It also imparts unique mineral flavours.

fat and ripe, the Pinot Noir ruined by rain. The north of the region might be perfect, the south disastrous. There are no rules about consistency of weather.

So a *chef de cave* is supposed to produce the same taste from very different ingredients. They do it by getting grapes from all over the region: the greater the variety of sources and styles, the more blending material they have. Reserve wines, with all the qualities of terroir plus the richness of age, fill the gaps.

The other side of the coin is good growers who challenge the conventions we've accepted from the big houses. Their wines are not the same year after year, and they rejoice in difference, in terroir. They may have lower yields and greater ripeness, and less chaptalization: the long-standing convention is to pick at 9–10% potential alcohol, then chaptalize (build up the alcohol by adding sugar). Cynics, and top growers, say this is because sugar is cheaper than grapes.

These top growers have led Champagne's slow tiptoe to biodynamics via sustainability; they've led the fashion for zero-dosage champagnes, which sommeliers adore even if most consumers still find them a bit challenging. They've led forays into the region's older grape varieties, like Petit Meslier and Arbane; they may have concrete eggs, or amphorae in their cellars, and they may rejoice in the risks of wild-yeast fermentations. They're a determined, perfectionist, sometimes cussed lot.

Champagne is a northerly, marginal wine region. Climate change and warmer summers help it, but the acidity from a cool climate and chalk are the foundations of the wine's flavour. In Champagne, chalk's damp, water-holding, water-draining whiteness is everywhere. The main grapes are the same as in Burgundy: Pinot Noir and Chardonnay, plus Pinot Meunier (now more often referred to as 'Meunier'), which is frequently found in non-vintage blends, where its immediate juiciness works well, more so than in vintage wines intended for longer ageing. You can find brilliant, stony *blancs de blancs* (made from just the white grape, Chardonnay) and richer, broader *blancs de noirs* (made solely from red Pinot Noir and Meunier grapes), but for complexity a blend usually does a better job.

How much do the still wines resemble burgundy? Not much, but they're not really meant to. The process of turning juice into champagne is only part-done when the new *vins clairs*, the still wines, are on the tasting table in January. A novice finds it harder to tell Mesnil from Avize at this age than Puligny from Meursault.

There are four main regions: the Côte des Blancs, the Vallée de la Marne, the Montagne de Reims and the Aube or Côte des Bar. If you think of the Côte des Blancs as growing Chardonnay, the Montagne for Pinot Noir and the Vallée and the Aube for Meunier you won't go far wrong, but there are exceptions. Villages are rated Grand Cru or Premier Cru in their entirety, which is absurd, because nowhere in the wine world is a village homogeneous in quality. Aÿ, one of the most important Pinot Noir villages, consists of four separate valleys. Aÿ produces Pinot Noir of weight and fatness, but it's not all identical. Curiously, Chardonnay from Aÿ has a distinct flavour of Pinot.

Roughly, Pinot Noir from the north of Montagne de Reims, from villages like Verzy, Verzenay or Mailly-Champagne, gives fresh, austere wines, while Pinot from the southern part of the Montagne and the Vallée de la Marne, from villages like Bouzy, Ambonnay, Aÿ and Mareuil-sur-Aÿ, have more heft. As for Chardonnays, the north of the Côte des Blancs gives dark fruit, minerality and a firm body. Southern villages, like Le Mesnil or Vertus, give saltier, racier wines. Avize Chardonnay has a lead-pencil note; Oger is more stone fruit.

There's a lot of chalk, and it goes very deep. The cellars were dug by the Romans, and have been used for shelter as well as storage. In World War I the people of Reims hid in the cellars while the city was being shelled – they lived, worked, and went to school and hospital in the chalk cellars. There are over 200 kilometres of chalk tunnels under Reims alone.

There's also clay, alluvial sand and flint. The Aube is largely clay and limestone. But chalk's acidity seems different. The experience of the infant English sparkling wine industry – which makes fizz from many different soils, including the same chalk as in Champagne – is that acidity from chalk isn't different analytically, but *is* different on the palate – finer, softer, longer.

The chalk has formed itself into gentle, pillowy hills and ridges: this is an open, welcoming landscape. Vines sweep across slopes in barely broken swathes;

hilltops are forested. Montagne de Reims is topped with woodland. It's a national park; you can walk here for miles. When you come to the edge you'll look down on vines and villages, villages and vines, in pleasing contrast. There are medieval churches, and even a few medieval bits of villages; but villages are often at their most picturesque from a distance. This has been one of Europe's battlefields.

In the Middle Ages, before anyone thought bubbles would improve Champagne's thin, austere wines, the area was famous for cloth. Sparkling wine arrived later. In Hautvillers, one of the most beautiful villages, they'll tell you the 17th-century monk Dom Pérignon set out to invent champagne. In fact, he wanted to make still wine to rival burgundy and never made sparkling wine, as far as anyone knows. Fizzy alcoholic drinks were pioneered in England, with cider. Champagne is one of the world's great unintended consequences.

Dom Pérignon looked to Burgundy. Modern growers increasingly do the same in their search for greater precision, perfect aromatic ripeness and for perfecting Pinot Noir. Burgundian attitudes to terroir, to biodynamics, to returning life to the soil, to picking dates, are permeating Champagne. Louis Roederer aims to be entirely biodynamic. Veuve Clicquot has introduced big oak vats in its cellars, for the most subtle seasoning of creaminess. Dom Pérignon is obsessed with ever-great tension, via perfect aromatic ripeness. They try to emphasize differences of terroir site to site – even if they blend them away.

The other strain of Champagne's history, trade, explains why the food you'll be offered – most of it very good – may not have very deep local roots. Champagne was for other markets – London, Paris, Versailles, New York. Visitors didn't want the sturdy, unglamorous traditional food of northern France: they wanted something to suit the wine's pizzazz. Champagne is a centre of good food, but its ideas are taken from everywhere.

Another vignette: a carpaccio of artichoke with curls of foie gras and a touch of Parmesan, cooked by star chef Joël Robuchon and matched with 2006 Veuve Clicquot Grande Dame Rosé. Or marinated Atlantic sea bass, betel leaves and golden caviar, invented by chef David Thompson to match 2008 Dom Pérignon. This sort of thing, rather than chalk on your shoes, is the reason most people visit Champagne; but it's the chalk that makes it all possible. That and the rain dripping through the electric fittings.

First published in *Gourmet Traveller* in 2018. Reproduced here with kind permission of the author.

THE MÉTHODE CHAMPENOISE

Within the walls of its sturdy green bottle, champagne undergoes a second fermentation: carbon dioxide is produced but can't escape, so is instead absorbed quietly into the wine, later to burst forth as bubbles in our glass. This the heart of the *méthode champenoise* – a process that has changed little in 200 years...

1 Quality starts in the vineyard

Chardonnay, Pinot Noir and Meunier, Champagne's classic grape trio, are traditionally harvested at a low potential alcohol (10–11%) so that they create a wine with structure and gentle (rather than overt) fruit flavours. The region's cool northern climate ensures they give a fresh, vibrant acidity, but they must be ripe, and not 'green' when harvested – and brought to the press house quickly, handpicked and uncrushed, so that no colour is leached from the red grapes, nor harsh flavours developed from oxidized juice. The grapes should be pressed carefully too, in whole bunches, so that the juice drains away quickly via the stems and stalks which act as conduits. Pressing the grapes too heavily results in the release of bitter tannins. By law, only the first 2,550 litres of juice from 4,000 kilograms of grapes are allowed for champagne production.

2 The first fermentation

Next, *débourbage*: the juice is gently chilled so that particles of grape skin and impurities can settle to the bottom of the vat. Once clarified, yeast is added and the first fermentation will take place quickly, usually in stainless-steel vats, to create a simple base wine, or *vin clair*. Champagne's complexity and character depends on the quality of these base wines – which will be fermented separately, in batches – and on the way they react, later, with the yeast in bottle (in a process called

autolysis, whereby spent yeast cells break down, releasing creamy, bready flavours). Any use of oak barrels or malolactic fermentation (the transformation of sharp malic acid into buttery lactic acid) at this stage must be carefully judged so as not to overshadow the delicate flavours that will develop in bottle.

3 Blending, bottling and capturing the sparkle

Assemblage, or blending, can involve the merging of many hundred different base wines, each varying according to its grape variety, village and vineyard. For non-vintage champagnes, 'reserve wine' (a special combination of wine from previous fine vintages) will be used, but 'vintage' wines will contain *vins clairs* from only one supremely good harvest. Blending is an intricate process that needs to result in a consistent – but adolescent – version of the house wine, the true balance of which only emerges after the all-important next stage…

A mixture of yeasts, sugar, clarifying agent and champagne (*liqueur de tirage*) is now added to the blend. As the yeasts awaken, the *prise de mousse* – the second fermentation – will begin. To contain it, the wine is quickly bottled, sealed with a crown cap and transferred to racks in a cool, 10–12°C, cellar. Champagne bottles must be specially toughened to contain the 6 bars of pressure this process will generate over the next 10–90 days. As fermentation takes place and the sugars are transformed, carbon dioxide is created and absorbed into the wine. The wine in its bottle is now ready to sparkle. All that is left is for it to gain in elegance, and the longer it remains with its lees (the used-up yeast cells), the more 'autolytic' complexity it will develop, and the finer and more persistent its mousse (or sparkle) will become.

The resting bottles now stay *sur lattes*, resting on their sides, for months or even years. Once the winemaker (*chef de cave*) decides that the champagne is ready, the bottles will be transferred to *pupitres*, the wooden frames in which they can, with a gentle twist each day, be gradually rotated

and upended, thus encouraging the lees sediment to make its way into the neck of the bottle. (This is *remuage*, a painstaking job now frequently performed by mechanical 'gyropalettes', that handle the bottles with greater efficiency than humans can.)

4 Ageing, disgorgement and corking

Disgorging (*dégorgement*) is one of the most critical stages in the life of a champagne. Once the ageing period is over, the collected sludge of dead yeast must be removed from the bottle with a simple, if fiddly, extraction technique: the neck of the wine bottle is placed in an ice-cold brine solution; the liquid inside freezes; the bottle is then uncorked and a yeasty ice-pellet is swiftly ejected. The whole process must be rapid, and the bottle swiftly recorked so as not to lose the wine or its fizz. Crucially, the space left by the yeast must now be filled with replacement wine and a topping of *liqueur d'expédition*: this solution may or may not contain sugar (or dosage), the inclusion of which will have a strong bearing on the style of the wine. Champagne's sweetness levels range from 'brut zero' (dry, with no dosage) via extra brut, brut, extra dry and dry at up to 35 grams per litre residual sugar (not 'dry' at all, but notably sweet), then demi-sec (30–50g/l) and *doux* (50g/l).

Chefs de caves argue endlessly over whether it's best to age a champagne before disgorgement, or afterwards. Storing and ageing a wine on its lees will help retain freshness; its acidity will also round out with time, requiring less dosage to balance it. But late-disgorged wine can be less stable when it comes to disgorgement, and may disintegrate quickly thereafter (especially if over 25 years old). Alternatively, while every wine needs a period of adjustment after disgorging to let the added sugars integrate and ameliorate, for many winemakers this is the ideal time for developing complexity through the 'Maillard Reaction', which is when the amino acids left by the lees and the reduced sugars (without oxygen) in the wine begin to react together to create highly desirable toasty, nutty, caramel characters.

Finally, a champagne cork must be inserted with some force (*see* the hefty mallet wielded in mosaic 4, on the previous page) and kept in place with a wire cage to avoid it succumbing to the pressure of the champagne inside the bottle. The cork must not be porous if the champagne is to retain its fizz; so agglomerate cork is used to block the leakage of CO_2. This is supplemented by two layers of natural cork for a faultless seal.

5 Labelling and packing

Champagne's *habillage* – the foil wrapping, the gold-embossed labels and smart packaging – marks the final stage of preparation, and while this differs dramatically today as the wines adapt to changes in winemaking, marketing demands and consumer taste, the processes that make the wine in the bottle are essentially the same as those illustrated in the mosaics that adorn the entrance to Jacquart's old cellars, pictured on pages 18 and 19.

ON YOUR MARQUES

Champagne's major houses are the source of everything we expect this wine to be. Masters of the old techniques and at the forefront of the new, their winemaking is exceptional, their champagne reliably magnificent. Such glamour comes at a price, but never lacks the ability to surprise…

FIZZING FORWARDS
Adam Lechmere (2022)

JEWEL IN THE CROWN
Fiona Morrison MW (2022)

HOMAGE TO THE WIDOW…
Elin McCoy (2022)

KING OF CHAMPAGNES
Tyson Stelzer (2020)

BOLLY AND POL
Jay McInerney (2013)

FOR THE GODS ONLY…
Tim Triptree MW (2022)

Adam Lechmere (2022)

FIZZING FORWARDS

Craftsman, Showman, Scientist, Visionary… Frédéric Panaïotis has the top job at Ruinart. As winemaker for one of Champagne's most distinguished houses (founded in 1729), he has all the skills necessary to guide this great wine into its next quarter-century. Adam Lechmere finds out exactly what it takes to propel a *grande marque* into the future…

Frédéric Panaïotis, the *chef de cave* of Champagne Ruinart, is at pains to point out that he's a craftsman, not an artist. You might distinguish the two like this: a craftsman makes the same thing over and over again, only better each time; an artist makes something different every time. The description works to an extent, though as Panaïotis says, in Champagne 'it's not exactly the same because you can change over the years'.

Ruinart is part of the Moët Hennessy Louis Vuitton (LVMH) empire and a stablemate of Dom Pérignon, Veuve Clicquot, Krug, Moët & Chandon and Champagne Mercier. All these houses have their unique personalities but Ruinart has the distinction of being the oldest (in 1729 Nicolas Ruinart was the first to set up a company to export champagne), and the only one to use exclusively Chardonnay grapes in its vintage wines.

It's a venerable institution. Nicolas Ruinart's uncle, a Benedictine monk called Dom Thierry, was a contemporary of Dom Pérignon himself; legend has it that Nicolas was inspired by his uncle's tales of a wondrous sparkling wine. Ruinart's foundations lie not only in the apocryphal stories handed down from generation to generation, but also in the bedrock of Champagne: chalk. The house (in common with a handful of others) sits on miles of chalk cellars – the famous *crayères* of Reims – hewn out by the Romans and now home to hundreds of thousands of bottles.

With such a history (literally) underpinning it, there should be something immutable about an institution like Ruinart, but it's more complicated than that. While the job of the *chef de cave* is to achieve consistency of style, they

Frédéric Panaïotis' dream career changed the night his uncle brought a bottle of 1976 Richebourg to dinner. He no longer wished to be a vet to lions and tigers; wine was now his fantasy, champagne his mission.

must also ensure that that style evolves. 'Modernity is as important as tradition. You might aim to be modern, but if you don't change, then after five years you're not modern any more. You need to be on the move without making a revolution, but slightly and consistently evolving to achieve your goal.'

It's rather like the famous analogy of the swan: serene and unruffled on the surface while underwater its legs are paddling for dear life. Panaïotis gives an example of the sort of fine-tuning his job necessitates. When he became *chef de cave* in 2007 he decided the dosage (the additional shot of wine and sugar that's added before corking) was slightly high in the Blanc de Blancs and 'R' de Ruinart, the two non-vintage cuvées. The wine was a little too sweet – 'I thought it was becoming a little too comfortable,' is his phrase. 'It was around 12 or 13 grams per litre so I brought it down to nine grams. Then I started getting letters from our older customers.'

So he quickly readjusted the sugar level. 'I went back to 11, and then began to gradually lower it. We're now at seven grams per litre for the non-vintage, and we may go even lower, to six or five.'

Dosage levels are changing across Champagne. 'The balance of the wine is changing and we can do the same job with less dosage,' Panaïotis says. There are many reasons for this. Climate change is one of them: it is now easier to achieve ripeness, harvests are routinely earlier, and grapes are brought in with lower levels of acidity. 'The wines are not as lean as they used to be, so we need less sugar to balance them out.' Then there are changes in the vineyard, such as more use of cover cropping, resulting in more competition for nutrients which means thicker-skinned berries. In short, Panaïotis says: 'We're getting better at winemaking.'

Winemaking is an incredibly precise business, but it is only a part of the job of the *chef de cave*. Ask Panaïotis to describe a typical day and he laughs. 'There's no such thing. It can be anything.' On the day we meet over Zoom, for example, he has been in the vineyard surveying progress on Ruinart's biodiversity project: the planting of 25,000 trees and shrubs in its Taissy-en-Champagne vineyard. 'Then later on today I will be tasting this year's releases and writing the tasting notes.'

On other days he might be meeting with Ruinart's resident artist. At the time of writing, this year's appointment has not been announced ('It's someone super-famous'); in 2020 it was the British artist David Shrigley. Panaïotis will spend a good deal of time with whoever is appointed. 'We'll visit the cellars and the vineyards, there will be lunches, dinners. I met David in London a couple of times.' He finds the process fascinating. 'An artist has such an acute visual sense, whereas for me it's more the nose and the palate. Talking to the artists is a source of inspiration to me.'

If meeting an artist is inspiration, then the actual blending of the *vins clairs*, the base wines – this happens before the second in-bottle fermentation takes place – is 'excitement'. 'The whole year coming to the glass to see how well we've done, what nature has given us.' Sessions take place between October and December, with the team typically tasting 25 to 30 samples over an hour. During the winter they will taste up to 350 samples. It's a routine, Panaïotis says. 'I don't want to share our secrets but we're looking for purity and precision, no trace of oxidation or lactic character, though a bit of reduction is normal and even welcome in the early stages.'

The team also looks for the key differences in style between the non-vintage wines (the Blanc de Blancs and Brut, and the 'R' de Ruinart) and the vintage wines (led by the flagship Dom Ruinart). The non-vintage, Panaïotis says, should be a '9am to 9am' wine – one that you can drink at any time of the day or night. 'They have to be clean and dry but lovely and bright, with a rounder and softer balance, in order to be perfectly approachable in two-and-a half-years when they go on the market.' For vintage wines, ageing capacity is key.

Then there is harvest, which Panaïotis describes as the most challenging part of his job. 'The days are very long, you have so little time, you have to deal with human factors and natural factors, and you have to make quick decisions under stress that have huge impact.' Ruinart owns 25 percent of its vineyards (unusually for Champagne) and so Panaïotis has a measure of control over growing conditions – but for the rest of the vineyards he has to call on his diplomatic skills. 'You have to be very good at managing those relationships – the grower has to trust you and you have to trust them.' Here, though, as in every aspect of the life of a vigneron, things are changing: the sons and daughters of long-established growers are now taking over; a new generation that 'knows more about sustainability, about new methods in the vineyard'.

The *chef de cave*, then, understands craft, and art, sustainability, biodiversity and diplomacy. He must also be a scientist – the great Champagne houses are obsessive collectors of data, especially if they are part of an operation the size of LVMH, which last year opened the Robert-Jean de Vogüé Research Centre in the Champagne village of Oiry, a €20-million project dedicated to research around sustainability. 'We are at the cutting edge of science. We use every single technology possible to understand what we do, and how to

Frédéric Panaïotis believes that to move champagne forward, its vineyards need to go back in time: at Ruinart, trees, shrubs and hedges are being reinstated as natural wildlife corridors, reconnecting the vines to the local Montbré forest. Fauna vital to the health of the land is flooding back.

reproduce it. Intuition is all very well, but intuition backed up by science is robust and dependable.'

And he must be something of a showman as well: the *chef de cave* is an ambassador for the brand. Some take to it as to the manor born: Richard Geoffroy, the former head of Dom Pérignon, was an indefatigable traveller, famous for his philosophical musings as he entertained critics from London to Shanghai. Panaïotis is the same, if not as gnomic as his old colleague. 'I spend maybe 25 percent of my time thinking about the markets and promoting Ruinart. It's something I always have in mind because I see my job as not only making champagne, but also bringing happiness, giving people a good time. I enjoy that part of it.' He's delighted to be travelling again after the pandemic – he says a trip to Japan, or China, or any one of the house's many markets, is another valuable source of inspiration. 'There's no better way of understanding what's going on than travelling, and being open and curious.'

For Ruinart to evolve, it's obviously crucial to have a curious, enquiring mind at the top. It's something of a paradox: the very history of the house must carry it forward. 'I'm always thinking, how can I embrace the future? You have to have a vision as a winemaker, especially for a house like us, which is so old. We have to work out what is the future for the next generation.' He is cellaring wines now that he will not see reach maturity – 'We're laying the ground for the next generation so we have to make sure it fits'. Perhaps 'futurologist' is another responsibility that should be added to the job description.

Fiona Morrison MW (2022)

JEWEL IN THE CROWN

Fiona Morrison falls in love with the Vieilles Vignes Françaises, Champagne's most mysterious wine, from a tiny walled plot of Pinot Noir vines in the Grand Cru village of Aÿ. Treasured possession of the house of Bollinger, this is a site that's been admired for its wines since medieval times, but is it the age of these '*vieilles vignes*' or the precious nature of this terroir that confers such luxury status?

My first encounter with this champagne was when I was handed an anonymous glass. It was like a blind date. I had absolutely no idea what I was about to meet. The colour was rich, golden; not burnished or coppery, just warm and glistening. The nose was gentle, discrete, quite floral but there were tantalizing, intense notes of lime, nougat, blossom and quince.

I kept on wanting to go back to the glass. At first, smelling it was enough: hazelnut here, linden and fennel there; fleeting glances of orange peel and cinnamon. Then I became inextricably drawn in by the flavour, fascinated by the structure and the impressions that the champagne left in my mouth – salt, fruit, tingling sherbet sensations, and at the end of the palate a wild savouriness that I found utterly beguiling. I couldn't wait for the second date…

Before then, I do some research; I go to Aÿ to inspect the old vines – the *vieilles vignes* of the wine's name. I expect old, gnarled, twisted trunks with rugged barks and sturdy branches. So imagine my surprise at being greeted by rows of skinny, tall, gangly Pinot Noir vines. I have difficulty hiding my disappointment from my hosts at Bollinger.

I scratch my head, not wanting to appear stupid. Theses vines look young, I'm told, because they *are* young. But the vine canes are from last year's growth, so the term *vieilles vignes* is surely a misnomer? Is this some devilish Bollinger marketing ploy? *Mais non*. These adolescents are trained so that the year after they have produced grapes, they are bent down and replanted into the soil leaving three fledgling buds above ground. The next year, the wood that is buried develops new roots and those three buds develop new canes which will bear that year's grapes. This is a very old, traditional method of vineyard training that I have never seen before. It is called *marcottage* (layering) or *'en foule'* (meaning 'in a crowd'); an appropriate enough term because over the years, as the canes are folded back into the ground, together the vines move slowly through the vineyard, like Macbeth's Birnam Wood. The 'old' in these *vieilles vignes* refers not to the age of the vines but to this ancient method of vine propagation.

The magic of these vines is that they are ungrafted; they are grown on their own rootstocks, unlike most of the world's grape vines which have been grafted onto American roots to save them from the killer bug, phylloxera, which decimated the vineyards of Europe in the 19th century. If it has its chances, this aphid can still wreak havoc today: one of the three parcels of the Vieilles Vignes Françaises, Croix Rouge, tragically succumbed to phylloxera recently and is no more. Usually, ungrafted vines can only survive in sandy soils as the bugs get asphyxiated by the grit. I bend down, searching for the tell-tale, coarse, beachy grains. Again, to my surprise, instead of sand, I find some dusty topsoil and the classic chalky rock of the region. Another mystery to solve.

So, whose hairbrained scheme was it to preserve these vines *'en foule'*? History points its finger firmly at Lily Bollinger, one of the redoubtable widows of Champagne who kept their houses running throughout the difficult war years and beyond. Persuaded by British wine writer Cyril Ray, who always loved this vineyard, Lily decided to save these special Pinot Noir grapes and make a separate cuvée in 1969. Interestingly, the fruit from these vines ripen earlier than grafted vines, so Bollinger is often ready to pick here before the official start of the harvest. In the height of summer, as I am standing in the Clos Chaudes Terres – a tiny 15-acre plot behind the Bollinger house – I see that the grapes have already begun to change colour to a deep magenta. This is the best known of the Vieilles Vignes plots which total only 36 ares (a little less than an acre) yielding around 2,000 bottles each year. These delicate vines need lots of loving care. Where it usually takes 500 hours a year to manage a hectare of vines in Champagne, for these parcels it takes 1,500 labour hours to bring the vines to fruition.

The unusual trellising method, in which last year's wood is buried under the soil, is one of the keys to protecting the vines from phylloxera as well as encouraging the development of organic matter. Another key to the magic is that these two remaining parcels are 'clos', surrounded by walls which shield the vines, keeping them well aerated and exposed to the sun (hence the *Terres Chauds* or

The 'Vieilles Vignes Françaises' may not look 'old', but, behind the high stone walls of the château, safe from all aphid predators, their ancient root systems continue to yield Pinot Noir grapes for what many believe to be the finest *blanc de noirs* champagne in the world.

'warm soils' name). Slightly elevated temperatures mean the vines can suffer from lack of water. All sorts of efforts are taken to preserve the climatic balance using permaculture, where straw is spread under the vines to protect them from the sun; fruit trees are planted around the clos to encourage biodiversity, giving life to an insect population and shade to the vines; small sheep graze in the winter months to add manure, and horses are used to till the soil to keep it strong. If all these methods sound medieval, they are. Yet very efficient and precise too, and if they add to the nostalgia of the Vieilles Vignes so much the better.

Talking to Charles-Armand de Belenet of Bollinger brings me fully into the 21st century. He talks about the research projects and laboratories. He speaks about trials to understand the magic of the Vieilles Vignes: where does that incredible salinity in the mouth come from? Why is the maturity level of these vines so high? How come the terroir of the clos is more pronounced than the vintage differences? It is easy to imagine why today's oenologists are so fascinated.

So, is it worth all this effort for a couple of thousand bottles of champagne every few years or so? At north of £1,000 a bottle, the answer is probably yes. De Belenet smiles ruefully and stresses that it is wonderful to be a part of living history in growing vines in this forgotten style. Later, as I am lucky enough to sip a prized bottle of the 2008 vintage, with its notes of quince, figs, brioche, sea salt and summer blossom, I delight in the fact that an important part of Champagne's heritage is being preserved in such an extraordinary vineyard. Was it love at first sight? Perhaps, and this is a relationship I would like to continue.

Elin McCoy (2022)

HOMAGE TO THE WIDOW

In no other wine region have women played such a visible and formative role. Many of Champagne's *grande marques* – Veuve Clicquot, Pommery, Laurent-Perrier and Henriot among them – bear witness to those who have conquered markets, blazed trails and created the wines that now bear their names. Elin McCoy traces the widows, pioneers and winemakers who have shaped Champagne's early history and those who bring acclaim to its leading houses today, finding that their influence is shining as brightly and continuously as ever…

In 2020, Vitalie Taittinger became president of her eponymous family Champagne house. Her earliest memories of growing up in the region are smelling autumn on walks in the woods and sipping leftover warm bubbly from the tables in the *salon* after the grown ups had adjourned to the dining room. When she took over, her father left two letters on her desk; one proclaiming his full confidence in her, the other telling her to take all the hard decisions she would have to make with her heart.

That same year, Julie Cavil was named the first female *chef de cave* at the prestigious Champagne house Krug, one of the top winemaking jobs in the region. She'd shadowed Eric Lebel, the former *chef de cave*, for 13 years, absorbing intangible aspects of craftsmanship, his intimate knowledge of vineyard plots, the taste and smell of reserve wines from many vintages. And she now leads a six-person winemaking team of three women, three men, each bringing something unique to this famous *marque*.

Both their stories are part of a larger comeback tale as well as something new in Champagne: a generation pushing to create a more equitable future for women in the cellar, the vineyard and the boardroom, and convey a new idea of bubbly to drinkers.

The 19th-century pioneers

Yes, men have owned and managed the vast number of wine estates in the region throughout history, and they've also mostly been the winemakers. But Champagne's past has included a surprising number of strong-minded women who built famous *grandes marques* and exerted a profound influence on the region's wines through bold investments in technical innovations that resonate today. Highly attuned to the desires of consumers at the time, they revolutionized marketing, just as their female counterparts are doing today.

The route to their responsible positions, though, was highly traditional, through the untimely deaths of young husbands, with no grown sons to leap in. For 100 years, and more, running an estate almost required becoming a widow first.

Barbe-Nicole Ponsardin   Apolline Henriot   Louise Pommery   Mathilde Emilie Perrier   Lily Bollinger

I've always been fascinated by Champagne's forward-thinking widows, starting with Widow Clicquot. In old drawings and paintings, she appears solid and formidable, a broad stately figure with a lace cap on her hair, layers of petticoats and dresses, and a serious, impassive look on her face that seems to say: 'Don't mess with me. I know what I'm doing.'

Today, things are different; belonging to a Champagne family helps, and, for many, formal education in oenology is essential. But determination still turns out to be a must.

Barbe-Nicole Ponsardin created Veuve Clicquot from the modest wine *maison* owned by her husband, François Clicquot, after he died in 1805 from typhoid fever. Only 27 at the time, she insisted on holding onto the enterprise despite her doubting father-in-law, ran it while looking after her young daughter and rebranded it under her own name: Veuve Clicquot-Ponsardin. Her future-oriented innovations and canny business decisions made it a success. In the dark days of the Napoleonic Wars, she experimented, eventually inventing the riddling process to improve her wines' clarity and taste that's still standard procedure today. In 1811, the year of the Great Comet, she created the first vintage champagne, Le Vin de Comete, and risked shipping more than 10,000 bottles to Russia to capture the market there. She astutely snapped up vineyard after vineyard. By 1821, she was producing 280,000 bottles annually, and her fizz was a staple of royal entertaining.

Ever since, she has been a touchstone for the important role women have played in Champagne: a reminder that a glass ceiling was broken there more than 200 years ago.

More entrepreneurial, innovative widows followed. Young, newly widowed Apolline Henriot founded Veuve Henriot Aîné in 1808 and created its first cuvée by consulting a book on winemaking written by her great uncle, a monk. Louise Pommery, whose husband died in 1858, was left with a new wine venture and a new baby. She saw a way forward by shifting from producing red wine to sparkling and responded to the English thirst for dry champagne by creating the very dry Brut style that is by far the most popular one today. By building an elaborate château to welcome visitors she kickstarted wine tourism.

In 1887, the widow was 35-year-old Mathilde Emilie Perrier, whose husband, Eugene Laurent, had inherited the Champagne house where he was cellar master. Mathilde combined their names to create Veuve Laurent-Perrier and developed the first zero-dosage champagne a century before the style grabbed attention.

Wars also pushed women to the forefront of Champagne brands as men went off to fight, leaving women, as usual, to keep things going. The female connection at Laurent-Perrier picked up again in 1939, when Marie-Louise Lanson de Nonancourt bought the house. Her sons joined the French Resistance; she shepherded Laurent-Perrier, walling up her stock in a cellar to hide it from the Germans.

Lily Bollinger's husband Jacques, who died in 1941, had been coaching her for 20 years, cross-examining her on which vintages she preferred and why, writes author Cyril Ray in his book *Bollinger* (1971). It was a bad time for Champagne, but she was determined to preserve what her husband had entrusted to her. She was called Madame Jacques, which tells you she started as simply a stand-in for her husband. But she bicycled around the vineyards, asked questions, inspected vines, and launched the idea of a late-disgorged cuvée in 1967 with the 1952 vintage.

In the late 19th century, points out Kolleen M Guy, author of *When Champagne Became French* (2003), using the word *veuve*, or 'widow', on labels turned out to be a huge plus, key to the way champagne was marketed. In a rapidly changing world, the word provided 'a sense of continuity with the past and a certain nurturing reassurance'. So powerful was it as a marketing tool that many male-owned firms created labels featuring the names of fake '*veuves*' as well as using labels with images of Queen Victoria in black mourning.

The connection between women and champagne echoed widely in French culture. Madame de Pompadour, Louis XV's mistress, made fizz fashionable by insisting it was the only wine that left a woman more beautiful after drinking it. Her breast, supposedly, was the mould for the long popular champagne coupe.

Bubbly even became something of a gendered drink. Although Louise Pommery created the first very dry cuvée, it was sweet ones, contends Guy, that were considered 'particularly appropriate and respectable for "ladies" to drink' in the late 19th century. Men drank dry.

But the *grandes marques* luxury brands are only one of the region's several worlds.

As they do on farms everywhere, women and daughters played an integral part at small family houses that made bubbly from their own vineyards. Women helped with the harvest, kept the account books, performed administrative tasks, fed the harvest workers. Often, they were 'invisible', given little credit for their work. Few took on skilled jobs in the vineyards, or in the cellar. They didn't vinify.

And so it went.

There were always exceptions, such as the family-owned J Lassalle artisanal house on the Montagne de Reims, one of the first independent growers to be sold in the US. After Jules Lassalle's widow, Olga, took over the estate in 1982, a tradition of *une femme, une esprit, un style* was established. Now the third-generation woman, Angeline, is the winemaker, preserving what the house describes as a delicate, feminine style.

The early new wave and the 21st century

Fast forward to the 1990s. With a generational shift in the region, things were changing. Champagnes from small, independent producers and growers who had decided to launch their own labels – so-called farmer fizz – were on the rise, finding their way outside France. Daughters of owners were establishing themselves in important careers outside the region. The easiest roles for women to grab at a Champagne house were in marketing, but when it came to a woman running the show, that still happened primarily because of dire family circumstances.

That's the story of Anne Malassagne of family-owned, century-old grower house A R Lenoble, with 18 hectares of vines. When her father became ill in 1993, she was 28, on a fast track in Paris as a financial director at L'Oréal. She was the only family member able to take over, though she had no idea how to make wine. 'It was really difficult,' she told me a few years ago at a conference held at A R Lenoble. 'I had to fight for credibility.'

It was an era in which women struggled for their voices to be heard.

Carol Duval-Leroy, whose husband died in 1991 at the age of 39, once said that no one thought she could succeed when she didn't sell to one of many potential buyers; but she'd promised her husband to keep the house family owned. She had little support for her decision. Yet she eventually became the first female president of the *Association Viticole Champenoise* and promoted the first woman in Champagne to *chef de cave* – at her own house.

These women, and others who headed their own houses, such as Evelyne Boizel, helped spur change in the 21st century.

Based on her experiences, Anne Malassagne decided that what was needed was an all-female organization to make women more visible, promote them as professionals, and offer guidance for how to move up in the industry when you have children. So began *La Transmission: Femmes en Champagne*. Her first attempt, in 2011, fell flat. When she tried again in 2016, joining up with dynamic Maggie Henríquez, then head of Champagne Krug, the idea resonated, possibly because a new generation was coming into positions of influence at their family properties. It was a place where they could speak 'without power struggles'.

Today, the women members mirror Champagne's diversity, highlighting women owners at grand and tiny domaines, of different ages, in different parts of the region. Besides Malassagne and Boizel, it includes Alice Paillard, Vitalie Taittinger, Charline Drappier, Chantal Gonet, Mélanie Tarlant and Delphine

La Transmission Femmes en Champagne: 1 Mélanie Tarlant 2 Maggie Henríquez 3 Vitalie Taittinger 4 Charline Drappier 5 Chantel Gonet 6 Delphine Cazals 7 Anne Malassagne 8 Evelyne Boizel and 9 Alice Paillard. Their goal: to 'transmit a living, rich, diversified knowledge of champagne to others'.

Cazals. 'We're not about ego,' Maggie Henríquez told me two years ago. 'It's about mentoring the next generation of female leaders in Champagne.'

Working outside the region has been one way some of them gained the necessary confidence. Tarlant, for example, returned to Champagne Tarlant, which she co-owns with her brother, after proving herself in film production. She was the first woman in 12 generations to have an official job in the family business; she learned from her mother and grandmother, but like so many women of their generation, their work went unremarked. Tarlant was one of the first to understand the value of a blog and explore social media, and to research global warming.

A second women's collective *Les Fa'bulleuses,* whose name is a play on the words fabulous and bubbles (*bulles*), formed at about the same time, pulling together seven young women winemakers at independent small growers.

To highlight women in the region, both stage their own tastings at high-profile events like *Le Printemps de Champagne,* a five-day extravaganza pulling together dozens of small grower-producers. Charline Drappier, co-owner of her family's Champagne Drappier says she still feels that she has to bring up reams of technical details to convince tasters that she knows what she is talking about.

Different areas of Champagne have different cultures. In the Côtes des Bar, two hours from Reims, where Drappier is located, Charline Drappier says there is more of a spirit of women working in the fields. 'When you are part of a family business, I think it is easier for women to be accepted,' she adds, though she admits it's not always easy to work with some male egos.

In another era, sons, not daughters, took over. Now the opposite is often true, as at Champagne Bruno Paillard, where 39-year-old Alice Paillard, not her brother, is co-owner and took responsibility as director in 2018. She sees more women in technical jobs, and as vineyard managers. 'Education has been one route,' she says: 'Anything that gives you trust in yourself helps you.'

At Laurent-Perrier, the two daughters of Bernard de Nonancourt, Alexandra Pereyre de Nonancourt and Stephanie Meneux de Nonancourt, are co-CEOs.

Women *chefs de caves*

While women were becoming power players in their family houses, it remained more difficult until recently for women with no family vineyards to find a foothold outside of a marketing department. The tiny number of female *chefs de caves* is a 21st-century phenomenon. It's a big job; the chief winemaker is responsible for blending the cuvées, introducing new ones, perpetuating the house style and much more. All those in the role today are the first women ever to hold the title at their respective houses. Education and mentors have been key.

The first was Sandrine Logette-Jardin, who ascended in 2005 to the role at Duval-Leroy, owned by a woman. When she graduated with an oenology degree in the early 1990s, women were not generally allowed in cellars, and it was hard to find a job at all. She started in the lab before advancing to quality control.

Though more women have joined the ranks in the past decade, figures in 2019 show that only 13 of the 76 major houses had a woman heading the winemaking. Caroline Latrive, whose lips first touched champagne as a newborn, has held the position at Ayala since 2011. After working in her father's oenology lab, she headed for a degree. 'It was a way to prove I had the competency to grow.' One of her biggest challenges was managing a team of 10 people, all men.

In the past couple of years, the tempo has picked up. Champagne-born Severine Frerson credits memories of playing between the rows of vines and the smell of wines in the cellar for igniting her passion for wine and determination to study oenology. She always dreamed of being a *chef de cave*. After gaining experience under the great Régis Camus at Piper-Heidsieck for 15 years, she became deputy *chef de cave* and then, in 2018, the first woman cellarmaster. Four months later, she moved to the same position at Perrier-Jouët, which, she says, 'had a heritage of a woman'.

That reference point was important to Frerson, who read books about the dynamic Rose-Adélaïde Jouët, who co-founded the company in 1811, was closely involved in the vineyard management and winemaking, and recognized the value of Chardonnay grapes. Once again, it was a link to the powerful women of the past.

Alice Tetienne, *chef de cave* at Henriot since 2020, also piled up degrees, with a master's degree in vines and terroir, followed by another in oenology. Eventually, she landed a winemaking job at Nicolas Feuillattte, then at Krug, where she was responsible for vineyard relations before arriving at Henriot. 'Women were always part of the landscape,' she says, 'but they didn't have official roles. More women today are in those official roles.' She, too, looks back to a 19th-century woman founder, Apolline Henriot. 'The two-century-old story becomes part of you,' she says. 'When her husband travelled, she made the wine.'

But to reach the top remains very difficult. Women generally say they have to work harder than men to prove themselves, to prove that they can actually do the job.

Floriane Eznack, one of the youngest women to become a *chef de cave*, joined Jacquart in 2011, at the age of 30, but in 2019, she stepped down. She told *The Drinks Business* that it was exhausting to constantly have to fight to prove she was capable of doing her job, that men she worked with did not take her seriously.

The future

The culture in Champagne changes slowly, but the numbers of women in key positions is speeding up. Today, 60 percent of the oenology students in Champagne are women, according to the BBC. Initiatives like *La Transmission* and *Les Fa'bulleuses* have created a buzz around the women of the region, shining a light on what they are doing. Alice Paillard is convinced it will be easier for women in the future. 'The rules of working are becoming different.'

Charline Drappier believes the younger generation of women is more confident, that sometimes being a woman is an advantage, but worries that not enough women are encouraged to study science, which is essential for those who want to pursue oenology. 'We have a different perspective on how we work, with recognition that we want to pick up our children, not work long hours. And we are speaking that out loud.'

There is still a long way to go, and the bigger challenges for the future in Champagne include global warming and climate change. The region has declared a goal of zero herbicides by 2025. Many woman-run domaines are already there.

Tyson Stelzer (2020)
KING OF CHAMPAGNES

Tyson Stelzer believes Krug is the greatest sparkling wine estate on the planet. He has been visiting its hallowed halls for 19 years, assessing its wines over a span of four decades. Cuvée for cuvée, his ratings declare it to be a Champagne house in a league of its own. And there is something mystical about it, too…

To those of us gazing in from the outside in wide-eyed wonder, Krug is to Champagne as Domaine de la Romanée-Conti is to Burgundy and Petrus is to Bordeaux. It possesses a grandeur, an other-worldliness, an amplitude that is as lofty as its mesospheric price. Krug's grand hierarchy of prestige begins at a higher price than any other in Champagne, and its single-vineyard wines rank among the most expensive in the world.

I've always wondered if the magic of Krug is real. If one worked there for long enough, would the sparkle evaporate, the cellar turn into just a dank, dark hole, the barrels become just dirty old kegs, the cracks in the walls reveal these old buildings for what they are, and the day-to-day reality expose the hyperbole of one of the most clever of all French marketing spiels?

I'm not the only one who has wondered. Julie Cavil, who leads Krug's talented young winemaking team, made a flippant passing comment when I first met her in 2010. 'When I joined, I went behind the scenes because I suspected that not everything was done as it is said to be. But I found that it is,' she said. The magic, it seems, is real.

For sixth-generation director, Olivier Krug, the revelation came in 2011 with the discovery of a book buried in the company archives for more than 160 years – the personal notebook of Olivier's great-great-great-grandfather, Joseph, written to document the philosophy of Krug just five years after he founded the house in 1843. In it he expounded the principles of creating a champagne of great richness and yet extraordinary elegance, of selecting only the finest elements from the greatest terroirs, rejecting mediocre fruit and, revolutionary

Olivier Krug has directed operations at Krug since 1999; the oldest of five siblings, he relishes his job leading the family firm. He says: 'There is no "sub-Krug"; only prestige champagne.'

Leaving her advertising career to study oenology was a risk for Julie Cavil, but when she graduated in 2006, Krug opened its doors to her. She is now its first female cellarmaster.

at the time, making both a non-vintage and a vintage cuvée. It sent shivers down the spine of Eric Lebel, then *chef de cave*, to read the philosophy that articulated everything that he had for so long aspired to achieve.

Perfectionism before tradition

'Joseph was not a non-conformist, he was a very serious German guy, but he was ready to go beyond the rules to create something different,' Olivier reflects. 'He left the stability of the largest house in Champagne in 1842, with a vision to create a champagne that didn't exist.' That same daring spirit flows in Olivier's blood, relentlessly pursuing the very finest grapes, regardless of variety, vineyard classification or village reputation, and fanatical vinification, regardless of cost.

Meunier is prized, even in these wines of untiring longevity. Classification tastings are conducted blind, with no regard for a vineyard's *cru*. Krug purposely does not constrain itself to Grand Cru, nor even to Premier Cru vineyards, and its reach has extended as far even as the village of Les Riceys at the most southerly extreme of the Côtes des Bar, on the border of Burgundy.

Krug owns just 21 hectares, less than 35 percent of the vineyards required to meet annual sales of an undisclosed figure somewhere in the vicinity of

650,000 bottles. Olivier says that Krug is not selling any more bottles today than it was 15 years ago, though production has increased by an undisclosed amount to facilitate a slow future growth in sales. My estimation is that Krug is currently producing between 900,000 and one million bottles annually.

Estate vineyards are supplemented with fruit from 73 hectares owned by 100 loyal growers, some of whom have supplied the house since its foundation. More than 90 percent of Krug's contracts are signed according to individual plots. 'Ten years ago, people laughed at us, as most growers will not commit to a plot,' Olivier reveals. Flexibility is upheld to maintain quality in difficult vintages.

'One grower called us in 2010 and said: "I have a different plot for you because yours was done by rot",' he says. Few champagne houses can claim such loyalty. Olivier personally visits the vineyards every day during harvest.

Krug pays a premium for higher-quality grapes, and pays its picking teams mostly by the hour rather than the usual rate by the kilogram, an important distinction in ensuring stringent selection in the vineyards. Pickers are instructed to drop anything with rot and burned or weak berries. I was surprised by just how much fruit was dropped in the mid-rows of Clos d'Ambonnay.

Growers of Krug grapes are able to taste the wines made from each plot of their vines so they can follow their evolution – the best will be selected for Krug's reserve wines.

Krug is working with its growers on an internal sustainability program to achieve *Viticulture Durable en Champagne* certification in biodiversity and carbon and water footprints. Olivier admits it is very difficult to encourage growers into a programme of sustainability, with its inherent risks. 'Certification costs money and takes a lot of paperwork, so we are building a programme to manage this for our growers,' he says.

'This is a collaboration, and it is our objective to show our growers the road and help them achieve this,' adds Julie. 'We do the administrative stuff and help them with the audit, so they can concentrate on their field.' One-fifth of growers are certified to date, with the hope of having the majority on board within four or five years. The company has been herbicide-free for three years.

Obsessed with detail

Krug's long-ageing style begins with fruit harvested with more acidity and less sugar, so pHs are usually lower than the rest of the region. When I visited mid-harvest in 2017, Krug finished harvesting Clos du Mesnil on the same day everyone else in the village started. This is a polar-opposite approach to the riper style of houses like Louis Roederer, whose *chef de cave* Jean-Baptiste Lécaillon told me unprompted later that very same day: 'I told Olivier I think he picked Clos du Mesnil a little too early!'

'In 2010 we started in Clos du Mesnil two days before the official regulated start of harvest,' Olivier recalls. 'Everyone in the village said we were mad, but they were all watching us!'

Grapes are selected plot by plot and pressed individually by their growers. 'Even if a grower chooses grapes from the same part of the village, we ask them to press as many parcels as they can.'

Olivier's late father, Henri Krug, told him: 'If you have a chance to vinify a wine on its own, you will express more of its personality. The more individuality you get, the more precise you can be with your selection.'

'It is as if I have a friend who paints the most beautiful panorama covering a wall, so lifelike and so detailed that it is as if the wall is not there,' says Olivier. 'And he paints the sky using 200 different shades of blue. Pale for the horizon, grey-blue for the east and deep blue for the west. But if he mixed all 200 shades of blue together and used the same proportions to paint the sky, it would have nothing of the same detail. So it is with blending champagne. We make 250 separate vinifications of parcels that could all be blended into just three vats.' To facilitate this, 36 stainless steel double vats of small capacity were installed in 2007, increasing the small-batch storage capacity of the winery. In keeping each plot separate, reserve wines can be kept fresher. 'Some plots have more potential to age than others, and if they were all vinified together, the blend would lose the freshness of the freshest parcels,' he explains.

Last year one of Krug's largest growers in Avize came to taste his six reserve wines back to 1998. 'He knows which plots are in each sample and we don't,' Olivier recounts. 'He went white when he tasted them. Out of 20 plots that he has supplied us over 13 years – more than 250 wines in all – five of those six reserves were from the same plot. None of us had any idea, because what we do is by taste, not by recipe. Such is our attention to detail in the tasting room.'

Krug's winemaking team admits to an obsession with numbers. Krug works with 200–250 very small parcels of fruit every vintage, all of which are tasted after vintage and again the following year. 'We know all of the musicians through pre-listening before we assemble the orchestra!' waxes Olivier, adding that Krug is the conductor. Any not up to Krug's exacting standards go somewhere else in the Louis Vuitton-Moët Hennessy (LVMH) group. Olivier and his uncle Remi join the winemaking team for the tastings, which comprise 15 wines each day. Olivier personally attends about half the tastings, between an increasingly busy travel schedule.

'The reserve tanks are the heart of Krug,' says Olivier. Since 1990, Krug has more than doubled its reserves, without increasing production. In 2006 alone it added 36 new double vats to house its growing reserve collection, which has grown from 60 to 150 different wines in 15 years. Reserves are kept fresh in 150 small tanks, deep in the cellar at a stable 11–12°C. At any time, all of these 'treasures' are under consideration for Grande Cuvée, and all are tasted annually. The final blend comprises more than 100 parcels, spanning eight to 10 vintages, reflecting a different recipe each year. 'Our job every year is to recreate the most generous character of champagne,' says Olivier. A particular 1995 reserve wine from Bouzy has been tasted every year for 16 years and is yet to be allocated to the blend. There are still two 2001 reserve wines in Krug's cellar. As always, taste comes before reputation. 'Even in a crap vintage, there are still great wines,' grins Olivier.

At any given time there are five million bottles in the cellar, 10 times the annual production, a massive ratio and testimony to this long-ageing style.

Magnificent longevity

Krug attributes its longevity to the primary fermentation of all its wines in more than 4,000 small, 205-litre oak barrels. When I arrived in September 2015, I was confronted by a sea of barrels in preparation for vintage packed tightly into Krug's large courtyard. And Krug has more barrels on site at its Clos du Mesnil and Clos d'Ambonnay vineyards. It uses these not for oak flavour or aroma, but to build richness, complexity, balance and a 'high fidelity' not possible in stainless steel.

This is achieved by using old casks of average age 20 years, currently dating back to 1964. They are decommissioned after about 50 years, when they become too difficult to repair. Seguin Moreau barrels were used exclusively in the past, but Taransaud have been introduced recently. 'It took six years of tasting trials to establish the best coopers for Krug,' Julie tells me. All barrels are purchased new and are seasoned for a few years by fermenting the second and third press before it is sold for distillation. A waste of a new barrel, but that's Krug!

To uphold freshness, Krug's wines spend just a short time in cask and are transferred to tanks following the first fermentation. When I visited in

Walled since 1698, owned by Krug since 1979, Clos du Mesnil is Champagne's most prestigious plot of vines. The pure chalk soils of this tiny, protected 1.84-hectare site produce a long-ageing Chardonnay that is released only in the finest vintages and in tiny quantities.

early January 2019, half of the 2018 harvest had already been racked to tanks. Contact with oxygen during fermentation in barrel furnishes Krug with a resilience as it ages, infusing its wines with rock-solid consistency. I have not seen the degradation of freshness in Krug bottles that plagues many other champagnes as they travel around the world. These are wines capable of ageing magnificently for decades.

When a bottle in Krug's museum cellar popped as its cage was replaced a few years ago, the board and winemakers were immediately assembled to taste the wine blind. Vigorous debate ensued as to whether it was from the 1950s or the 1960s, but it was decided it was too fresh for the 1960s. It turned out to be 1915 – all the more remarkable because this was when the Côte des Blancs was under occupation during World War I and the wine was made exclusively from Pinot Noir, without the structural longevity of Chardonnay.

The age of Krug's cuvées is revealed, first thanks to an ingenious ID code printed above the barcode of every bottle, the first three digits of which indicate the trimester (first digit) and year (second and third digits) in which it was disgorged. Using this code, Krug.com and the Krug app reveal the season and year in which the bottle was shipped, the number of years over which it has aged, the blend and the vintage story for vintage wines. For non-vintage blends, it reveals the number of wines and each of the vintages. Eric has recently been elaborating wonderful insights into the *crus* and the seasons, making Krug.com an increasingly powerful and invaluable resource. There is even a Twitter robot that will reply with the details when you tweet #KrugID with the code.

Secondly, in 2016 Krug began printing the edition number on the front label of every Grande Cuvée – though this has been discontinued on half-bottles, because the house doesn't want to encourage people to age these. Edition 166 is based on the 2010 harvest, the 166th release in its history. This edition number comes with another exciting promise from Krug: the release of older editions of Grande Cuvée in the future.

Such disclosure ushers in a brand-new era for Krug, initiated by Maggie Henríquez, Krug's dynamic CEO since 2009. 'I was resisting the concept of disclosing the disgorgement date,' admits Olivier. 'But the world has changed. People want to know. I have changed. And we are keen to be more transparent now.' Bravo, Maggie.

Extract from *The Champagne Guide 2020–21, Edition VI*, by Tyson Stelzer (Brisbane, Australia) 2019

> Jay McInerney (2013)
>
> # BOLLY AND POL
>
> Jay McInerney praises two of his favourite, family-owned Champagne houses, each de rigueur in Great Britain – where champagne is 'viewed more as a necessity than a luxury' – suggesting they should be essential drinking in the States too…

The recent history of Champagne can be summarized thusly: the big get bigger and the small get street cred. The *grand marques* are increasingly coming under consolidated ownership – you could be forgiven for thinking that luxury brand group LVMH owns all of them – even as the small-grower champagnes, very few of which were available on these shores five years ago, have become the darlings of critics and sommeliers.

Somewhere in the middle are a handful of venerable family-owned brands, including two of my favourites, Bollinger and Pol Roger, both of which have long been immensely popular in Great Britain, where champagne is – quite correctly, I feel – viewed as more of a necessity than a luxury. Fortunately, both firms send enough bubbly to these shores to ensure that most of us should be able to find some for the holidays.

One of the smallest of the big houses, which has remained in the same family since its founding in 1849, Pol Roger has always been a connoisseur's champagne. Its most famous patron was Winston Churchill, who declared its headquarters, at 44 Avenue de Champagne in Epernay, 'the world's most drinkable address'. In fact, the address has recently been changed to 2 Rue de Winston Churchill, though my GPS didn't seem to have been apprised of this change as of my visit in October.

'I cannot live without champagne,' Churchill famously declared. 'In victory I deserve it and in defeat I need it.' Pol Roger was his favourite champagne and he became close with the family. After Churchill's death the company created a special cuvée in his honour. Released only in exceptional years, beginning in 1975, the Pinot-heavy cuvée has been called 'burgundy with

Pol Roger's cellars – a network spanning seven kilometres, on three levels – delve further than any in the region. At 34 metres, the *cave de prise de mousse* (fermentation cellar) is the deepest.

bubbles', and it's almost always one of the greatest champagnes of the vintage, though I sometimes almost prefer the intricately subtle vintage *blanc de blancs*, made from 100% Chardonnay, especially in its youth.

Touring the seven-kilometre maze of cellars underneath the streets of Epernay with urbane managing director Laurent d'Harcourt – which in mid-October were overwhelmingly fragrant with freshly fermenting must – I experienced first-hand one of the alleged secrets of Pol Roger's success: at more than 30 metres below ground, the cellars are deeper than those of its neighbours, which makes them as much as a degree and a half Fahrenheit (nearly one degree Celsius) cooler, and prolongs the fermentation and maturation process. The depth of the tunnels may be explained by the collapse of the former cellars in 1900, resulting in the loss of a million and a half bottles.

Another factor in the quality of Pol Roger wines is the collective 'family palate', represented by Pol Roger descendants Christian Pol-Roger, Christian de Billy and his son Hubert de Billy. Although the winemaker, Dominique Petit, formerly of Krug, vinifies more than 30 different lots from Pol Roger's own 200-plus acres of vineyards and purchased grapes, the decision on final blend is made by family members.

The jovial, gregarious Hubert de Billy, great-great-grandson of Pol Roger, is the latest incarnation of the family palate. I managed to catch him on a layover between planes in Paris the day before I visited Epernay. He remembered that I'd told him when we first met that the 1914 Pol Roger was the greatest champagne I'd ever tasted. 'It's probably my favourite as well,' he said. 'We have a few left in the cellars.' The vintage was unique due to the combination of spectacular weather and man-made catastrophe: World War I had just broken out in August, and by the time of harvest most able-bodied men had been conscripted. 'The grapes were picked by women and children,' de Billy told me. De Billy's grandfather Maurice was the mayor of Epernay at the time: he was the only official to stay on after the Germans occupied the town, and he remained there facing the threat of execution. In an attempt to boost morale, he offered to buy any and all the grapes from his neighbours. 'He said: "Pick as much as you can and I will buy it all!"' de Billy told me. 'When he ran out of money, he printed IOUs.' Such was the mayor's prestige, the IOUs were accepted as currency in the region until he was able to pay them off years later. 'Due to the bombardment, the harvest was small but quite a bit of it ended up at Pol Roger,' de Billy said.

After the war, Maurice, an avid hunter and sportsman, forged close ties with the British aristocracy – an on-going association highlighted by the selection of Pol Roger as the official bubbly at the wedding of Prince William and Catherine Middleton in 2011. But Pol Roger has a powerful rival in Bollinger, which received a royal warrant in 1884 from Queen Victoria, making it the official champagne of the British court. Whatever other flaws we can attribute to the British aristocracy, bad taste in champagne is not one of them.

While it's not easy to pin down exactly what makes Pol Roger exceptional, Bollinger's appeal is unmistakable: it's rich and powerful and Pinot Noir-heavy – the Château Latour of champagnes. If vintage Pol Roger might suggest a Jaguar, Bollinger – to stick to British automotive analogies – is more of a Range Rover. (Although Pol's Pinot-heavy Cuvée Winston Churchill is somewhat Bolly-like.) Bollinger's Special Cuvée is one of the biggest non-vintage champagnes on the market and the complex Grand Année is really a food wine more than an apéritif.

Based in the Grand Cru village of Aÿ, long recognized as among the best towns for Pinot Noir, Bollinger owns more than 162 hectares of prime vineyards, supplying over 70 percent of its own needs, an important aspect of controlling quality. Bollinger starts with great fruit, but it's what happens in the cellars that defines the wine's style: specifically, the reliance on used wooden barrels, some of them up 100 years old, for fermentation. (Pol Roger, like most houses, uses stainless-steel tanks.) Bollinger employs a full-time cooper to keep these gnarly, ancient-looking barrels functional. Fermentation in barrels, which breathe, results in a smoky, slightly oxidative character – a pre-ageing of the wines, in a sense. These wines are eventually transferred to magnums, where they mature, separated according to their village of origin, until the time of blending.

Bollinger's methods haven't changed much since German immigrant Joseph Bollinger teamed up with Paul Renaudin and a French aristocrat named Paul Levieux Renaudin to found the house, although it was Lily Bollinger, the steel-willed wife of Joseph's grandson, who consolidated the firm's reputation for quality. When her husband, Jacques, then the mayor of Aÿ, died during the German occupation in 1941, she took over all aspects of management, travelling the vineyards on her bicycle and later touring the world to promote the brand. Among her many accomplishments was one of the great paens to champagne: 'I drink it when I'm happy and when I'm sad. Sometimes I drink it when I'm alone. When I have company, I consider it obligatory. I trifle with it if I'm not hungry and drink it when I am. Otherwise, I never touch it – unless I'm thirsty.'

As powerful as Bollinger's Special Cuvée and vintage Grande Année bottlings are, nothing can compare to the turbo-charged, over-the-top vinous power of Bollinger's Vieilles Vignes Françaises, made from ungrafted Pinot Noir vines from two tiny vineyards enclosed by stone walls adjacent to the winery – with an average production of around 2,000 bottles.

For a more accessible experience, Bollinger's big, smoky non-vintage Special Cuvée provides an interesting contrast with Pol Roger's leaner and fresher Brut Reserve, though the choice is strictly a matter of taste. Both houses make very good rosé, although both Lily Bollinger and Maurice Pol Roger were adamantly opposed to the concept, perhaps in part because rosé was long associated with brothels. Happily, their descendants overcame their scruples, though in other respects both families have close hewed to the traditions that made their houses exceptional. This holiday season, you would be well advised to drink as the Brits do, though you may find yourself developing an on-going habit. Champagnes like these really deserve to be drunk year-round.

First published in *The Wall Street Journal*, November 2013; reproduced with permission of the author.

> Tim Triptree MW (2022)
>
> # FOR THE GODS ONLY...
>
> Tim Triptree is often asked which champagne he sells most at London's pre-eminent auction house, Christie's. Invariably it is the most luxurious wines, the 'prestige cuvées' – the pinnacle of production from the region's major houses – that bring the highest bids... But how much better are these wines really? And what does it take to be the best? (2022)

A prestige cuvée is the finest bottling from a champagne producer – the pinnacle of its production, the flagship of its range. For these wines no expense is spared: the utmost care is taken in viticulture and winemaking, and every attention is lavished on the design of the bottle and luxurious packaging. They are the height of luxury – and invariably the most expensive in a producer's range.

But there is no official definition. The CIVC (*Comité Interprofessionnel du Vin de Champagne*, or the Comité Champagne as it's now known) has no set guidelines for these wines and it is up to each producer to define and determine their composition – they have the freedom to create their own finest expression. It can be a wine from a single year's harvest, an exceptional vintage in which the quality of the grapes is deemed high enough to produce a superlative wine; it can be from one Grand Cru village, or from a single specific vineyard. The uniting factor will be that it is the most expensive, exclusive and desirable wine produced.

Here are some of the pioneering wines that are emblematic of each of these categories:

The single-vintage, multi-vineyard prestige cuvée...

Louis Roederer's Prestige Cuvée was created in 1876 when a special edition champagne was crafted for Tsar Alexander II and the Russian Imperial Court. It was produced in a lead crystal bottle, giving rise to the now-famous name of 'Cristal'. The bottle was unique: its flat bottom enabled the crystal to withstand

Still true to Tsar Alexander's original request, Cristal's traditional clear glass bottle shows the 'luminous' golden colour of champagne in all its glory.

the pressure of the sparkling wine inside – and doing away with the traditional 'punt' (the hollow 'dimple' or dent underneath a champagne bottle that back in the days of glass blowing was contrived to make the glass stronger) also meant that the Tsar could rest assured no bomb had been hidden there, as assassination attempts were a constant worry. To this day, the bottle still features the Russian Imperial Coat of Arms, although glass is now used instead of the more fragile crystal. It was not until 1924 that Cristal was available for general consumption in Europe when the 1921 vintage was offered to customers. Prior to this, every bottle of Cristal was destined for the Russian court.

Today, Cristal is produced exclusively from 45 plots of Grand Cru grapes on vineyards owned by Louis Roederer, and is a blend of slightly more Pinot Noir than Chardonnay. Only vines older than 20 years are allowed to produce fruit for Cristal, as it takes this long for the roots to grow down to the bedrock, where they tap into different flavours, finer textures and better concentration. Louis Roederer is at the forefront of biodynamic and organic viticulture in the appellation, and the 2012 Cristal is its first vintage to come from certified organic vineyards.

Winemaker Jean-Baptiste Lécaillon believes a prestige cuvée should have a 'long history of excellence', be 'linked to great terroir' and have significant ability to age and evolve. There's no doubt that Cristal ages superbly but its deliciousness in youth means that far too much is drunk before it has had the chance to develop bottle complexity. As Jean-Baptiste explains: 'Cristal has to be luminous, fresh, full of fragrance, with fantastic lightness and delicacy.' In other words: it's hard to resist!

Cristal has a very subtle autolytic character, which is achieved by leaving the wine for a shorter time on its lees after fermentation in bottle, compared to some of its peers. The idea is to allow fruit characters to be more pronounced, with less emphasis on toasted brioche notes. Delicacy, power, subtle fruit and floral aromatics are combined with a chalky, saline minerality and the structure to evolve in bottle. The highlight is the 2002 – an excellent vintage with rain and sunshine exactly when needed, and according to Jean-Baptiste Lécaillon: 'The perfect champagne year… easy… a gift.'

Cristal Rosé is even rarer and more expensive than Cristal (a common theme for rosé vintage champagnes which are typically positioned at a higher price point for most producers). It was launched in 1980 by Jean-Claude Rouzaud with only 9,000 bottles of the 1974 cuvée. 'Cristal Vinothèque' is long lees-aged, late-released and rarer still.

From the house of **Moët & Chandon**, Dom Pérignon is undisputedly the most famous of all prestige cuvées. One reason for this is that production levels exceed all others. The exact number of bottles made is a closely guarded secret but could potentially be up to four million from 800 hectares of vineyard – enough for a wide global distribution and easy recognition of the iconically shaped bottle. What is in no doubt, however, is the impressive quality of the wine.

Only Chardonnay and Pinot Noir are used in the blend, in almost equal proportions; the wine is aged for on average eight years on lees. Dom Pérignon often has an initially reductive smoky and toasty autolytic character on the nose. It manages to combine freshness and maturity with a rich textural sensation on the palate.

The first commercial vintage was the 1921, released in 1936. There was a pre-cursor to this, as in 1935 the house produced a special bottling specifically for its distributor which featured the 1926 vintage. It was here that the iconic bottle was introduced, but the wine was not called Dom Pérignon until the 1921 was released the following year. Extensions of this iconic prestige cuvée have been released with Dom Pérignon Rosé 1959 and the Oenothèque series (since renamed as the Plenitude 2 & 3) of late releases with extended lees ageing.

The single-vintage, Grand Cru vineyard prestige cuvée

Salon Le Mesnil is one of the most highly coveted vintage champagnes. This house produces only one wine, from only one single Grand Cru village in the Côte des Blancs – Le Mesnil-sur-Oger. This rare champagne is a *blanc de blancs*, made solely from Chardonnay, and is produced only in exceptional harvests. Only 43 vintages have been produced since its inception in 1905 to the current release being 2012.

Today Salon Le Mesnil is produced from 10 hectares of vineyard (in all, 20 parcels of vines), with on average 60,000 bottles per vintage. For the years Salon is not produced it is declassified as 'Delamotte' (released by the Laurent Perrier Group, owners of Salon since 1988). Salon is vinified in stainless steel with no malolactic fermentation and aged on the lees for an average of 10 years prior to release. Salon is mineral and delicate, taut with freshness and nuanced with almonds, citrus and brioche, the epitome of elegance, finesse and harmony, with exceptional ageing ability.

The single-vintage, single-vineyard prestige cuvée

Clos des Goisses is the pinnacle of production from the house of **Philipponnat**. An Extra Brut with low dosage, enabled by the ripeness of the grapes from this famous 5.83-hectare walled vineyard with an ideal southerly exposure. Some of the warmest temperatures recorded in the region are here, producing fantastic Pinot Noir and Chardonnay. The wines are fermented in a combination of oak and stainless steel which gives them texture and a hint of spice.

For Charles Philipponnat: 'Clos des Goisses is like a Burgundian Grand Cru: it is all about the terroir.' Clos des Goisses was the first of Champagne's single-vineyard expressions (subsequently others have appeared, including Krug's Clos du Mesnil (1979) and Clos d'Ambonnay (1995)) and is typically intensely aromatic, opulent and generous, with rich flavours of red fruits and hints of spice and lime. Clos des Goisses production is limited due to the size of the vineyard, with, on average, 25–30,000 bottles produced each vintage.

There are many other excellent prestige cuvées and far too many to name them all here, but among the most famous and certainly worth seeking out for your collection are Pol Roger's Sir Winston Churchill, Taittinger's Comtes de Champagne, Bollinger's Vieilles Vignes Françaises, Perrier-Jouët's Belle Epoque and Charles Heidsieck's Champagne Charlie, which has been relaunched as a multi-vintage blend in 2022. The wines of Krug are also superb, age-worthy and powerfully intense, from its multi-vintage and multi-terroir Grand Cuvée to its vintage expressions and superb, very rare single-vineyard wines, Clos du Mesnil and Clos d'Ambonnay. Julie Cavil, the *chef de cave* at Krug, concurs with Jean-Baptiste Lécaillon, saying 'the most important characteristic of a *prestige cuvée* is that it will gain beautifully with the passage of time'.

Prestige cuvées are now a key component of a serious wine aficionado's collection. The recognition of the ability to age and evolve and be considered a serious fine wine for laying down has led to the increasing popularity of this segment of the fine wine market. My advice, stock up now before the prices rise even more!

Pol Roger's Cuvée Sir Winston Churchill, first released in 1984 (with the 1975 vintage): named after the great statesman, who had been a customer of the firm since 1908, and blended according to his preference for a full-bodied, characterful wine, with relative maturity.

BEAUTY OF ITS OWN

2

Everyone has a favourite. Follow champagne by colour, by vintage, by grape variety, or via its variations of added sweetness. Each delicious style offers a range of flavour opportunities, but they're none of them straightforward…

THE RISE AND RISE OF ROSÉ
Victoria Moore (2022)

SUGAR RUSH
Jane MacQuitty (2022)

TRILOGY OF CHALK LOVERS
Essi Avellan MW (2022)

VINTAGE GLAMOUR
Serena Sutcliffe MW (2022)

Victoria Moore (2022)

THE RISE AND RISE OF ROSÉ

To allow a champagne to sparkle, or to take on the natural 'pink' hues of Pinot Noir and Meunier, were possibilities investigated only by Champagne's most frivolous – or forgetful – early cellarmasters. How things have changed… Victoria Moore tells the story of rosé champagne and its ascent to graciousness.

Rosé champagne is highly prized now. The colour, tinged a burnished bronze or wild salmon, and the reflections that fall from glass to tablecloth aren't just admired for their beauty; they also key up a sense of anticipation for the flavours that might be found in the wine.

It has not always been so. Still 'Rozé' was made in the Champagne region long before the advent of sparkling wine, but enthusiasm for rosé champagne has wavered considerably over the centuries. In the beginning, pale pink champagne was known locally as *taché* – 'stained'. '[The word] was not a positive compliment,' says Mathieu Roland-Billecart of Champagne Billecart-Salmon (a house whose best-known wine is pink), emphatically: 'It was a sign of bad winemaking.' Even if the intention is to create a white wine, much champagne is made using at least a proportion of red grapes. If these are handled roughly or hang around before being pressed, pigment from the skins leaches into the white juice 'and you are left with a tainted rosé'.

It's not clear which early tastemakers habilitated its social status but order books from the time show that, in the 18th century, rosé champagne was not just being made deliberately, its pinkish hue and delicate, red-berry flavours were much appreciated by European aristocracy. The House of Ruinart has the earliest known written record of an order of rosé champagne: an account book entry showing that, on March 14th 1764, 60 bottles of '*oeil de perdrix*' champagne were shipped to Baron de Welzel in Germany who ordered them on behalf of His Serene Highness the Duke of Mecklenburg-Strelitz. Incidentally, *oeil de perdrix* is a French term that is still often used to describe rosé wine. Not

Pinot Noir and Meunier grapes don't just lend colour. Whether added at the press or in the blending room, they will gently lower the acidity of a rosé champagne so that it's perfect for drinking while young, perfumed and fresh.

quite as romantic as it might at first appear, it refers to the colour of the eye of a dying or recently shot partridge.

Records also show Ruinart rosé was despatched to Maria Theresa, archduchess of Austria and queen of Hungary and Bohemia. A few decades later, in 1801, at a rival Champagne house, Jean-Rémy Moët noted down an order for 100 bottles of sparkling pink for Napoleon Bonaparte and his mother Letizia.

Yet, somehow, for much of the 20th century, rosé champagne was little appreciated. Jean Roland-Billecart, the great-uncle of Mathieu was going out on a limb when, in the 1970s, he decided he wanted to make, 'The finest rosé ever made in Champagne,' says Mathieu. 'I'm sure you've noticed rosé champagne is very popular now but it wasn't very popular then. But he went against the flow.' Rosé was beginning to move. Krug released its first rosé around this time, in 1983, and Bollinger launched its Grande Année Vintage Rosé (a 1976 wine) the following year (Bollinger didn't release a non-vintage rosé until 2008).

Even so, to most wine drinkers, rosé champagne in general remained, for the rest of the century, a distinctly second-class wine, pigeonholed as a gimmick,

Not every champagne house takes rosé as seriously as Dom Pérignon. With its assertive notes of Pinot Noir and beguiling sweetness, this is one of an elite set of wines that tantalizes when young but also improves with age. It was first released in 1959.

like a heart-shaped Valentine balloon. Some winemakers say it still felt like that even to the Champenois themselves. 'I think there was a perception that maybe it was a bit frivolous. OK we'll make one but that's all,' says one. Then the whole conversation around rosé wine changed. Pale rosé from Provence became aspirational, a drink sipped on the decks of superyachts or on villa holidays amid the umbrella pines and jasmine of the Côte d'Azur, and much desired for all its associations with blue skies and relaxation. Still rosé got serious, and rosé champagne was drawn into the limelight.

Its ascent has been dizzying. Benoît Gouez, *chef de cave* at Moët & Chandon, says that when he arrived at the house in 1998, rosé accounted for only two to three percent of Moët & Chandon's production. Just over two decades later, it was a fifth. Moët & Chandon punches above its weight in this respect but the new appetite for rosé is clear. In 2020, 8.4 percent of all champagne sold in the European Union was pink; in non-European countries the figure was 11.5 percent, with Americans showing a particularly keen enthusiasm for the colour – rosé accounted for 18.2 percent of champagne in the US in 2020, according to figures released by the Comité Champagne.

It's a peculiarity of champagne that rosé may be made – and is commonly made – by the *assemblage* method of mixing separately vinified red wine with a white cuvée. Alternatively, it can be made by leaving grape skins in contact with their juice for just long enough to impart the desired colour – and flavour – to the wine. This latter method is favoured by Fleur de Miraval, a very high-end collaboration between the actor Brad Pitt, the Perrin family of Château de

Beaucastel in the Rhône, and the Péters family of Champagne Pierre Péters. 'When you vinify Pinot as a red wine you get more tannin and we felt that didn't go well with the aromatics of Le Mesnil-sur-Oger Chardonnay so we made a *saignée* Pinot Noir and that's the blend,' says Marc Perrin. The very existence of Fleur de Miraval shows just how far rosé champagne has come: Fleur de Miraval launched its debut champagne in 2020, becoming the first ever Champagne house to be exclusively dedicated to rosé.

One factor that helped rosé champagne to move upmarket is its ability to pair well with food and make its way onto restaurant wine lists. '[Establishing Billecart-Salmon Rosé] started with us talking to the top Michelin-starred chefs and showing them that even if they thought they didn't like rosé champagne, ours was different,' says Mathieu Roland-Billecart. Rosé champagne can be good with sushi, smoked salmon, raw meat (such as veal tartare) and the fruitiness of fuller-flavoured wines can take on richer foods such as duck or fillet of beef.

Another is its range and its vinosity, attributes that have proved attractive to wine nerds. There are some very different wines out there. For instance, Fleur de Miraval is an elegant marriage of old Chardonnay and young Pinot Noir. But rosé has also inspired some winemakers to play with the more spicy, fruity notes of the Meunier grape. An example of this is Laherte Frères Rosé de Meunier, a darker-coloured, structured wine made from Meunier that has been vinified in three ways: as a white, as a *rosé de maceration* and as a red.

Rosé champagne today has true cachet at the very highest level. Accordingly, it is increasingly traded on the secondary market. In January 2022, Liv-Ex (the London International Vintners Exchange), which tracks the prices of the most traded fine wines on the market, added new wines to its Liv-Ex 100 index 'to reflect the growing demand for rosé champagne, the expansion of Burgundy and shifting brand power within Bordeaux'. Louis Roederer Cristal Rosé 2012 and Taittinger Comtes de Champagne Rosé 2007 both joined the index after rising in value during the previous year and setting new trading highs.

A good question for rosé champagne is where will it go next? The expectation is that it will continue to be taken seriously, evolving in all directions. As Frédéric Panaïotis, *chef de caves* of Ruinart Champagne, says: 'A great rosé has conviviality. For me it's a very seducing wine in the way that it fits any circumstance.'

Jane MacQuitty (2022)
SUGAR RUSH

From the ambrosial wines of the tsars to the startlingly sugarless cuvées of today's fashionistas, Jane MacQuitty explores the magic of champagne from ultra sweet to ultra brut with a myriad dosage possibilities in between the two…

What could be more magical, after all that fumbling with the foil and wire muzzle, than the pop of a champagne cork and the whoosh of bubbles? So magical that I spent one very happy spring and summer writing a book on the subject and tasting my way through every non-vintage, vintage and prestige champagne from all the major houses. Bliss! Since then, my enthusiasm for Le champagne, the wine, from La Champagne, the region, has not dimmed. The Rolls-Royce of sparkling wines is still my desert island bottle of wine by a country mile. Madame Lily Bollinger got it right when she said: 'I never touch it – unless I'm thirsty.'

Revelling in the golden age of champagne, now the quality from every *grande marque* Champagne house, single grower and co-operative has never been better, it's hard to remember the era when all was not as it should be. Yet sloppy standards and unprecedented demand in the mid- to late 1980s, led Christian Bizot from the grand old Aÿ house of Bollinger, worried by the poor image and low quality of some of the Champagne region's wine, to launch a Charter of Quality: Bollinger's 1991 superior code of practice, emblazoned on the back label of its non-vintage Special Cuvée, was chiefly concerned with the finer provenance of its grapes and this house's insistence on the long ageing of its wines on lees prior to sale.

Moët & Chandon and others soon followed suit, aiming for longer than the statutory minimum of 15 months' bottle ageing for non-vintage champagnes and three years for vintage champagne. Lowering yields, axing the notorious third pressing[1] and setting aside a sizeable proportion from bumper crops as reserve wines to help regulate stocks also boosted quality.

As the '90s unfolded, top-drawer producers, using finer grapes and wine, started to respect the complex, heady yeast autolysis aromas of brioche and toast that decent ageing brought with it. Champagne had turned a corner. Quality was on the up and has remained up more or less ever since. No mean feat given that Champagne's acreage since the war has leapt up from 11,000 hectares to around 34,000 hectares today.[2] Heck, even multi-million-case producers like Lanson and Piper-Heidsieck, on sale in every supermarket, have raised their game with increasingly tasty non-vintage fizz. Of course, escalating champagne quality is partly due to the Champenois realizing that if they didn't jump to it, classy New World *méthode champenoise* competition from California and Australia would take their shelf space.

Treating champagne as an elite wine, not a sparkler, with the emphasis on terroir and better vineyard management with superior clones and rootstocks, including finding the best patch of dirt for Chardonnay, Pinot Noir and Meunier, has paid off. Improved winemaking has helped, and global warming has also had a useful knock-on effect of producing naturally riper grapes. Perhaps the most obvious aspect of the new golden age of champagne is the steady decline in the sugar levels in the dosage of non-vintage and vintage examples. Hard to believe it now, but back in 1860, Pol Roger's standard dosage was a whopping 56–70 grams per litre (g/l), while other leading champagne houses plumped for twice that, weighing in with a gum-torturingly sweet 150g/l. The latter was the favoured level of the tsars and the Russian Imperial Court who guzzled sweet champagne with glee, often to the tune of 1,000 bottles at a single swanky event, although how they sunk all that sugary fizz is beyond me. Roederer's 1876 Cristal, in its clear crystal bottle, a special order for Tsar Alexander II, weighed in with 100g/l.

Surprisingly, Ayala, a great, old-fashioned champagne name, beloved by Queen Victoria's son Edward, when Prince of Wales, was ahead of the curve

---

1 In Champagne, the first pressing, the *tête de cuvée*, by law only 2,550 litres of juice per 4,000 kilograms of grapes, yields juice with the finest balance of sugars, acids and fragrance; the second press, the *taille*, allows the next 500 litres of juice – many producers sell this on, or vinify it separately. The final, third pressing (the *rebêche*) may, by law, only be used for distilling or vinegar and cannot be used for champagne production.

2 The original appellation law (in 1927) permitted production of champagne grapes from 46,000 hectares of vineyards. A wartime slump in the markets led to the area of production being limited to 34,000 hectares in 1951. But through the 1960s, normal trade quickly resumed; global demand for champagne soared, and the 34,000 hectares were soon found insufficient to meet requirements. It then became impossible to overturn the restriction for fear expansion would undermine quality. Only in 2003 were tentative plans for re-expansion allowed…

when it comes to dosage. In 1865, Ayala released what they described as a 'dry champagne' with just 21g/l. By the 1880s the standard dosage of champagne was somewhere between 14 and 42g/l, the lower end used by Pol Roger and other top houses in the late 19th century. Laurent-Perrier followed suit at the end of the century with a 'Sugarless 1893 Grand Vin'.

The heros at zero

It's not just sugar to balance champagne's naturally high acidity that plays a part in each Champagne house's dosage, but wine. The latter could be oaked, unoaked, venerable reserve wine, or just the same wine that's in the bottle; whatever the selection, it gives the *chef de cave* a final chance to emphasize the house style of their champagne. In the bad old days, many houses added a dash of cognac to their dosage to bump up the alcohol content and give the impression of age but all that stopped in the mid 1950s.

The shift to drier styles, where there is little or no sugar to hide behind and a greater use of reserve wine – around 40 percent for some producers – has been steadily gathering steam since the '90s. Back then, 12g/l for non-vintage brut from the big producers was the norm, now it's more like 9g/l. For comparison's sake it's worth noting that most popular Prosecco weighs in at around 15g/l. Although as Didier Mariotti, Veuve Clicquot's cellarmaster, points out, the creamy roundness necessary to balance the acidity in a good champagne: 'Can be created by adding sugar, or created by ageing wines, or by the use of reserve wines. Thanks to ageing we can lower the dosage to create roundness, body, texture and creaminess.' Veuve Clicquot fans, according to Mariotti, like most modern champagne drinkers: 'Want to know more about champagne and are looking for drier champagnes, for niche cuvées, for more ageing and more diversity. Our clients are treating champagne as a wine, not just a fizz.'

Over at Pol Roger, James Simpson MW who heads up the UK office notes that: 'Pol Roger has been flying the flag for dry, full-bodied champagne for a long time now. The dosage in Pol Roger's non-vintage White Foil has dropped from about 12g/l to 9g/l to 8g/l in the past 20 years to reflect drinkers' changing tastes. Natural acidity is lower and the grape parcels are riper than in the past, so with more ripeness and less acidity, the stage was set in 2008 for us to release our zero-dosage Pol Roger, Pure. Partly, this was because conditions meant that we were able to do this, but it was also to prove that we could make a zero-dosage better than anyone else.'

It's hard to dispute James Simpson's claim because Pol Roger Pure is a mouth-wateringly crisp, zingy, nutty, citrus-edged, beautiful, bone-dry bubbly, made from all three champagne grapes. It's a very different beast from the first modern zero-dosage champagne that was launched here in 1981, Laurent-Perrier's Ultra Brut. So mouth-puckeringly tart was my first sip of Ultra Brut's inaugural cuvée that I was reduced to adding my own sweet Sauternes dosage. Luckily, Ultra Brut has evolved: now a blend of almost 50:50 Chardonnay and Pinot Noir, but only from ripe vintages and with six years minimum on its yeasty lees, it's a still fresh but biscuity mouthful, beloved by calorie-counting models like Kate Moss.

Laurent-Perrier's Blanc de Blancs Brut Nature is its latest champagne, launched in 2019, and as a Chardonnay-dominant house is spot on, with 40 percent reserve wine, four years on lees and, though mostly a mix of 2012 base wine, has an enriching 40 percent wallop from the sunny 2009 vintage. The result is a svelte, crisp, tangy, Cox's apple orchard crunch. Louis Roederer's

Champagne as nature intended? Roederer's zero-dosage Champagne Nature is softened by time, not sugar; it spends six years on the lees before disgorgement.

sparky, greeny-gold, citrus-blossom-scented 2012 Brut Nature was born in 2019 as a collaboration with the famous French designer Philippe Starck and is another no-dosage gem. Sourced exclusively from Coteaux de Cumières Premier Cru vineyards, Roederer's Brut Nature is principally Pinot Noir, with around a quarter each of Meunier and Chardonnay, unusually pressed together, and then aged for six years in the cellars.

Dosage, but not so you notice it…

Not everyone is convinced that Brut Nature and Zero Dosage, at less than 3g/l, and Extra Brut (under 6g/l) work. The former's less than 3g/l means that no sugar has been added but there may be some natural residual sugar left in the wine from the grapes. But chances are, if you splash out regularly on Dom Pérignon, you have been enjoying Extra Brut champagne without realizing it; lots of Dom Pérignon's low-dosage vintages fit into this category, even if it doesn't say so on the label. Moët & Chandon, Dom P's sister-ship, followed suit from around 2002, but the 2009 vintage was the first to have the words 'Extra Brut' on the label, instead of Brut, just as the recently released 2013 vintage does.

Zero-dosage bubbly is champagne, if you like, in its purest form, and it has to be said is very much a niche style for the adventurous drinker. David Gleave MW, founder chairman of Liberty Wines, is not completely convinced: 'On one hand you've got the sommeliers and the geeks who love no dosage, and talk no dosage, but they don't actually drink it. Separating the trend from the noise is difficult but there's no doubt that dosage is coming down.' Gleave goes on: 'Really, ripeness and balance is the key, rather than the dosage. These days, a good champagne *chef de cave* is just as likely to be in the vineyard, as in the cellar, on the hunt for better fruit and better fruit balance. It all starts there. My view is if you notice the dosage, the wine is wrong.'

A sweet step further…

Before everyone gets overexcited about the rise of Brut Nature and Zero Dosage champagnes, it's worth remembering that these bone-dry bubbles have just a few percent of the champagne market. Confusingly, the Extra Dry champagne category with 12–17g/l doesn't really taste dry at all and is actually sweeter than

Brut champagne, but nowhere near as sweet as the sugary end of the champagne scale. Here, the sweetest styles of Sec (17–32g/l), Demi-sec (32–50g/l) and Doux (at over 50g/l) are rare, but still collectively sell twice as much as the Brut Nature and Zero Dosage brigade.

However, Moët & Chandon has done well with its sweet Nectar Imperial, launched in 2011, a Demi-sec with 45g/l dosage, and a Pinot Noir-Meunier blend, topped up with a dab of Chardonnay and perked up with a good dollop of around 20–30 percent reserve wine. Instagram-friendly Moët & Chandon Ice Imperial, in its brilliant snow-white livery, the first champagne created to be drunk over ice in large glasses, has made even more friends – again it has around 45g/l dosage and roughly the same mix of grapes and reserve wine component as Nectar Imperial. Imitation is the sincerest form of flattery and five years later Veuve Clicquot went one sweet step further than Ice Imperial by launching the snazzy, silver-bottled Rich, a 60g/l dosage bubbly, with the same blend as Nectar, designed to be drunk as a cocktail with ice and a slice. *Sacre bleu*!

Unsurprisingly, Brut champagne, with less than 12g/l of dosage, accounts for the vast majority of champagne sales. Everyone has their favourite champagne house, whether it's beefy, broad-shouldered Bollinger and Krug, honeyed Louis Roederer, or the creamy pin-head mousse (foam) and bubbles of Pol Roger, fruity Veuve Clicquot or the classy, contemporary, Chardonnay-chic of Laurent-Perrier. But as Brut champagne has got drier and quality more transparent, the *chefs de caves* of the leading *grandes marques* have to work harder every spring after the vintage to put their non-vintage blends together. In theory, a non-vintage blend like Moët could contain 100 different wines; in practice, it's usually less. Most non-vintage Brut champagne, from the better houses, is a blend of lots of reserve vintages and has at least three years' bottle-age after disgorgement. The average non-vintage cuvée is a blend of two-thirds black grapes to one-third white. Still, the permutations are endless, as all the elements must be orchestrated into one perfectly polished piece, above all to reflect the typical taste and style of each house. *Vive le champagne!*

Essi Avellan MW (2022)

TRILOGY OF CHALK LOVERS

Champagne author and Finland's first Master of Wine, Essi Avellan, introduces the famous Champagne grape trio – Chardonnay, Pinot Noir and Meunier – describing the role each plays individually, in *blanc de blancs* and *blanc de noirs* wines, and in the makeup of a blend. The hallowed three, she reveals, can legitimately be joined by five more…

The soils of Champagne have seen a wealth of grape varieties come and go. In the 19th centry, the grape mix was plentiful but the ravages of phylloxera followed by the official birth of the Champagne appellation in 1927 made the region focus its varietal effort. Today, Pinot Noir with its 39 percent proportion leads the way closely followed by Meunier (31 percent) and Chardonnay (30 percent). But there is more to the varietal mix of Champagne than this famous grape trio. The historical varieties Arbane, Petit Meslier, Pinot Blanc and Pinot Gris are being revived and now, with climate change in mind, Champagne is authorizing a wholly new variety, Voltis. But let's start at the top…

The rising star, Chardonnay

Chardonnay is well established in Champagne today. It is strongly present in the Grand Cru vineyards and in increasingly high demand for its lightness and vibrancy, with its proportion of the plantings creeping slowly but steadily upwards. It is a highly welcomed component in a champagne blend, imparting a single-minded 'linearity', freshness and elegance, but it also excels on its own, as *blanc de blancs* (white of whites). In practise, *Blanc de blancs* in Champagne means Chardonnay, but it could just as easily include the region's other white varieties, of which more later…

Chardonnay is a relative newcomer in Champagne with first written mentionings of it dating back to 1851. Its real vogue commenced in the first half of the 21st century when the *grands marques* Salon, Taittinger, Laurent-Perrier

Chardonnay grapes account for only around 30% of the total Champagne grape plantings, and cover 25,000 acres.

Pinot Noir is the region's most planted grape, at 32,000 acres (more than in its ancestral home, Burgundy) and 39% of the total.

Meunier (often referred to as Pinot Meunier) is a rising star, now occupying 31% of the vineyard area, 26,000 acres.

and Ruinart started to embrace it as a framework for their house styles. Salon practically launched the *blanc de blancs* category in the 1920s, but the other Chardonnay houses followed with equally charismatic Chardonnay prestige cuvées. Taittinger first made its Comtes de Champagne Blanc de Blancs in 1952 and Ruinart crafted its inaugural Dom Ruinart Blanc de Blancs in 1959.

A rather unfussy grape variety in the vineyards, Chardonnay isn't particularly vulnerable to Champagne's major viticultural hazard – rot – and it brings home generous volumes. It thrives on chalky and other well-drained soils, enjoying eastern aspects with the morning sun. Thus, the east-sloping and predominantly chalky Côte des Blancs vineyards south of Epernay are planted almost exclusively with Chardonnay. The Côte de Sézanne is a continuum of Côte des Blancs and here too Chardonnay prevails, but the wines are much more open and fruit-forward in style compared to the tight and lean wines of the Côte des Blancs. The east-facing Montagne de Reims villages such as Trépail and Villers-Marmery also produce first-class Chardonnay with a more structured and vinous profile. Vitryat southeast of Epernay is another up-and-coming, premium area, together with Montgueux down south near Troyes in the Aube.

Examples of great *blanc de blancs* growers include Pierre Gimonnet, Suenen and Pierre Péters; from Côte de Sézanne, Marie Copinet; from Montagne de Reims, Arnaud Margaine, and from Montgueux, Jacques Lassaigne.

Blanc de blancs in the glass

Lime, lemon, pear and Granny Smith apple are typical Chardonnay fruit characters in champagne when the grapes are grown in the coolest terroirs, but the warmer sites' wines may come across peachy and apricotty or even tropical. The fruit aromas are often supported by fragrant white flower notes and also chalky mineral whiffs. On the palate, Chardonnay tends to be linear and racy and comes with a seemingly light feel. *Blancs de blancs* are often described as 'apéritif style' champagnes.

As racy and steely-acidic *blancs de blancs* can be aggressive in youth, some houses are producing these wines at lower pressure. This kind of gently bubbling champagne was once called *crémant*, but nowadays this name is reserved for traditional-method sparkling wines from French and other European wine regions. Thus, regrettably, no common labelling term exists for these creamier *blancs de blancs*.

Even if *blancs de blancs* may sometimes be razor-sharp and acidic in youth, they can become luxuriously toasty, nutty and creamy over time, amply rewarding one's patience.

The mighty Pinot Noir

Pinot Noir arrived in Champagne in the 1500s and by 1860 it had become the most planted variety. As bubbly wine from Champagne gained popularity, the variety's suitability to the style was realized and it became the 'king' of champagne grapes. Still, today, most of the traditional houses, from Veuve Clicquot to Moët & Chandon, Lanson and Bollinger, are considered Pinot Noir houses with the grape responsible for framing the features of their famed house styles.

Pinot Noir is the muscular base of champagne, bringing richness, breadth and poise to the mouthfeel. On the aromas, red berries, red apple, undergrowth, fruitcake, mushrooms and spiciness prevail. Pinot Noir champagnes are solid and powerful, even chewy wines, with a round and vinous mouthfeel. The ageing capacity of the very best is universally appreciated, with the wines of the likes of Krug, Bollinger, Louis Roederer Cristal and Philipponnat Clos des Goisses being among champagne's most collectible.

Pinot Noir is the ruling grape on the Montagne de Reims with Grand Cru villages housing it on both their warm south-facing and cool north-facing sites. The second major Pinot Noir district of Champagne is in the *département* of Aube, some 150 kilometres southeast of Epernay. Here, Côte des Bar presents a notably different landscape, climate and soil from the Champagne vineyards of the Marne. Pinot Noir represents an 82 percent share of plantations here and, being the warmest part of Champagne, the Côte des Bar adds a more supple, fruit-forward and easier-to-approach style to Champagne's palette of Pinot Noirs.

However, Pinot Noir is notoriously fussy both in the vineyards and winery. It is prone to rot in the humid Champagne climate and its picking window is painfully short. In the winery, pressing, handling and use of barrels must be carefully orchestrated to prevent the wine becoming prematurely oxidized.

The number three, Meunier

Meunier's path in Champagne has been short of glory, even if its suitability to the region has earned it a popularity that now rivals that of both Pinot Noir and Chardonnay. It may come as a surprise to many that in the mid-1950s, no fewer than half of Champagne's vineyards were planted to Meunier vines.

The variety's exact birth date remains a mystery, but we can trace this age-old genetic mutation of Pinot Noir at least as far back as the 16th century, when it was referred to as Morillon Taconné. Meunier's later budding and earlier ripening are its assets in the frost-prone parts of Champagne, notably the Marne Valley. Due to its sluggishness in the spring, it may escape damage when early-season temperatures dip below zero. Equally, its speedy ripening in the autumn may save it from the perils of rainy weather.

The dusty or 'flour-covered' underside of Meunier leaves has given the variety its name, *meunier* being French for 'miller'. In Champagne, the variety was traditionally called Pinot Meunier but that was merely a local usage, and 'Pinot Meunier' was never registered in the French catalogue of authorized grape varieties (issued by GEVES, the French Variety, Seed Study and Control Group). Relatively recently, the Comité Champagne decided to align its practice with that of INRAE (the National Research Institute for Agriculture, Food and the Environment) and has abandoned the local nickname in favour of the official 'Meunier'. Long-established customs die hard, though, and many Champenois do still refer to 'Pinot Meunier'.

Even if the variety is considered a 'workhorse' grape by many, its masters agree it to be the most difficult grape to grow. Greedy yields are the real culprit when it comes to lack of quality and personality. For one of its strongest champions, Benoît Tarlant, Meunier is positively 'resistant to industrialization', since it requires such tender loving care from its growers. Nor is Meunier an easy child in the winery. One needs to be cautious, especially with oxidation and barrel work.

It is much more difficult to define Meunier's varietal characters than to describe the well-understood qualities of Pinot Noir and Chardonnay. Generally, many Meuniers may lack the depth and structure of Pinot Noir and might fall short of the elegance and drive of Chardonnay. Instead, most come across as fruit-forward and easy to drink. Because the Meunier component of a blend typically peaks earlier and falls away relatively quickly, it is widely used, especially for non-vintage cuvées. When grown at lower yields, however, in top locations such as Sainte-Gemme, Leuvrigny, Merfy and Hautvillers, Meunier can excel and does then have the capacity to age – a fact that has long been cherished by Krug, among others.

Many Meuniers are generously fruity, soft and amply bodied, but there are also much more reserved styles that emphasize mineral characters over fruitiness. The common aromas range from flowers to red apple, red berries, confected fruit, pastry, smoke and soft spiciness. Sometimes the expression can even be one of dark berries, but orange and Mirabelle plum may also be found in the bouquet.

The rare and demanding *blancs de noirs*

Blanc de blancs's counterpart is *blanc de noirs*, literally meaning white wine from dark grapes. Made of Pinot Noir or Meunier or both, these wines are much less common than *blanc de blancs*. Still, as white grapes have always represented a minority share in Champagne, most champagnes were historically *blanc de noirs*, even if the name remained almost unknown until the 1980s.

While *blancs de noirs* can have depth, they often miss the finesse and liveliness that Chardonnay brings to a blend, so remain less popular than their white counterparts. Their vinosity, richness and power, as well as the oxidative tendencies, can make them heavy and melancholic, and much more challenging to master. But, at best, they are superb, perfectly suited to the dining table. Most *blancs de noirs* are fleshy and muscular, with an autumnal aroma profile of ripe apples, spices and notes of undergrowth. They make great gastronomic partners with mushroom and meat dishes.

The best-known Pinot Noir *blanc de noirs* include Bollinger's Vieilles Vignes Françaises, Krug's Clos d'Ambonnay and Billecart-Salmon's Clos Saint-Hilaire. As the style increases in popularity, these have been joined by successful new cuvées from Bollinger, Philipponnat and de Venoge, as well as wines from grower-producers like Egly-Ouriet, Ulysse Collin, Clandestin, Nicolas Maillart and Pierre Paillard.

Meunier has become familiar to us as a blending component rather than as a varietal star, but 100% Meuniers have also started to emerge on the market, the most shining examples including Jérôme Prevôst's La Closerie Les Béguines, Chartogne-Taillet Les Barres, Huré Frères 4 Elements and Moussé Fils's Spécial Club.

The five spices

Even if Chardonnay, Pinot Noir and Meunier rule, a third of the vineyard area still grows Champagne's historical grape varieties: Arbane for its savoury herbal flavours; Petit Meslier for racy acidity; Pinot Blanc (locally called Blanc Vrai) for crispness and floral notes; and Pinot Gris (or 'Fromenteau') for its intense fruitiness.

While their share shrank dramatically after phylloxera in the late 19th century – especially Arbane and Petit Meslier as these grapes were considered difficult to grow – today, the Côte des Bar holds 102 hectares of plantings and counting, with the last two decades seeing a real return of interest, and the surface area slowly creeping up by 24 hectares. Pioneering advocates Drappier and Famille Moutard have been joined by Alexandre Bonnet, Cédric Bouchard, Fleury, Olivier Horiot, Vouette & Sorbée and Château de Bligny in making champagne solely or partially from these varieties. In the Marne producers like L Aubry Fils, Laherte Frères, Tarlant and Agrapart have followed suit.

Additionally, Champagne has recently accepted trial of the mildew-resistant grape variety Voltis. Following 20 years of research, Voltis will become the first grape hybrid to be included in a French appellation. It has been of interest for its resistancy to both downy and powdery mildew, allowing the producer to drastically reduce phytosanitary treatments. If the ongoing process is accepted by INAO, Voltis will be included in the testing frame of VIFA (*Variétés d'intérêt à fin d'adaptation*) for a five-year trial, limited to a maximum of 10 percent of the champagne blends.

Serena Sutcliffe MW (2022)
VINTAGE GLAMOUR

Honorary chairman of Sotheby's International Wine Department, Serena Sutcliffe, explains the pulling power of the champagne vintage. Released only in years of exceptional quality, these precious wines from a single harvest differ from non-vintage cuvées in that they are not blended but gain their richness and character as they age in bottle, in contact with their yeast lees….

What is it about vintage champagne that absorbs and beguiles me? Vineyard vintages are a fascination anywhere but, in Champagne, they are a conundrum, combined as they are with the implications of blending grape varieties, villages and *crus*, vineyard ownership and grape contracts, century-old Champagne house styles and traditions, all allied to the phenomenal climatic changes we are seeing in our lifetimes. What could be more straightforward?

Then there is the human, and corporate, element. The skills of viticultural research and improvements; the myriad details in the cellar that can be tuned and modified; the characters and perceptions of owners and winemakers; and, it has to be admitted, sometimes the aims and ambitions of big business: these are all in the mix. Above all, there is the variation in the weather each year, common of course to most wine regions and a vital part of the rich tapestry, which is added to the magic of the bubble in this most seductive of liquids.

Perhaps it is this bubble, this fizz, that adds another emotional dimension to how one views vintage champagne? There is, first, the anticipation of a vintage: will, or won't, this wine be 'declared'? – an announcement that is keenly discussed as not every Champagne house or grower follows the same policy. Then there is the first tasting of each vintage, the reflections on other vintages, the guessing game that is assessing the age potential and, naturally, the assiduous study of its development over many years. Anticipation becomes reality and, finally, the vintages in their turn become nostalgia.

I think this nostalgic element is stronger in Champagne than for other classic regions, however grand and majestic the wine is, probably because nostalgia for the champagne itself is intertwined with the circumstances in which it was drunk. However seriously one takes the subject of champagne – and I do – it is also at the centre of joyous occasions, fabulous moments both private and public, and at the heart of tremendous celebrations and landmark events. At our first meeting, my husband and I talked into the early hours over half-bottles of Roederer vintages from the 1960s – and we are still carrying on the conversation over vintage champagne.

One cannot talk about 'vintage' without circling round to global warming, especially in a vinous area as far north as Champagne. When I first knew the vineyards of the northern part of the Montagne de Reims, those that face east and north, the local term for these villages, especially after some libation, was 'Siberia'. Somehow I do not hear this any more. The talk now is about ripeness and all that this brings, notably changed phenolics and distinctive lowering of dosage levels. Some vintages of the past had a dosage of 12 grams per litre (g/l) sugar, now it is 8g/l or less. Yields still vary considerably, but high yields do not necessarily mean modest wines – think 2004 and 1982, both glowing with exceptional champagnes. For the future, the 2018s are sure to prove the point.

Before I reveal the vintages I most admire, I should set them in context by answering the question: 'How long do these wines age?' The answer can only be subjective. Even some non-vintage wines mature well and I like to age them and watch them gain in gravitas. For vintage bottles, though, I would say the 10-year point is when to start trying them, then, after that, rely on personal taste to choose your drinking window. I often hover around the 15–20-year mark, but the greatest wines will go on for decades longer than this. You should factor in the style of the vintage, storage conditions (as cold as possible) and whether you are drinking your vintage as an apéritif or with food.

When looking back vertically, and sometimes vertiginously, to vintage champagnes of the past, by far the greatest impact on their taste came with the switch to tank fermentation in the first part of the 1960s. Stainless-steel tanks became modus operandi in the first part of the 1960s for the ease and control they brought to the first part of the *méthode champenoise*. But so many of the absolute greats come from the years of labour-intensive barrel fermentation before this (and from barrel fermenting in general): vintages with astounding vinosity, all honeyed brioche, orange and walnut flavours.

Heading this triumphal march were those two miracles, Billecart-Salmon's Cuvée Nicolas François 1959 and 1961, first and second in the historic 1999 Stockholm tasting to bring in the Millennium, when the greatest champagnes of the 20th century were judged over three memorable days. They happened to be my two top wines as well as the jury's, and I shall never forget their originality, nobility and sheer firepower. This, of course, is a stunning epoch and one could wax lyrical (at the risk of becoming extremely boring), but there is also Dom Pérignon 1959, 1961 and 1964; luscious Krug 1959, 1962 (the first of Henri Krug's great reign) and 1966, Olivier Krug's birth year. Then there is Moët's 1959, 1961 and 1962, the last year at Moët where all the wines were fermented in barrel, going to half for the show-stopping 1964 vintage and no barrels at all in 1966.

In a different register but equally amazing, there is Salon Le Mesnil Blanc de Blancs 1959. Here one is in the field of fables and fairytales, for this wine is both frustrating and frivolous in equal measure. Even if it could be unearthed, it, like us, has changed with time; it is no longer the same – although carbon dioxide is a famous protector of beauty…

It would not be possible to work in this 'game' (as rather envious friends occasionally call the wine trade) if one did not have favourites, even fetish vintages that always appeal and really 'talk' to one's senses on a personal level. In the 1980s, it was, and remains for me, 1988, followed by 1985: who could forget the polemic around those two vintages at Bollinger, both of them remarkable, but the 1988 touched by stardust?

This was the first of a trio of great champagne vintages – 1988, 1989 and 1990 – comparisons with which have remained incredibly exciting during every decade since. It started for me with a telephone call from Rémi Krug asking: 'Serena, when will you next be in Paris?' Fortunately, it was soon after I put the 'phone down! I met a serious-looking Henri and Rémi in the entrance of Alain Dutournier's mouthwatering restaurant, Carré des Feuillants, and they sat me down before two glasses and asked my opinion. I loved them both, but pronounced one much more ready to drink than the other – I favoured the structured, sublime 1988 but the delicious, tempting 1989 was the wine for 'now'. The brothers stood up, embraced me and said words to the effect of: 'That does it, we launch the 1989 before the 1988!' I am sure they had already made up their minds to do this, but it was the first time a great house had declared a vintage out of chronological order.

Since then, there has been Dom Pérignon 2009, launched and tasted in 2017, ahead of the 2008 – this was the first time the vintage release order was not chronological at DP, and with perfect judgement, as the 2008 was still at the beginning of its life. It was a similar approach for Cristal, with the 2009 appearing '*sur scène*' before the 2008, both divine in their quite different ways.

The 1985s line up in admirable fashion, with the leader of the pack being Cristal 1985, to which I gave 100 points in the Stockholm tasting and continue to revel in its creamy nuttiness. Clicquot's La Grande Dame is sensational, as is Perrier-Jouët's Belle Epoque, and Pol Roger is perfection.

The 1990 came in with a roar and I have loved (and, unfortunately, lost) many of these vintage wines as they were just so drinkable, never more so than the Cristal, Clicquot's La Grande Dame, Dom Pérignon, Belle Epoque and Salon. Then things did not go too well in Champagne, although Pol Roger's 1993 transcended the weather in delectable style – I wrote that it was '*enivrant*', as well as floral and tempting. It is the place, here, to digress (which is always permissible when discussing champagne) and say that I find Pol Roger the most consistently excellent purveyor of vintage style, day in and day out, plus evenings of course. It is the esprit, the élan and the fruit of the wine that enchant – this is a champagne that never puts a foot wrong: charming in years like 2000, magical in 2002, pure in 2004, grand in 2008… One could go on….

I now pick and choose my 1995s and 1996s: the latter vintage always a talking point, with its hot days and cold nights giving acidity that sometimes led to over-compensation by dosage. Belle Epoque did magnificently in both vintages and Salon's 1996 has a marine note to it that is just opening out. The 1998 has never pretended to be top of the class, but Moët's certainly is – I love its verve and flavour. And Pol Roger's Cuvée Sir Winston Churchill is flawless. For the most part, 1999 does not have huge character but, needless to say, Pol Roger provided it!

The new millennium heralded a parade of the best – bringing in the Platinum Age of champagne now upon us. One downed the 2000s with great alacrity and then embraced the vintage that, for me, outshone everything: 2002, complete and captivating, is my outright winner. I do not think I have ever tasted a bad 2002 and a list of all these stupendous champagnes could become a litany. Seize every one you can. The 2004s are crystalline, the 2006s sumptuous, the 2007s appetizing and great for Chardonnay – look at Taittinger's Comtes de Champagne (superlative throughout the decade) and

Amour de Deutz. The 2008 defines the description of a classic vintage style, 2009 is soft and welcoming, 2010 a tad edgy and 2012 is splendidly majestic. Beg, borrow or (preferably not) steal Bollinger Grande Année 2008 and 2012, just for a glimpse of heaven.

> **Bollinger Grande Année 2008**: 71% Pinot Noir, 29% Chardonnay, 18 *crus* and 8 grams per litre dosage. A fantastic, complex champagne, with its wonderful, saline, aromatic Bollinger bouquet. Great freshness on the palate, expressive and with immense character. Youthful vinosity, with glorious texture and a touch of toast at the end. This has it all!

I rest my case, and raise my glass to these gems. Broaching bottles of vintage champagne opens the door to exuberance and straight-up hedonistic pleasure, while we anticipate, and then pounce on, new vintages, as one yearns for the arrival of the first asparagus and native oysters!

CHAMPAGNE'S STRANGE WITCHERY

3

Champagne is a wine for many occasions and any table, but which gastronomic setting suits it best? How do we taste it to understand its strangeness? Is it true that bigger bottles are better? Do there have to be bubbles? And how do we serve it… safely?

THE COLD, SINGING FIRE
Andrew Jefford (2017)

DEATH TO THE FLUTE!
Robert Walters (2022)

THE MAGNUM EFFECT
Tom Stevenson (2015)

BEYOND THE ICE-BUCKET
Natasha Hughes MW (2022)

LITTLE BOMBS EVERYWHERE…
Kelli White (2022)

Andrew Jefford (2017)

THE COLD, SINGING FIRE

Andrew Jefford weighs up the strangeness of champagne and suggests that, to understand it fully, we should peer inside the bubbles and admire this wine for the authenticity of its flavour – we should look beyond the sparkle and the ritual.

No wine is more sipped, but less tasted, than champagne. For many of its drinkers, it's a social marker. Clutching a flute of champagne is a secular rite – to denote achievement, happiness, success, or to shine a light on any of the significant way-marks in life. What it actually tastes like is secondary, perhaps irrelevant. Indeed, given its high acidity levels and ever-decreasing levels of dosage, I suspect that many of its bright-eyed celebrants must secretly suffer it rather than relish it.

To those who are interested in tasting champagne rather than merely enacting a ritual, I'd say this. Notice what a strange sort of wine it is. As you hold it in your mouth, try to see the wine inside the bubbles, shocking though that experience may be.

The greatest wines often have a kind of lovely unloveliness at their heart – the fierce tannins of the Langhe, the austerity of classic Médocain beauty, a mocking, stony-sour slenderness in red burgundy. So with champagne, and champagne's structural acidity. It is unreasonable, and in and of itself, almost impossible to like.

Visitors to the region who get a chance to taste the *vins clairs* (the still base wines) before blending will often find them painful, challenging, inscrutable and tooth-jangling. You can experience something of this for yourself by sampling a still Coteaux Champenois white wine. Only the ripest wines from the most favoured villages will be used; even so, it's hard to call them 'balanced', or to see how they could justify their luxury pricing. Climate change, it's true, is moving the regional fulcrum a little, thus balances are easing, but the acid challenge remains; indeed, those whose lives are spent crafting champagne struggle to find ways to nourish and retain acidity as the sinister warmth advances like an algal bloom.

This might lead us to conclude that the beauty in champagne is a matter of acquired externalities: the sinew of malolactic fermentation, the nutty resonance which comes with a little controlled oxidation (via cask fermentation), the tongue-teasing texture of tiny bubbles, the bready scents and creamy palate fullness of autolysis, the chamfering brought by the addition of finely judged dosage, the gathering harmony that is the legacy of cellar years. Those elements must constitute the secret, no?

I don't think so: these externalities can be mimicked by any skilled sparkling-wine craftswoman or craftsman anywhere. And they do; and they are. Other regions making champagne-style sparkling wines nonetheless struggle to match the greatest champagne (though both England and Tasmania glide impressively close). Either champagne craftspeople are simply more skilled than everyone else – which seems improbable – or we are back to the raw materials themselves: champagne grapes, champagne must, the *vins clairs*.

That's where champagne's quality lies. An understanding of this strange wine consists in paring away the externalities to see, to smell, to taste and to weigh up the intrinsic nature of the lunging fruit beneath. The region's muddy, chalky soils are not the primary cause; the magic lies above all in the grey, fretful, hesitant Champagne season, and the flavour maturity so painstakingly acquired over the length of that season winning out, finally, over the two-sided hazard of deficit sugars and unreasonable acidity. That is where the perfume, the nuance and the lift of truly great champagne lies, although it is necessarily buried in raw young acidity at the *vin-clair* stage. It's when the balancing externalities are in place that we drinkers are finally able to unlock the resonance of champagne's slow-season grapes and (now the bright chalk can play an additional role) very finest vineyards.

That's what I'd urge you to seek in champagne. There should be nothing sweet, nothing bitter, nothing short, nothing hard, nothing too creamy, nothing too fizzy, nothing evident. It's by looking into the cold, singing fire of its acid profile that you'll find the allusions we love most in this wine: orchards, fields, mists and the half-hidden, grass-covered fruits they surrender.

First published in *Decanter* magazine in December 2017; updated for this book, in 2022, by the author and reproduced here with his permission.

Robert Walters (2022)

DEATH TO THE FLUTE!

Robert Walters questions the use of the tall, tapered flute – that elegant showcaser of champagne bubbles – finding its shape wanting when it comes to the serious appreciation of today's fizz. And, he asks, do we really need the bubbles anyway…?

The flute is clearly not dead yet; the vast majority of restaurants around the world still use this glass shape to serve sparkling wine to their clients. Is at least dying? I am not so sure. Certainly, when it comes to the finest wines of Champagne, there is a growing band of drinkers around the world who are rejecting this glass shape.

The reason is quite straightforward: the flute is a terrible glass if you wish to fully appreciate the wine being served. You can't swirl the wine effectively in order to release the perfume, and the mouth (or rim) is too small, making it impossible to get your nose into the glass in order to appreciate the wine's aromatic capacity (or WAC[1]). The perfume of a wine is, of course, the carrier of much of its pleasure impact potential (or PIP[2]). The restricted rim also directs each sip onto only a small area of the palate, so that only a fraction of the wine's texture and flavour can be registered. Try drinking a quality still wine from a flute and the limitations of this glass shape will be immediately apparent.

In fact, any glass that's sold as a 'champagne glass' will tend to limit the WAC and PIP of the wine being served. This is because its narrow, straight sides will have been designed to preserve the bubbles in the wine for as long as possible – and tapering the rim of a glass can keep the bubbles popping for up to 30 percent longer. But it turns out that, beyond a certain point, there is an an inverse relationship between bubble retention and wine appreciation. The smaller the rim, the less the wine can 'show'. Simply put, champagne glasses cramp the wine's style.

[1] This is an acronym I have just this moment made up…
[2] And here's another one!

The coupe (*left*), the flute (*centre*) and the favourite among wine professionals, the tulip-shaped swirling glass (*right*). Each has its advantages for tasting champagne, but to savour this wine fully, there needs to be ample room to 'nose' the aromas and a modest surface area to avoid losing the fizz. Champagne lovers these days opt for the tulip shape for the best of all worlds.

The coupe, that wide-mouthed vessel, forever associated with grand, Gatsbyesque parties, was banished from serious wine tables decades ago. This, too, is a useless glass in terms of its ability to transmit the full personality and pleasure that any wine has to offer. But its problem is largely the opposite of the flute; its rim is too wide, causing much of the wine's perfume to dissipate before it can be savoured by the drinker. Of course, if you want to build a champagne fountain, that's quite another story...

Today, we can roughly split champagne drinkers into two camps; those who prefer to drink from flutes, or some recognized form of champagne glass, and those who insist on using standard wine glasses of the kind they might use to serve any other fine wine. The first group tend to be drinking for fun and celebration and are keen to see their bubbles last as long as possible. The second camp could not care a fig for bubbles, and even encourage them to dissipate by serving the wine in large glasses, by decanting, and even by splashing the wine around after it's been poured. This latter group, of which many in the wine trade are now a part, is still a tiny minority, yet they are growing in number, especially among those who drink the region's finest wines on a regular basis.

As you may have guessed, the question of glassware is not really about the drinker, it's about the wine being served. The two camps of drinker above broadly reflect two, quite distinct, wine styles that are emanating from the vast region of Champagne today.

The first, and still dominant, wine style produced in Champagne is the kind that made the region famous. This wine will typically be a blend of many vineyard plots, located across a vast area. Such wines will be typically high acid, yet will be dosed with a generous dollop of sugar, not only required to try to balance the high acidity, but also to give the wine much of its texture and character (notes of toast, caramel, baked bread, etc, that have long been associated with such champagnes are, it turns out, a winemaking artefact directly linked to sugar additions – *see* Maillard Reaction, page 20). Finally, these wines will be marketed under global, or aspiring-to-be-global, brand names.

The second category of Champagne is produced mostly, but not exclusively, by the region's finest grower-producers. These wines derive from lower yields, considerably riper fruit, and often from a specific vineyard or commune. The ripeness of the fruit used to produce these wines means that lower levels of sugar are generally required (sometimes none at all), and so, in general, these wines tend to be far drier and more vinous, yet also more fruit-driven (as they came from riper fruit). They also tend not to have any of the toasty, biscuit-like notes that we have long been told champagne is supposed to have.

Even if most of these latter wines come from the finest growers of Champagne, it is a mistake to understand the two categories of wine outlined above as simply 'growers' vs 'houses'. This is a false dichotomy; the correct distinction to be made is between those who farm in a certain way and those who don't, between those who aim to maximize terroir expression and those who prioritize house style.

There are, of course, degrees to this distinction, the world is always blurry around the edges. Yet it's nonetheless one that holds up remarkably well when surveying the wines of Champagne today. Some might add a third category: one made up of the better, so called, prestige cuvées of the houses. These are certainly the best-quality examples of the first category above, yet they still tend to sit comfortably within this grouping. Regardless, once you understand which of the above camps you sit in, and once you have acknowledged whether or not the bubbles in the glass matter to you, then the choice of glassware becomes simple.

If you're serving your champagne simply as a refreshing, luxurious apéritif, or simply because you want to celebrate, and if you want your wine to remain bubbly for as long as possible, then you will serve your wine chilled (serving a sparkling liquid cold slows down the loss of gas) and in a flute, or any other form of tapered champagne glass.

If, on the other hand, you believe that the champagne you are serving is a great artisanal wine first and foremost, a great wine that just happens to be sparkling, and if you want to maximize your appreciation of the wine 'behind' the bubbles, every bit of the WAC and PIP, then you will use a classic wine glass and serve your wine at cellar temperature, in the right company and with the right food. In other words, you will treat your champagne as you would any other great wine.

Today, I serve my champagne at cellar temperature both for the expression of the wine and also because it allows the bubbles to dissipate more quickly. I serve the wine in a burgundy-shaped glass (the largest glass possible) and swirl it in a way that encourages the gas pressure to diminish rapidly, before starting to enjoy the wine on offer. I do not say that the bubbles are bad. I know that they are part of a process that has helped reveal the personality of the invariably marvellous wine I have before me. But I simply don't need them as much. If they are too forceful, they distract from the wine; and anyway, there will always be some fizz: there are as many as two million bubbles in every glass of champagne, and a bottle of champagne can stay fizzy for days after opening (even without any closure).

Another approach is to ask the following question: what would this wine taste like if it lost all of its gas and was served unchilled, at room temperature? If your answer is: 'It will taste even better!', then you know you are dealing with a category-two champagne, and you can bravely go forth and ask for a larger wine glass!

Tom Stevenson (2015)

THE MAGNUM EFFECT

We now understand more of the theory of why champagne bottled in magnums (with twice the capacity of a standard 75cl bottle) will taste so much better than the same wine presented in an everyday bottle… Tom Stevenson finds incontrovertible and irresistible proof when he samples the bigger format…

At its most basic, the magnum effect infers something so intrinsically superior about magnums that they will always taste significantly better. The commonly accepted reasoning behind this phenomenon has always been that the smaller ratio of oxygen to wine in magnums causes the same wine to age more slowly and more gracefully. This is indeed true. But when it comes to sparkling wine there is more to it than that.

Some time in the 1990s (I forget exactly when), I was enjoying a one-to-one tasting of bottles and magnums of Croser sparkling wine at the Bridgewater Mill in the Adelaide Hills with the great man himself,[1] when he asked me whether I thought the magnum effect occurred before disgorgement as well as after. He did not seem to think so, but it was an intriguing question and one that I would eventually pick up and run with.

Even before Brian Croser had planted that line of enquiry in my mind, it was evident that although large bottle formats of red wine are favoured by collectors, the magnum effect is more noticeable in sparkling wine than it is in any still wine, whether it is red or white. Furthermore, although Jéroboams of sparkling wine are clearly superior to regular 75cl bottles, the jump in quality

[1] Brian Croser, the winemaking visionary renowned for his outstanding contribution not just to Australian wine but to the global wine scene, is founder of the Petaluma and Tapnappa wine estates in South Australia. He has been a maker of premium Australian sparkling wine since 1987.

from magnum to Jéroboam is far less than it is from the 75cl bottle to magnum. Typically, champagne and sparkling wine bottled in magnums is smoother, has more finesse, and can quite often be devoid of any oxidative character, even when the 75cl bottles of the same wine are highly aldehydic.[2]

So what is it specifically about magnums and sparkling wine?

When corked, a sparkling wine produced by the traditional method is in a highly reductive state, unlike a still wine. At the time of disgorgement (which is to say just before final corking), all the oxygen in a bottle-fermented sparkling wine has been scavenged by the yeast, whereas in a regular still wine – Bordeaux or whatever the wine happens to be – there will be dissolved oxygen. The neck and the diameter of the opening for a 75cl bottle is exactly the same as it is for a 150cl magnum (whereas they are much bigger for a Jéroboam), thus the headspace in both will contain the same volume of oxygen, and therefore the future rate of oxygen ingress will also be roughly the same. For those who find the notion of oxygen entering a sparkling wine against a pressure of some six atmospheres counterintuitive, please be assured that it is true (*see* Boyles Law, partial pressures, and so on). Since a magnum has double the ratio of wine to oxygen, both in situ and in the future by ingress, its potential for oxidation will be approximately half that of a 75cl bottle. This is the magnum effect explanation in a nutshell. Or used to be until Brian Croser raised the issue of whether it exists before disgorgement, as well as after…

Above Champagne Taittinger's special millennium magnum stands proud in its 4th-century *crayères. Opposite* Tom Stevenson assesses the results of a magnum vs 75cl bottle comparison.

Altered biochemical pathways

As it turns out, the magnum effect does exist before disgorgement. In fact, the magnum effect starts before the second fermentation.

There is a radical difference in the progress of the second fermentation of exactly the same wine in both 75cl bottles and magnums. The second

---

2 Aldehydes are chemical compounds formed by the oxidation of alcohol in wine. In some wine styles (for example, sherry) the nutty, butterscotch characters they give are seen as an advantage, but in champagne their presence divides opinion.

fermentation in a regular 75cl bottle is relatively smooth and straightforward, with just a little dip towards the end, when the yeasts, which are voracious consumers of oxygen, have to scavenge the wine for sufficient oxygen to maintain their numbers and complete the fermentation. By comparison, the yeasts in a magnum have twice as much wine to ferment, yet virtually the same volume of oxygen with which to sustain their health, metabolism and thus numbers. (The difference in dissolved oxygen is inconsequential compared to the oxygen in the headspace.) This relative shortage of oxygen causes the fermentation to start two or three days later (because it takes longer for the yeast to build up a viable population of active yeast cells) and continues to be problematic for the yeasts, which seem to 'gasp for air' throughout the entire second fermentation, not just at the end; consequently, the whole process takes approximately eight days longer to complete. It should be stressed that the difficulties faced by yeasts in a magnum are not insurmountable and are not even serious, despite the restricted oxygen reserves. They are merely hurdles that the yeasts can overcome if they work a little harder and a little longer. However, because the yeasts have to work harder and longer, some of the biochemical pathways in a magnum fermentation are altered, effectively producing an altered sparkling wine from exactly the same base wine in a 75cl bottle. So magnums of sparkling wine are not only fresher and smoother, with much more finesse than the 'same wine' in 75cl bottles, but they are also different.

Personal perspective

I routinely taste bottles and magnums of the same champagne or other sparkling wine and, like most *chefs de caves*, winemakers and oenologists, I am totally convinced by the so-called magnum effect. There will always be exceptions for good reasons. But generally magnums have more finesse. This is primarily the result of less and much slower oxidation, but can also be due to lower pressure. The lower pressure is either because the wine is a non-vintage blend and magnums on the shelf often lag one blend behind the standard 75cl bottles of the same cuvée, or because the magnums are given longer to rest after disgorgement. Sometimes both. The slower rate of oxidation not only produces a smoother-finished wine with no or less aldehydic aromas, but the lower the acetaldehyde, the less debilitating effect it can have on the primary fruit flavours, so there is generally more fruit in a magnum and that fruit will have more finesse.

Many years ago, I installed magnum racks in my cellar and switched exclusively to magnums for long-term storage, but in recent years I have begun to use magnums for everyday drinking, which last me two days instead of one. Magnums are a barometer that clearly indicates how serious (or not) a sparkling wine industry is. If an individual producer or region rarely produces magnums, it illustrates just how far that producer or region has to progress to compete with other sparkling wine producers and regions in the world. It also restricts the potential of its customers to respect the age-worthiness of the sparkling wine produced, because serious sparkling wine consumers like to cellar their wines. Too many producers feel trapped in a catch-22 situation when deciding whether to begin magnum production, believing they have no demand, and yet they cannot create any demand without first selling magnums. Eventually the most serious sparkling wine producers realize that customers cannot break out of this, only producers can, but the only producers who do are those who have as much belief in the potential of their customers as they do in the potential of their sparkling wine. That is why magnums are such an effective barometer.

First published in *The World of Fine Wine* in 2015. Reproduced here with permission of the editor.

Champagne bottles, from smallest to largest: Piccolo (197ml), Demi (375ml), Standard bottle (750ml), Magnum (1.5 litres), Jéroboam (3 litres), Réhoboam (4.5 litres), Methuselah (6 litres), Salmanazar (9 litres) and Balthazar (12 litres). Above this (not pictured) bottle sizes continue up to the Nebuchadnezzar (15 litres), Solomon (20 litres) and the unwieldy Melchizedek (30 litres).

Natasha Hughes MW (2022)

BEYOND THE ICE BUCKET

Champagne shines when sipped solo. Accompanied by little more than a salty snack, it does nothing but please us. But, urges Natasha Hughes, we should take it off ice and consider the 'swoon-worthy' partnerships its major styles offer across the menu…

If champagne were a human being, it would probably end up as tabloid fodder – a wine with a reputation for turning up at one glamorous party after another, the oenological equivalent of a posh, good-time girl. It's hard to imagine any wine lover celebrating a birthday or an anniversary without toasting the occasion with a glass of champagne. I even find it tricky to invite friends round for dinner without opening a bottle or two of non-vintage (NV) to get the evening off to a convivial start.

But there is a flipside to champagne's festive froth, and it's this. Despite the fact that these wines are – in theory at least – terrific partners for all kinds of food, very few of us ever carry our flutes on past the last round of canapés and over to the dinner table. So it's well past time to take a second look at champagne's diversity of styles and ask what the wines can offer in terms of food pairing.

Before we do, though, a couple of thoughts on serving champagne as a food wine rather than as a prelude to the main activity. The first thing to mention is those flutes. Ditch them, please! Their tall, narrow shape may work wonders in terms of channelling fine bubbles onto your palate, but does little when it comes to helping the wines express their full aromatic range. Think about serving temperature as well. Most fridges are set to a temperature of around 4–7°C, but simpler NV champagnes benefit from being poured at temperatures closer to 8–10°C, while richer *blanc de noirs*, vintage styles and rosés fare even better at temperatures closer to 12°C, as a little more warmth allows them to reveal their generous flavours.

Most champagne is straight-up, no-nonsense **Non-vintage fizz**, but within this catch-all definition lies a world of variation that depends on the percentage of each of the different grapes in the blend, the proportion of reserve wine used and the level of dosage. Nevertheless, most NV cuvées are bright and refreshing, with a little autolytic richness to complement their fruit, which allows them to be matched with a similar range of flavours.

Their brightness of character and those characteristically fine bubbles mean that these wines lend themselves well to balancing out the salty snacks that are often served as canapés, and help to explain why champagne is such a good partner for smoked salmon (or even smoked eel) and caviar as well as briny oysters. By extension, champagne's refreshing acidity also helps to cut through fat, whether that's present as an ingredient (think butter, cream, mayonnaise or hollandaise sauce, for instance) or by virtue of the cooking method (frying).

This is particularly true when the NV champagne in question is a **Blanc de blancs**. Here, Chardonnay's incisive acidity can provide a counterweight to the richness of the dish while not overwhelming any delicate flavours. Open a bottle to accompany dishes like dressed crab or chicken in a creamy sauce (this is particularly true if it's flavoured with mushrooms, whose flavours chime particularly well with the underlying yeastiness of the champagne). Or, for a truly decadent marriage, try pairing that most democratic of British national dishes, fish and chips, with a taut, linear *blanc de blancs* for a truly revelatory contrast of textures and tastes. A Japanese meal based around tempura seafood and vegetables would provide a slightly more sophisticated twist on the theme.

In fact, NV and *blanc de blancs* champagnes work in harmony with pretty much any seafood dish you care to throw their way, but, as ever, balance is key. The more delicate the fish, the lighter and crisper your champagne should be – think of the wine as being like a vibrant vinous squeeze of lemon rather than something that rides roughshod over the flavours of the food. Both styles also work well with the slightly more exotic raw seafood dishes, from delicate slices of sashimi to thinly sliced Italian crudos, especially when you spike your crudo with citrus zest and the merest hint of chilli.

If you're planning on sushi, though, a **Blanc de noirs** might make a better partner as, in addition to the fish itself, the wine has to stand up to the mild sweetness of the rice, as well as the savoury soy and the gentle fire of the wasabi, so a little heft is called for. In a broader context, richer, weightier fish – salmon or tuna in particular – are ideally matched by the richness and weight of a *blanc* *de noirs*. In summer you might even consider cooking the fish on a barbecue – you'll find that a touch of smokiness chimes well with the wine's flavours. Alternatively, try wrapping some bacon or pancetta around some scallops and flashing them under the grill for another sublime match that touches on similar flavour themes. Or, for the ultimate in brunch-time luxury, there's nothing quite like a chilled bottle of *blanc de noirs* and a full English, particularly when the latter includes a slice of dense, fudgy black pudding.

Rosé champagne is – like its still counterpart – an incredibly versatile wine to bring to the table. The sheer fruity joyousness of pink fizz is particularly welcome when exotic spices or complex Asian flavourings are brought into play. Chargrilled *yakitori* skewers, with their sweet *tare* sauce (sweeter and thicker than soy), are complemented by fruity rosés. Alternatively, pop a cork on a bottle when sitting down to a dim sum feast – nothing is going to harmonize perfectly with every morsel, but rosé champagne does a great job of rubbing along happily with pretty much everything in the standard *yum cha* repertoire, from *har kau* dumplings to *char siu* pork-filled buns. It's worth noting that straight NV will also work in both contexts, but provides more of a contrast to the flavours than a harmonious echo.

You can also ramp up the heat when you have a rosé to hand (although don't overdo it – high levels of chilli don't do favours to any wine). Some of my favourite partnerships include quail marinated in Ras el Hanout (a perfumed Moroccan spice blend) and mild seafood curries from Southern India, although it's worth experimenting with stir-fries too (try pork, spring onions and fresh ginger). Rosé champagnes can also be revelatory when teamed with the smoky paprika-driven warmth of chorizo sausage – I like to wrap mine in puff pastry to make sausage rolls for picnics (another great occasion for exploring the food-friendly nature of rosé). Or chargrill your chorizo slices and use these to garnish freshly shucked oysters – a wonderful start to an evening's barbecue and particularly delicious with a glass of pink fizz. And while you're out in the garden, you can carry on drinking that rosé with a generous platter of barbecued pork ribs slathered in a sweet, sticky Southern-style glaze.

Thanks to autolysis, champagnes typically have an umami character – a kind of savoury intensity that's hard to explain but is a common element in ingredients like aged Parmesan cheese, mushrooms, seaweed and soy sauce – and as a result, umami-led dishes work exceptionally well with fizz. This is true for NV blends, of course, but **Vintage champagnes** have an extra dose of

Tangy palate pleasers. A range of bite-size canapés all set to match a glass of fizz; *from left: pissaladière* (flatbread with anchovies, onions and black olives), oysters and caviar blinis. So far so sensible. But champagne's matchability doesn't stop here: there's a style for any dish on the menu.

autolytic richness that makes them superb partners for menus with their own umami component. Vintage wines are sublime when teamed with dishes like chicken in a creamy morel sauce or turbot with wild mushrooms or truffle, and a mushroom and truffle risotto scattered with Parmesan shavings can be taken to the next level with a glass of vintage fizz. And, as far as I'm concerned, when it comes to the cheese board, you might as well jettison the received wisdom about pairing dairy with red wines and save a glass of umami-rich champagne for the end of the meal, especially if you're serving a selection of washed-rind or hard mature cheeses. Alternatively, you can bring the same characters together at the start of the meal – or for a light but extravagant supper – with the combination of a cheese soufflé and mature champagne.

The umami flavours so popular in Japanese cuisine means that vintage champagne is extraordinarily well suited to a traditional *kaiseki* meal – a succession of dishes that incorporate seasonal flavours and a range of cooking techniques. Vintage champagne can also provide a solution to dealing with the sometimes challenging range of flavours at a Chinese banquet. In both instances, the wine can cope with the more robust characters in these dishes while allowing more subtle elements to speak for themselves.

Famously, the author Jeffrey Archer used to feed guests at his South London penthouse parties with shepherd's pie and Krug, a NV wine but one so rich and weighty it might as well have been a vintage cuvée. I'd probably eschew the shepherd's pie myself, but richer champagnes can certainly take on meatier dishes than those you might marry with lighter NV styles. Roast chicken or pork could certainly feature on the menu in this instance, although I'm not sure I'd go quite as far as serving the wine with lamb or beef – it doesn't sit well with meat served rare, and although it can cope with well-done steak, no self-respecting gourmet should insult a good cut of meat by cooking the flavour out of it like that. **Vintage rosé** lends itself well to being paired with pork and sweet-sour fruity sauces – roast belly of pork, with its unctuous fattiness and crisp skin, served with a sharp rhubarb or plum sauce is a truly swoon-worthy combination.

These weightier wines are also perfectly at home with shellfish. In fact, vintage champagnes are often a better match for the richness of scallops and lobster than more delicate NV styles. Grilled lobster drenched in slightly browned butter and a side of fat fries sings even more sweetly when accompanied by a glass of rich fizz, as do pan-seared scallops in a butter and soy sauce. Vintage *blanc de blancs* combine weight with vivid acidity, and are particularly good in this context; they also work wonders with fish served with hollandaise sauce or, for that matter, eggs Benedict.

And what of sweet dishes? Generally speaking – and despite a widely held opinion in the Champagne region itself – rosé fizz doesn't tend to work well with pudding. You need a wine to be as sweet as the dessert itself to create a harmonious pairing, otherwise the fizz appears unnecessarily austere. Although **Demi-Sec champagne** has fallen out of fashion, it's the only style of sparkling wine that's worth opening at the end of a meal. It's vital to ensure, however, that the dessert is not overly sweet – *tarte au citron*, for instance, works well thanks to the combination of tangy citrus fruit and the buttery richness of the pastry. Truth be told, though, I'd probably hold fire on the champagne when it comes to the pudding course – it always feels a bit forced.

Despite stumbling at the last meal-time hurdle, champagne is clearly more than the wine world's equivalent of a party animal. Take a bottle out for dinner some time – you might be pleasantly surprised by both its gravitas and its versatile charms.

Kelli White (2022)

LITTLE BOMBS EVERYWHERE...

Kelli White takes a wry look at the theatre of uncorking champagne. Named as one of the top 10 US sommelier's in 2013, she has experience aplenty when it comes to serving this 'menace to society'…

Everything about that day was sticky – from the moment I woke to find the sheets fused to my skin, up to the evening shower where I washed off the dried wine. It was the hottest day of the year in Boston, and humid as a cup of tea.

This was the type of heat that strains even the steadiest of tempers. The kind of day where crime spikes and relationships end. It was also murder on appliances.

I was fresh out of college and working in a wine store on the outskirts of the city. Our air conditioning unit was fragile on the best of days, but what it lacked in mettle it made up for in metal. It was a giant, hulking thing that hung over the entryway like a threat. No one knew its exact age, but it was clearly a relic of a former time (the Stone Age, the Bronze Age, the Giantfuckingairconditioner Age). And on this most scorching of days, it expired.

We didn't need a mechanic, we needed an archaeologist. Sadly, neither was available on such short notice. All around us, the city of Boston crackled with the death rattle of large electronics.

The store heated up quickly. I dug out two flimsy desk fans from the basement, neither of which helped. Eventually, we decided to prop open the beer fridge and pray that the compressor didn't overload.

Bedraggled customers in search of frosty beverages streamed in steadily, and each swing of the door let in a breath of fresh hell. Just keeping the coolers stocked was a full-time job.

I was walking down the sparkling aisle when it happened – a loud BANG followed by a splash of red liquid that soaked my shirt. I hit the ground and waited for the drive-by to conclude. 'Odd,' I remember thinking to myself, 'only one shot'. I was bracing for the pain that never came when I noticed the smell.

It was heady and decidedly grapey, with hints of strawberries and roses. The cork on the floor by my knee brought the picture into focus: a bottle of Brachetto happened to blow its top just as I strolled by.

I looked up to see a man standing over me. As soon as he determined I was unharmed, he asked for a bottle of champagne. 'Are you looking for a particular style?' I enquired, staggering to my feet. The customer looked me up and down before replying. 'Cold.'

Sparkling wine was a menace. I already knew that, having been previously shot in the throat by a champagne stopper. But other than the suspicious bruise on my neck that caused my relationship momentary angst, the damage was minor. I was lucky. My trachea could have been seriously crushed. And while I learned to stop storing my open bubbles in the swinging refrigerator door, I never ceased reaching for champagne. I guess I feel like the risk is worth the reward.

I suppose we all do.

Some like it warm

Gay-Lussac's Law states that the pressure of a gas is directly proportional to its temperature. Heat up that gas and the molecules gain kinetic energy; this causes them to bump more frequently against the walls of their container, thereby increasing pressure. This law was formalized in 1802 but the relationship between temperature and pressure was first noted in the late 1600s by a French physicist, right around the same time champagne got sparkly. Coincidence? I can't help but wonder if our scientists discovered this association when trying to open warm bubbly.

However the link was uncovered, the challenges of opening all but the coldest bottles of champagne remain. Sometimes the results are dangerous, but other times they are charmingly embarrassing. Such is the story provided by James Lechner, whose colleague got himself in trouble when trying to open a slightly warm bottle of champagne during brunch service. 'Amidst the chaos of strollers and lattes,' recalls Lechner, 'and in mid-sentence description of dosage, *tirage*, etc, [my co-worker] gives in to the ineluctable pull to sip the rising foam emanating from the lip, as one would at home. Except he's not at home.' The entire table witnessed the blunder and responded, unexpectedly, with rousing laughter. Not only did they refuse his offer of a replacement bottle, they generously extended a glass to their bumbling server.

Sarah Bray's folly was less well-received. Though she had diligently stuffed her wine bag with ice packs that morning, the hot New York City sun had been going to work on her bottles of California sparkling wine, as it had on the subway stairs and uneven pavement. By the time she arrived at her destination, an upmarket, mid-town restaurant with a notoriously elusive buyer, her wares had turned into weapons. As she removed the stopper from the first bottle of Iron Horse, the entire contents erupted over her hair, outfit and the surrounding area. The sommelier politely offered a serviette which the mortified sales rep used to dry her face. 'After all that,' Bray is quick to chastise, 'he could have at least bought the wine.'

A chance of rain is always on the forecast when under pressure and operating a pressurized beverage. This is a lesson that Abby Oliveras, Champagne Ambassador for Skurnik Wines in New York City, learned back in her restaurant days. It was a particularly popular night for a certain Crémant de Jura rosé, which meant all the pre-chilled bottles had been served, so Oliveras had to ice one down quick. 'The bottle was wet, so the cork came out into my hand while the bottle flew backwards.' According to Oliveras, the bottle completed two somersaults in the air before she caught it by the neck. 'It was magical, and I inhaled in relief. But then the wine shot out like a geyser and starting raining on the customers,' she recalls with a laugh. 'The only thing I could think of was to aim it towards myself… I got completely soaked.' This would not be her last run-in with a slippery bottle. 'At an American Express conference, during a quiet presentation, another wet bottle escaped me,' she confesses. 'This one snaked across the floor 15 metres with me running after it before I could catch it.'

Shaken, not stirred

Sometimes, a perfectly cold bottle of champagne will still misbehave. In these instances, the problem is usually the cork. After all, the average bottle of champagne contains six bars of pressure. That can result in considerable oomph, especially if encouraged.

Susan Sueiro of Obsidian Wine Company had a memorable childhood Christmas. 'My mother and grandmother spent the whole day making a huge Christmas Eve dinner,' she recounts. 'As we sat down with the untouched food on the table, my Argentine Uncle, who looked, acted and drank like Dean

Martin, made a festive show of popping the cork with his thumbs.' Over the table hung a heavy Spanish chandelier with blown glass bulbs. 'The cork hit the chandelier and glass rained down on the whole untouched meal. Fortunately, no one was hurt, but it all went in the trash and I believe I had cereal for dinner.'

At least Sueiro's misfortune was confined to immediate family. Other champagne gaffes have more public consequences. In 2012, Madison Michael was working at a hotel in Napa Valley. 'I opened a bottle at a table during Mother's Day brunch,' she recounts. But the wily cork escaped her grip and cracked the plaster ceiling over the buffet table. Michael proceeds to paint a grim picture: 'A film of gypsum dust [showered down] on the lobster tails, devilled eggs, on the caviar service, and the poor guy at the omelette station, not to mention the guests in line at the buffet.'

Older champagnes present their own suite of problems, even though their pressure is typically diminished. Specifically, the corks have a nasty habit of fusing to the inside of the bottleneck, which can make extraction difficult. David Beckwith, a fine wine advisor based in New York City, recently did battle with a particularly recalcitrant magnum of 1975 Dom Pérignon at a private client's house. 'No matter what I tried, the cork wouldn't budge,' he explains. 'After five to seven minutes I'm sweating from the effort and my hands are turning red and then the top of the cork just breaks off.' Beckwith moved to examine the cork fragment stuck inside the neck when it suddenly rockets out of the bottle, missing his eye by an inch. He gathered himself, shook off the adrenaline and tasted the wine, which had more surprises in store for him. 'It was corked,' he reports, flatly.

Not all victims are virtuous; sometimes, sparkling wine can be weaponized against the wicked. Rachel Allison conducted a demonstration on the proper procedure for opening sparkling wine and managed to 'spray Prosecco all over the living room' in the process. Looking back, she suspects foul play. 'I still think someone shook it before giving it to me because I was being slightly insufferable,' she admits, adding, 'I like to think I learned my lesson about unsolicited lectures!'

For wine industry or restaurant veterans, champagne catastrophes are inevitable, and almost a rite of passage; with the measure of a true pro being not in how often you avoid disaster but in how you handle the recovery. In this regard, Melissa Smith is as professional as they come. She was working as a wine steward at a Relais & Châteaux dude ranch in Montana when a guest ordered a bottle of Perrier-Jouët that had been 'rattling around in the lit soda refrigerator for God knows how long'. Smith dutifully opened the frazzled bottle, only to have it shoot out of her hands, land on the floor and spray her guests. Without missing a beat, she turned to them and pronounced: 'If it's any conciliation, you've been showered with our finest champagne.'

#Sabertownusa

When I began researching this chapter, I put out a social media call for funny or scary champagne stories. The response led me to two conclusions. First: an unusually high number of people have opened champagne with a combination of port tongs and super-soakers. Second: sabering should be outlawed.

Sabering a bottle of champagne is a dramatic bit of performance art wherein a person runs an object down the seam of the bottle until it hits the bottom lip of the neck. (The 'object' in question is usually a sword or kitchen knife, though many claim to have used the stem of a wine glass or, in one particularly brazen instance, a hotel fire extinguisher.) This takes advantage of the weakest part of the glass and, ideally, causes a clean break that sends the top of the neck and cork flying off into the sunset and leaves the majority of champagne in the bottle.

But circumstances are hardly ever ideal.

Lauren Acheson was working at a Seattle restaurant with a particularly showy chef. 'He was the kind of guy that put foie gras on everything,' she

The ultimate way for a showy chef to wow the crowd: slicing the top from a champagne bottle with a sabre. It makes a sensational start to a meal, but all too often ends with a hospital visit...

Little Bombs Everywhere...

describes. And so, one New Year's Eve service, he forced the front of house staff to 'simultaneously saber a bunch of *tête de cuvée* champagnes in front of the restaurant'. Acheson was handed a Nicolas Feuillatte's Palmes D'Or. Covered in raised indentations, this iconic wine has long been nicknamed 'the grenade', and on this evening it earned its moniker. Despite being well-practised with a saber, Acheson was 'cut clear down to the bone on the thumb'. Though she seems to regret the loss of wine more than the loss of blood. 'This is why you only saber cheap bottles,' she advises.

Sabering has long been a popular sommelier trick, but Patrick Cappiello arguably took the practice to new heights (or depths) at his now-shuttered lower Manhattan wine bar, Pearl & Ash. There, sabering was a nightly affair. Upon a guest's request, Cappiello would ascend the bar, curved sword held high, and slash the throats of some of the world's rarest champagnes. The antics were often immortalized on Instagram, along with the hashtag #sabertownusa, a play on celebrity chef Guy Fieri's Flavortown.

Sabertown went viral, and even earned Cappiello a handful of TV appearances. At first, he relished the act, snarling with fresh enthusiasm at each swipe. But eventually, he grew weary of the repetition, like a seasoned musician in a prison of his own greatest hits.

One particularly busy night, Cappiello and another sommelier climbed up opposite sides of the bar to perform an act of synchronized sabering. 'We do it, and I look over at Kimberly, and she has this horrified look on her face.' His partner had cut her hand badly and had to run to the kitchen to patch it up. 'In retrospect, it was all pretty dumb,' Cappiello offers, then laughs. 'But it felt pretty rock and roll at the time!'

Lauren Acheson knows her way around fizz.

ELEVEN ERAS OF CHAMPAGNE

Champagne across 400 years... Over the generations it has confounded the experts, been pummelled by war, transcended the cocktail age and experienced revolution in its vineyards. Here are its eleven eras, 1662 to 2022:

1 THE ENGLISH INVENT IT...
Stephen Skelton MW (2021)

2 FRANCE PERFECTS IT...
Hugh Johnson (1989/2021)

3 CHAMPAGNE'S ARTISTIC DEBUT
Tom Stevenson (2020)

4 THE BIRTH OF MOËT
Henry Vizetelly (1882)

5 MOËT GETS INDUSTRIAL
Henry Vizetelly (1882)

6 GOOD TIMES IN THE BELLE EPOQUE
Serena Sutcliffe MW (1988)

7 WAR, RAGE AND THE 'ROARING TWENTIES'
Tom Stevenson (1986)

8 ESCAPE FROM THE WEINFÜHRERS
Don and Petie Kladstrup (2001)

9 FIZZ, BUBBLY, POP IN THE SWINGING SIXTIES
Evelyn Waugh (1964)

10 CHAMPAGNE, OUR SOCIAL SIGNIFIER
Joe Fattorini (2022)

11 THE PLATINUM ERA
Robert Walters (2022)

Stephen Skelton MW (2021)

| THE ENGLISH INVENT IT…

In four vignettes from his book, *The Knight Who Invented Champagne*, Stephen Skelton charts the origins of sparkling wine back to the 17th-century taverns of, not France, but England, via a sequence of events – a Royal warrant, the Navy in crisis, the discovery of a new 'toughened' glass – culminating in a scientific paper that changed everything.

Nobody needed to invent sparkling wine because carbon dioxide – the gas that accounts for the fizz – is one of the main by-products of an alcoholic fermentation. Allow yeast to start multiplying in the presence of sugar and three main things are produced: carbon dioxide, a small amount of heat and alcohol. Winemakers wondering whether a barrel of grape must they are hoping has started to ferment will typically hold their ear to the bung hole. If it has started fermenting, however slowly, they will hear the tell-tale 'pop, pop, pop' of carbon dioxide gas being produced.

The practice of making wine from fruit has been one of man's pursuits for at least 8,000 years and possibly longer. Crushed fruit, left in a suitable container and at a suitable temperature, will spontaneously ferment using yeasts either on the fruit itself or present in the atmosphere. One can imagine the delight of the first caveman or woman who realized that their container (perhaps a sheep or a goatskin?) of rather battered, bruised and perhaps partially crushed berries had produced a liquid that was slightly sweet, slightly sparkling and possibly quite alcoholic. What was this mind-altering substance and where did it come from? One can also imagine that this news would travel quickly and it would not take long before our inventive caveperson was selecting the ripest, sweetest and easiest-to-crush fruit, placing it into a suitable container (a hollowed-out rock perhaps?) and impatiently waiting for it to turn into wine.

Although winemakers have come a long way in the intervening millennia, the essentials of winemaking have not: take ripe fruit, crush it, ferment it, drink it. OK, so there is a bit more to winemaking than this, and getting it

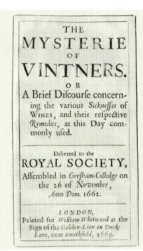

Christopher Merret (1614–95), English physician, scientist and polymath, was administratively controversial – he was expelled from the Royal Society in 1685 – but as a naturalist, his research was second to none. He was first to document the link between sugar and the sparkle in wine.

into a bottle so that it is stable and will keep, so that it can be enjoyed at some future date, takes care and suitable machinery, but essentially the job is the same. The production of sparkling wine differs from the production of still wine in that during fermentation, whether a primary fermentation or a secondary fermentation (where additional sugar and yeast are added to still wine), the carbon dioxide naturally produced is captured in the container.

The one thing that is common to all sparkling wines is the requirement to have a bottle strong enough to withstand the pressure created during fermentation and the often arduous journey from winery to customer. Shocks to the bottle during production, rough handling and changes in temperature can all cause a bottle with weaknesses to crack and explode. The story of the development of sparkling wine is therefore not so much one of how the wine was made sparkling – this was probably understood by the earliest winemakers – but how a glass bottle was developed which would withstand the pressures involved.

Setting the scene…

It is 1615. Shakespeare is still alive and the country is at peace. James I of England (James VI of Scotland) has been on the throne since the childless Elizabeth I died in 1603. The English Navy, which had been founded as a standing force by Henry VIII and had defended the country from several Spanish Armadas during the Elizabethan era, has been neglected. It needs rebuilding to face both the challenges from the Dutch, French and Spanish fleets, and to secure the trade routes to the new-found lands in the west: the Americas and the West Indies. This means new ships and a requirement for plenty of stout English and Welsh oak. Luckily for James, one of his closest advisors is an admiral, Sir Robert Mansell, who, having given up his naval career and become an industrialist and entrepreneur (as well as a Member of Parliament), saw an opportunity to secure his new-found business of coal mining and glassmaking. Mansell applied to the King to grant him a patent forbidding the use of timber for smelting (mainly iron and glass), and on May 23rd 1615 the papers were signed.

The document in question was called 'A Proclamation touching Glasses' and it prohibited the use of all wood and wood products (charcoal) in the glass industry. In a very few years, any process that needed massive amounts of heat, of which glassmaking and iron smelting were the main ones, turned them from being industries which had to be near their fuel source – basically in the middle of a forest where wood was abundant – to those that could settle in one spot, preferably near a port, on a navigable river or a canal, where fuel – coal, the necessary alternative to wood – could be delivered by ship. It is worth remembering that nowhere in Britain is further than around 65 miles from a tidal port, and most of the inhabited parts of the country are under half that distance from a navigable river or canal. It was this ability to access, readily and cheaply, a 'never-ending', high-quality source of fuel that turned glassmaking from a cottage industry producing rustic *waldglas* (the German term for 'wood glass') into an industrial one that produced reliable, perfectly formed, robust glass for domestic utensils, packaging and windows, the principal uses for glass in those early days.

Thus, with the stroke of his quill, the King started the Industrial Revolution that turned the British Isles from an agrarian economy, based upon wool, water power and wind power, to one where coal and steam brought about unimaginable developments in trade and industry. It was following the signing of the 1615 patent that glassmaking in Britain went from a peripatetic business which chased the fuel from clearing to clearing in the dwindling forests to one where the fuel travelled to the kilns. By virtue of the fact that kilns didn't have to move as the wood ran out, they could be bigger and better, brick-built with chimneys and flues, which made the glass more durable and therefore more useable. It was into this exciting, changing world of glassmaking that Sir Kenelm Digby (it is thought) developed his *verre Anglais* bottles which enabled the production of sparkling bottle-fermented ciders and wines.

Sparkling wine, by happy accident…
[a fictional account of the discovery]

It's 1632 and it's cold, very cold. King Charles I is on the throne and it's mid-February. George Blankpain is waiting outside the Rummer Inn in Newnham on Severn for the dray that is bringing eight barrels of wine up from the docks.

George is 17 and has been working at the Rummer for almost two years… The cellar of a busy inn is not a bad place to work. Cool in the summer and warm(ish) in the winter, and with no one to oversee him, George is his own master. As long as he makes sure the beer is fresh, checking each barrel as it arrives from Kemp's brewery and confirming that the barrels are marked with the date and used in strict rotation, Mr Jones (the landlord) has no complaints. George also has to look after the ciders, the meads and – his favourites – the wines.

George has decided that wine is strange. He knows that it varies from barrel to barrel and that this year's wines are very different from last year's. He has already had one delivery of the new wines from the 1631 vintage, and they have been well-received. Jones buys two types of wine: the light red wines known as 'Clairet' from the Gironde and white wines (in fact they are slightly grey – like the eye of a partridge) from Sillery, a village in the Champagne region.

The beer, of course, comes straight from the barrel – drawn through a wooden tap directly into tankards made of pewter or into serving jugs which are taken out to the customers. Cider and wine always used to be served like this, but in recent years things have changed. George has persuaded Mr Jones to put some of the wines into the new glass bottles that they are now making at the glassworks where his father works. This is one of Admiral Mansell's new coal-fired glassworks and one where Mansell's friend Sir Kenelm Digby has been involved with designing the new kilns. The bottles they are now making are darker, thicker and more robust than the bottles they used before, and are also of a different design to those previously made. They have a thick base, with a pronounced dimple in the bottom, and a long, slender neck which ends with a protruding ring which can be used to secure the bung with string to stop it from coming out. Why the bung would want to come out after it has been pushed home is a perplexing question and one that George has been thinking about.

When barrels of wine arrive from the ship, the first thing to be done is to get them onto the baulks of timber that sit on the cellar floor, make sure the bung holes are on top, and let them settle for a day or two. Then it's time to knock the barrels either side of the bung with the 'flogger', spring the bungs out and taste the wines. Most of them are really dry and astringent. The red wines are often a bit sharp and tannic, but so many customers, at least in the winter, drink these 'mulled' – with the addition of herbs, honey and usually served slightly warm – so they will be fine. The white wines from Sillery, on the other hand, vary quite a bit. George has noticed that some of them have a little touch of sweetness and are more pleasant to the palate. These barrels he marks with a chalk mark and makes sure that, once bottled, they are stored in a quiet corner of the cellar and kept for special customers.

It's now June 1632 and not far off Midsummer's Day. The beer and ciders keep on arriving, although cider from last year's apples is now getting scarce and is of questionable quality. Until the apples are ready to be harvested again in late September and October, the Rummer's customers will have to make do with ale – as long as there is barley there is always ale – mead and, of course, wine.

George has noticed that some of the 'special' wines he bottled in the spring have become slightly sparkling and that when the twine securing them is cut, the bungs fly out with some force, the wine foaming out of the bottle and sparkling in the glass as it is poured. He had asked the landlord why this might be, but in his mind he knew. It must have something to do with the touch of sweetness in the wines he had put aside. He hardly dare suggest this to Jones, but, plucking up courage, he did. 'Well, we can soon tell if that's the case,' Jones said without much conviction, 'go and get some lump sugar from the kitchen and put a small piece in some bottles and we will see what happens.'

At the next bottling, he did as he was told. Selecting the best bottles, those without any visible cracks or faults and with a good ring around the neck, he popped a piece of lump sugar about the size of a walnut into each of a dozen bottles and waited to see what would occur. It didn't take long to find out. With a July heatwave under way, the cellar warmed up and within two weeks of the bottling George walked into the cellar to see three of his 'specials' split in half, four without bungs and five still intact. He thought he ought to open one of the good ones to see what had happened to the wine. Taking out his pocketknife, he started to cut the twine, but before he was halfway through, the bung flew out and the wine foamed out of the bottle a yard into the air. He rushed up to find Mr Jones. 'Taste this and see what you think,' he said. He poured a glass of the sparkling, foaming wine and put it to his lips. 'My God, George, you have got something there – it's delicious. You get back down that cellar and get bottling. We've got a winner – sparkling wine!'

Lining the facts up

Thirty years later, towards the end of 1662 (six years before Dom Pérignon set foot in Hautvilliers), two members of the Royal Society, Dr Walter Charleton and Dr Christopher Merret, proposed to read papers on different aspects of wine and its treatment. On December 17th 1662, Merret read his paper headed: 'Some Observations Concerning the Ordering of Wines'. The opening paragraph states:

The mystery of wines consists in the making & meliorating of natural wines. Melioration is either of sound or virtuous wines. Sound wines are bettered by preserving and by timely fining and by mending colour, smel and tast [sic].

On the last page, Merret acknowledges that raisins plus sugar of some sort makes 'flat' wines 'recover':

Flat wines recovered with Spirit of wines, raysins and Sugar or Molassey and Sacks, by drawing them on fresh lees.

Flat is generally taken to mean still, that is, not sparkling, therefore adding a source of yeast (raisins) plus sugar would cause re-fermentation. He continues:

Our wine coopers of later times use vast quantities of Sugar and Molosses to all sorts of wines to make them drink brisk & sparkling & to give them spirit as also to mend their bad tastes, all which raysins & Cute & stum perform.

(Merret says: *'Stum is nothing else but a pure wine kept from fretting'* [fermenting]. 'Cute' is grape juice concentrate.)

This revelation to the members of the Royal Society that their wine was being sweetened and made to sparkle in the glass didn't raise any eyebrows or hackles. They were all men of the world and knew that most wines (and ciders) needed 'improving', especially late in the season when, getting tired, they had started to oxidize, or worse, turn to vinegar… But how much more conclusive it would have been if Merret had mentioned 'brisk and sparkling' in relation to bottled wine…!

Extracts from *The Knight Who Invented Champagne – How Sir Kenelm Digby developed robust glass bottles* (verre Anglais) *which enabled wine and cider-makers to produce bottle-fermented sparkling wines and ciders* by Stephen Skelton MW (London) 2021.

> Hugh Johnson (1989/2021)
>
> # 2 FRANCE PERFECTS IT…
>
> Champagne, before it sparkled, was a pale wine from black Pinot Noir grapes. At the Abbey of Hautvillers Dom Pérignon perfected its still form, but as he deplored 'instability' of any kind, bubbles came as an unwanted surprise. As Hugh Johnson observes, the fashion for '*mousseux*' took hold all the same, in the 1690s, far from the hands of the good monk…

Of all the world's great wines, only one is popularly credited with an inventor. The wine is champagne, and the man held responsible a Benedictine monk, Dom Pierre Pérignon, the treasurer of the Abbey of Hautvillers, which has overlooked the river Marne from its vine-covered slope since the time of the ascetic St Columbanus. Hautvillers was founded in 650 in the spirit of Columbanus, to be a place of untiring work and prayer. Its fame, as well as its holiness, was ensured by the possession of what were believed to be the remains of the body of St Helena, the mother of the Emperor Constantine. But since the archives of the Abbey disappeared in the French Revolution, neither allegation, the relics or the invention, is any longer capable of proof or disproof.

Many different claims have been made about good Father Pérignon. The easiest to dismiss is that champagne suddenly became sparkling in his cellars. Many legends about him, such as the idea that he was blind, that he was the first to use corks, that he said 'I am drinking stars', or that he could unfailingly name a precise vineyard by tasting a single grape, seem to have been inspired by the fantasies of the last treasurer of the Abbey, Dom Grossard, who was obliged to leave when the Revolution closed it down.

It may be argued that Grossard had had access to the lost archives (although nobody before him had told these stories), but it seems more likely that he simply rather liked to embroider the already lofty reputation of his predecessor. For Pérignon seems to have become almost the patron saint of Champagne within his own lifetime. It is intriguing that we can only surmise the reason why.

When Dom Pérignon was appointed treasurer of Hautvillers in 1668, at the age of 29, the Abbey was just finding its feet after a catastrophic 30 years of continual wars and military occupations. The position of Champagne on the map, at one of Europe's great crossroads, has made it perpetually prone to the tramp of armies since the beginning of history, as well as making it a natural centre for commerce: witness its pan-European fairs of the Middle Ages. The Hundred Years' War repeatedly devastated parts of the region. Then, in 1560, Hautvillers was destroyed in the Wars of Religion and its monks retired to Reims for 40 years. When they rebuilt and reoccupied the Abbey, a brief generation of peace was to pass before the marches and countermarches of the Thirty Years' War again turned Champagne into a great military parade ground. The civil wars of the 'Fronde' brought years of occupation by mercenaries up to 1659. Whichever side they were on, they were equally destructive. The troops of Marshal Turenne drank 600 barrels of wine at Hautvillers alone. 'It is not dogs that the king sends to guard his flock, but wolves,' wrote a miserable citizen of Reims.

In the 1660s, the people of Champagne had not seen the last of armies, although the battles were over for a while. Louis XIV's wars in the Netherlands and Germany kept troops continuously camped in or marching through the region. But however frustrating and menacing they were, this was the time when champagne made its great leap to prominence; a feat greater and more far-reaching even than the activities of the de Pontacs in Bordeaux in the very same years.

IN A SENSE CHAMPAGNE WAS ONLY RECOVERING LOST GROUND. It had been acknowledged in Paris in the 15th century that the wines of Aÿ (originally considered among the '*vins de France*', rather than coming from a distinct region) were of exceptional quality. In the early 16th century, King François I was glad to call himself 'Roi d'Aÿ et de Gonesse' – Gonesse was the place reputed to produce the finest flour for white bread in the north of France. The name of Aÿ came to be used as shorthand for the whole district, just as 'Beaune' was used for Burgundy. The same wines were alternatively known as '*vins de la rivière*': wines, that is, from the north bank of the Marne opposite Epernay. The vineyards here slope steeply up to the 'mountain' that separates the Marne valley from the district of Reims. 'Mountain' is a slight exaggeration for this substantial flat-topped hill, crowned with a forest of beech, but '*vins de la montagne*' was the term for the less highly esteemed production of the vineyards on its gentle northern slope.

In the later years of the 16th century the wines of the mountain also found a powerful advocate at court: Pierre Brulart, a privy councillor of King Henri III, a Parisian who had married the heiress of a great estate at Sillery, near Reims, with vineyards on its southern flank at Verzenay, Mailly and Ludes. Their son Nicholas became Chancellor of France under the great and benevolent Henri IV, the king who will always be remembered for desiring that every Sunday every peasant in France should be able to have a *poule au pot*. Nicholas's son was ennobled in 1621 by Louis XIII as Marquis de Sillery, and Sillery was to remain one of the great wine names of the world for nearly two centuries.

THE ABBEY THAT RECRUITED DOM PÉRIGNON as its treasurer had already set its sights on developing its wine business. The Brularts were an example of what could be done, and since the Wars of Religion Saint Helena was no longer the pilgrim-puller she had been. In 1661 the Abbot commissioned a great new vaulted cellar. Hautvillers possessed a modest 25 acres of vineyards of its own, but was paid tithes of grapes from villages around; most notably Aÿ and Avenay. The payment of these tithes was a matter for endless wrangling that raises the most fundamental question about the wine of the region at the time. We know that it was not sparkling. We know they were growing black grapes, the Pinot Noir among them. But was the wine red or white, or something in between?

The debate arose over tithes because they were collected in kind, in the vineyards, during the vintage. Small barrels called 'trentins' were distributed, and had to be filled with grapes packed tight by treading. In the case of Aÿ, the Abbey had the right to one barrel in 11. The citizens objected that if they trod their grapes into the trentins the juice would be stained red by the skins. It ruined their chance of making their best wine, which was white. They would prefer to pay in wine (or cash) when the wine was made.

The question of red or white was crucial because the region had deliberately set out to compete with Burgundy as far back as the days of the Valois Dukes. It was probably then, in the 15th century, that Pinot Noir was planted. And red was what was wanted. Reims was on the road followed by Flemish wine merchants travelling to Beaune; they were glad to be offered a cheaper alternative with a similar flavour and after a shorter journey. Their wines did not quite achieve the '*moëlleux*', the richness, of burgundy, but their colour could be (and was) deepened with elderberries.

Dom Pérignon was a skilled cellar manager but his greatest achievements lay in making wine white rather than in making it sparkle. There's little doubt, however, that his careful techniques paved the way for the perfection of the *méthode champenoise*.

Why then did the people of Aÿ want to make white? Because experience showed that if their red could never be truly first class, their best attempts at white wine could. This was presumably even more true of the Brularts' wine at Sillery, which does not have the advantage of a south slope to ripen its Pinot Noir. White wine made from white grapes had nothing like the same flavour and, they found, quickly turned 'yellow'. What they actually made was a very pale wine, varying with the vintage from claret colour to '*gris*' (grey), a slightly darkened white, but more often '*oeil de perdrix*' (partridge eye), a shade of delicate pink caused by the white juice having brief contact with the red skins. Hence the fuss about the trentins for the tithes. And hence, it seems probable, the first success of Dom Pérignon. He organized the harvesting in such a way as to achieve truly white wine, and at the same time studied the best vineyards, the best timing, the best techniques, and the best way of preserving the wine to make it as aromatic as possible, silky in texture and long in flavour.

The golden rules of winemaking that were established in Dom Pérignon's time, presumably by him, were set out in 1718, three years after his death, by the very precise Canon Godinot. First, use only Pinot Noir. The region's vineyards also contained Meunier, Pinot Gris (or Fromenteau), Pinot Blanc (or Morillon), Chasselas and perhaps Chardonnay, but Dom Pérignon did not approve of white grapes, partly because they increased a latent tendency in the wine to referment.

Second, prune the vines hard so that they grow no higher than three feet and produce a small crop.

Third, harvest with every precaution so that the grapes are kept intact, on their stalks, and as cool as possible. Work early in the morning. Choose showery days in hot weather. And reject any grapes that are broken or even bruised. Small grapes are better than big ones. Lay out wicker trays in the vineyard and pick over the crop for rotten grapes, leaves or anything undesirable. Even lay a damp cloth over the grapes in the sun. They must be kept fresh at all costs. If possible, have the press-house nearby so that you can carry the harvest in by hand, but if animals are essential, choose mules: they are less excitable than horses. Failing mules, donkeys.

Fourth, on no account tread the grapes or allow any maceration of the skins in the juice. An efficient and fast-working press is essential (peasants, therefore, stood no chance of making this kind of wine). The press must be used repeatedly and briefly, and the juice from each pressing kept apart. The first, the '*vin de goutte*', runs with the mere weight of laying on the wooden beams. Its wine alone is too delicate; it lacks body. The next two pressings, the first and second *tailles* or 'cuts' (because the cake of grapes must be cut up and replaced in the press) are of good quality. The fourth, the '*vin de taille*' is rarely acceptable, and any further 'cuts' are '*vins de pressoir*', but this time distinctly coloured and of no use to the perfectionist cellarmaster. The press-house workers were completely exhausted by the quick-fire work, day after day for three weeks or more. That was part of the price for extraordinarily fine wine.

ALL REPORTS AGREE THAT DOM PÉRIGNON studied his raw materials with the minutest care. It is true that he tasted his grapes. It was his habit to pick them in the evening and leave them all night by his open window before tasting them in the morning. Perhaps a very slight concentration of flavour took place overnight. He was a man of very abstemious habits. A newspaper reported after his death that 'this monk, whom one would expect to be a gourmet, never drank wine and lived almost entirely on cheese and fruit'. Could this explain the delicacy of his palate?

The blending of wines was a regular practice, but Pérignon, it is said, blended the grapes from different vineyards before they even went into the press. He had three press-houses at his disposal, and grapes from many different plots. It was his discovery that carefully judged proportions of grapes from a number of different vineyards, according to their ripeness and the distinctive flavours derived from their soils, made a better and more consistent wine than lots pressed individually. It is the exact opposite of the philosophy of Cîteaux, whose monks strove to distinguish and differentiate, letting the soil show through the Pinot Noir. At its simplest it could be explained as an attempt to guarantee quality and consistency, which makes it sound almost suspiciously like the public-relations patter of a modern Champagne house.

The more one learns about Dom Pérignon, the harder it is to decide exactly what he did to make his Abbey's wines as valuable as their invoices show that they were. In 1700 the 'most excellent' wines of the region sold for 500 livres a cask, but those of Hautvillers (and also of another Abbey, St-Pierre-aux-Monts at Pierry, whose treasurer, Dom Oudart, was a friend and colleague of Dom Pérignon's) sold for 800 to 900 livres. So famous was Pérignon by this time that Parisians took him to be a village like Aÿ or an abbey like Hautvillers, and looked for his name on the map. But the most impressive evidence of the advance of champagne in his lifetime is the fact that in 1706 it was reported that 'a recent traveller had drunk champagne in Siam and Surinam'. Such travels would have been impossible without the mastery of bottling. We should look in the cellar as well as the vineyard and the press-house to see what advances the famous monk was making.

His region's wine presented one great problem to Pérignon. It had an inherent instability: a tendency to stop fermenting as the cold weather closed in come autumn, then start again with rising temperatures in spring. This did no harm while the wine was still in cask in the cellar, but Pérignon was not enamoured of the cask. He found it 'tired' his wines and they lost all their famous aroma, unless they were bottled as soon as possible. Pérignon used intensive cellar work to prepare them. The abbot Pluche, who seems to have known his methods, wrote in 1744: 'Lees and air are the two plagues of wine'. To rid the wine of all lees needed repeated rackings into clean barrels, with the attendant risk of exposing the wine to too much air. The answer was laborious: as many as 12 successive rackings by the method that allowed the least splashing and contact with air, by forcing the wine from one cask to another with a bellows providing pressure from the top.

The lighter and greener the wine, experience showed, the more subject it was to fizzing in the spring. White-grape wine was fizziest; one of the reasons why Pérignon used only black grapes. But black-grape wine, made with his precautions, also lasted and matured for far longer. 'Formerly, the wine of Aÿ lasted hardly a year,' wrote the abbot Pluche, 'but since white grapes have not been used in the wines of Champagne, those of the mountain of Reims keep for eight to 10 years, and those of the Marne easily go five or six.'

IN ENGLAND, cellar work was not so meticulous. A treatise under the title 'The Mysterie of Vintners' was presented to the newly formed Royal Society in 1662. Its subtitle tells all: 'A Brief Discourse concerning the various sicknesses of wines, and their respective remedies, at this day commonly used.' A wine merchant was a wine doctor. Among the remedies were beetroot for colouring pale claret, elderflowers, lavender, cinnamon, cloves, ginger... To preserve Rhenish must, the author tells us, the Dutch 'rub the insides of the vessel with cheese'. More alarmingly, 'country vintners feed their fretting wine with raw beef', and most off-putting, 'herrings roes preserve any stum [that is, muted or stopped] wine'. These are the practices of honest vintners. 'Many other ways there are of adulterating wines, daily practised in this our (otherwise well-governed) City.'

Many wines are mentioned by name. Champagne is not among them. But one sentence is momentous in our story: 'Our wine-coopers of later times use vast quantities of Sugar and molasses to all sorts of wines, to make them drink brisk and sparkling.' In the very next year, 1663, the satirist Samuel Butler, in his *Hudibras*, makes the first English mention of 'brisk Champagne'. Champagne was not a normal part of the repertoire of the English wine trade. But it was already known in London, and coming into fashion, three years after Charles II took the throne (and six years before Dom Pérignon moved to Hautvillers). And there is an implication (although less than evidence) that it was rather fizzy. By 1676 it was specifically described, on stage, as 'sparkling'.

WE KNOW WHO WAS RESPONSIBLE for the prompt modishness of champagne in London at a time when it was still a rarefied taste in Paris. It was the Marquis de St-Evremond, a soldier, courtier and irrepressible satirist who had been threatened with a third sojourn in the Bastille for a malicious letter he had written about Cardinal Mazarin, Louis XIV's prime minister. In Paris, St-Evremond and his friends were known as Epicureans, or laughingly as the Ordre des Coteaux because they would drink nothing but 'Coteaux d'Aÿ', 'Coteaux d'Hautvillers' or 'Coteaux d'Avenay'.

In London St-Evremond made himself the unofficial agent of champagne, with immediate effect. In 1664 the Earl of Bedford ordered three *tonneaux* of Sillery for his palace at Woburn. Buckingham, Arlington, all the grandees of the day took to the new taste. With it they ordered bottles and corks: the new strong bottle invented by Sir Kenelm Digby. Unlike the vintners, they probably did not 'use vast quantities of Sugar and molasses'. But they did find their champagne, bottled on arrival, was perceptibly fizzy, if not downright frothing, when they opened it months, perhaps even years, later. What is more, to the disgust of St-Evremond, they were delighted with the fizz, and rapidly noticed its uninhibiting effect. The old Epicure was as repelled by bubbles in his favourite wine as we would be by bubbles in our claret. Dom Pérignon was fully in agreement. It was his life's work to prevent champagne having bubbles, and make a white wine the court would prefer to red burgundy.

Needless to say, the bubbles won. It took much longer in France. Paris was already in love with the glorious white wine whose 'perfume so embalms the senses that it could raise one from the dead'. In 1674 champagne was 'so frantically fashionable that all other wines scarcely passed, in smart circles, as more than "*vinasse*"', or as we might say, plonk. Louis XIV had simply never drunk anything else. He was a great conservative. He never tried coffee or chocolate or tea, or spirits, until in 1695 his all-powerful physician Fagon put him onto a mixture of old ('*usé*') burgundy and water. The Burgundians were no doubt delighted, but by this time champagne was permanently established.

In 1691, Louis XIV gave the signal for the start of regular commerce in champagne. He created the office of '*courtier-commissionnaire*', giving (for a hefty price) the right to set prices, arrange purchases and take commissions, although not actually to buy and sell. This essential activity was still done by personal courtiers or at an open market: buying to hold stock was not unknown, but it was illegal. It was also illegal to sell or transport champagne in anything but barrels. A trade in sparkling champagne was therefore strictly speaking impossible. Admittedly, wine was delivered in bottles by, among others, Dom Pérignon. He wrote in 1694: 'I gave' (he does not say sold) '26 bottles of wine, the best in the world'. It was also impossible up to this time for another reason: France did not have bottles strong enough to take any pressure. Her glassworks were still wood-fired. There were many experiments with different shapes, from globes to pears, and English glass blowers went to work at Ste-Menehould, the nearest glasshouse. But the problem remained until the 1730s: if champagne became really '*mousseux*', the bottle would probably burst.

The precise Canon Godinot gives us the best indication of when the fashion changed. In 1718 he wrote, 'for more than 20 years French taste has preferred *vin mousseux*'. To reconcile the state of taste and the lack of bottles is a problem. The solution, perhaps, is that '*mousseux*' is a relative term. Given only the natural tendency to referment (and no English-style addition of sugar), wine bottled in March (the full moon was preferred, when high atmospheric pressure helps to keep the wine 'tranquil' and clear) would be variably fizzy, but probably most often in the condition known today as '*crémant*' with just enough gas to pop the cork.

An English play of 1698, about the date Godinot indicates, seems to confirm the state of sparkle. The play is *Love and a Bottle* by the Dubliner George Farquhar. Club, the valet of the fashionable Mr Mockmode, pours out his champagne. 'See how it puns and quibbles in the glass,' he says: a marvellously apt image for the jostling of random bubbles in a *crémant* wine, less apt for the racing streamers of bubbles in a fully sparkling one. The French used various terms for this slightly foamy wine: '*sablant*', '*pétillant*' or '*mousseux*' all meant the same thing.

BY THE TIME DOM PERIGNON WAS 60, fashion was demanding more and more of the sparkling wine he had spent his career trying to avoid. Nobody knew more about it than he – his experience of cellar work would have been invaluable whether you wanted bubbles or not. He certainly knew, for example, that the cooler the vintage and the lighter and more acidic the wine, the less fully it fermented in autumn; therefore, the more potential it had for sparkling the following year. White wines from white grapes were lighter and more prone to referment, so, to follow the trend, a proportion of them was increasingly added. At first the desire for sparkle led makers into overdoing the under-ripeness. The Epernay landowner and one of the first champagne merchants, Bertin de Rocheret, described one champagne in about 1700 as 'green and hard as a dog, dry as the devil'. 'Montagne' wines were rarely used: the famous Sillery remained '*vin gris*', and utterly tranquil, until the early 19th century; the champagne of old-fashioned, unfrivolous connoisseurs. Increasingly, the best white-grape wines came from certain villages on the hills south of Epernay: Cramant, Avize, Le Mesnil were recognized for qualities of their own.

A most important factor, increasingly so with sparkling wines, was good cellarage. Deep cellars with unchanging temperatures could make all the difference between bottles bursting or not. The sub-soil (and indeed the soil) of Champagne is solid chalk. 'Spreading the butter of vegetation on the dry bread of chalk', is how one writer describes agriculture in the region. Chalk, happily, is the ideal material for excavating deep, capacious cellars that have little risk of collapse. It is said that Dom Ruinart, another religious colleague of Dom Pérignon's, made the momentous discovery, under the city of Reims itself, of gigantic, funnel-shaped chalk quarries dug by the Romans for building stone and long since forgotten. Ruinart's nephew Nicolas founded what is considered the oldest surviving Champagne 'house', using these '*crayères*', in 1729. In 1716 an even more familiar name had made its appearance: Claude Moët, a grower of Epernay, bought himself the recently created office of a *courtier-commissionnaire*. Now that champagne-making was becoming so complicated, involving capital to buy and bottle wine, the development of a specialized manufacturing side to the business was inevitable.

STILL THE FIZZINESS OR OTHERWISE of the wine remained a hit-and-miss affair, and the sufficient strength of the bottles extremely uncertain. So much so that once an order was placed the risk of '*casse*', of the bottles bursting, was borne by the purchaser. Depending largely on the vintage, anything between 20 percent and 90 percent of the bottles exploded. It was then the height of folly to walk through a champagne cellar without wearing an iron mask to protect your face from flying glass.

By 1735 the business was well-enough established for a royal ordinance to dictate the shape, size and weight of champagne bottles, the size of cork they should use (stipulated as being an inch and a half long) and the way they should be tied down with strong pack thread to the collar of the bottle. Since the pressure was unpredictable, all champagnes, whether sparkling or not, were lashed down in the same way.

There remained the question of sediment. Any refermentation produces a residue of dead yeast cells, which are trapped in the bottle and will look unsightly in the glass. Modern champagne-making, which involves adding both sugar and yeast to achieve a high degree of sparkle, produces so much sediment that removing it is an essential part of the process. But when there was only a little yeast left naturally in the wine the sediment was usually tolerable. Early 18th-century champagne glasses, elegant conical 'flutes', were often made with a dimpled surface to hide any slight sediment in the wine. In years when the sediment was substantial there was nothing for it but the uncertain and wasteful process of '*dépotage*', or decanting the wine into another bottle, losing a great deal of the precious gas en route. The modern system of '*remuage*', indeed the whole process understood by the term *méthode champenoise*, was not to begin for almost another hundred years. Throughout the 18th century the majority of champagne remained still wine (and much of it red). It was only a minority of light-minded customers (and rich ones, too) who became addicted to the '*saute-bouchon*'.

JUST HOW LIGHT-MINDED is made remarkably clear in the memoirs of the Regency that followed the death of Louis XIV in 1715. The later years of the Sun King's reign had been less than brilliant. Although Paris was enjoying an economic boom, life at Versailles was austere and boring. The Regent, Philippe d'Orléans, held a very different court at the Palais Royal. He surrounded himself with ladies of high rank and no morals at all, and the '*roués*', who were defined as 'men of the world, who have neither virtue nor principles, but who make their vices seductive, even ennobling them with elegance and wit'. Philippe himself coined the term *roué*; they were so wicked, he said, they deserved to be broken on the wheel.

The nightly '*petits soupers*' at the Palais Royal deserved all the scandalized gossip that surrounded them. The Duc de Richelieu laid all the blame on the fashionable wine: 'The orgies never started until everyone was in that state of joy that champagne brings.' The games were led by the Regent himself, who liked to see his mistresses (including the Duchesse de Berry, his own daughter) perform tableaux as Greek goddesses, although less modestly dressed. The candles were taken away to give free reign to the emotions provoked by champagne. Sometimes the host would wait until the darkness was full of sighs and then throw open a cupboard full of lighted candles to illuminate the luxurious scene.

NO OTHER WINE, no other drink, had ever created, by its special qualities, a whole mood that almost amounted to a way of life. We can speculate about what those qualities were, but it seems likely that we would recognize them. The perfectionism preached by the Abbey treasurer had given the world its first wine of unmistakable, irresistible quality: a model that all other wines with pretentions to excellence would have to emulate.

Extract from 'The First Perfectionist', Chapter 21 of *The Story of Wine, From Noah to Now*, by Hugh Johnson, Académie du Vin Library (London) 2021. Reproduced here with kind permission of the author.

Tom Stevenson (2020)

3 CHAMPAGNE'S ARTISTIC DEBUT

Tom Stevenson brings a magnifying glass and an analytical eye to Jean François de Troy's *Le Déjeuner d'Huîtres*, painted in 1735. This first depiction of sparkling champagne reveals a wine that is both the height of fashion and something of a novelty…

It could be said that Jean François de Troy's *Le Déjeuner d'Huîtres*, or *The Oyster Luncheon* (1735), is more famous in the world of wine than it is in the world of art, since it represents the first sparkling champagne to be captured in paint, the photography of its time.

Not that this is meant to infer de Troy (1679–1752) was a slouch as an artist. He was very successful and had been famous in his own lifetime, which is more than some grand masters could claim. He was one of France's leading historical painters and also painted frescos, including one in the north aisle of the ancient basilica of *Santi Bonifacio e Alessio* in Rome. Moreover, this particular painting was commissioned by none other than Louis XV, who wanted something that would express a *joie de vivre* for a new private dining room in his *petits appartements* at the Palace of Versailles, for which he paid De Troy 2,400 livres (about $28,000 by today's value) according to the king's fastidiously kept accounts.

At least one author has suggested it was commissioned to be hung in the room where Louis XV entertained Madame de Pompadour, but he did not meet her until 1744, the year before she became his *maîtresse en chef* (official chief mistress).

Le Déjeuner d'Huîtres is some 1.8 x 1.2 metres (6 x 4 feet) and currently hangs in the *Musée Condé* at the majestic Château de Chantilly, just north of Paris. It is compelling viewing, so if you are visiting the capital or make a dog-leg diversion when motoring from the UK to Champagne, it is well worth the 30 Euros entry fee. Château de Chantilly is also the most spectacular racecourse in the world and home to two of the most prestigious races in the France Galop, the Prix du Jockey-Club and the Prix de Diane Longines).

Jean François de Troy pioneered the *tableaux de mode*, a genre that diligently depicts the contemporary fashions and manners of the higher social classes in 18th-century France. In *Le Déjeuner d'Huîtres* we see the diners, just back from a hunt, eating oysters and drinking champagne in a sumptuously decorated room. Oysters were very fashionable among the elite at that time, and although medical books of the day alluded to the belief that they had aphrodisiac properties, the diners are exclusively male.

The round table is covered by a rectangular tablecloth, upon which we can see the bread, butter, salt, pepper and wild garlic, the traditional accompaniments to oysters in those days. There are young servants with a towel at their waist, shucking the oysters for the guests. Full oysters are arranged on the table in silver platters, while empty shells litter the floor. Older servants open and pour the champagne into stemmed glasses, which when not in use are overturned in painted porcelain bowls. Two bottles of unopened champagne are chilling in ice and water in the lead-lined compartments of a small *cellarette* in front of the table.

Finally, the fresco reproduced at the top of *Le Déjeuner d'Huîtres* is a pastiche of his own work, *Zéphyr et Flor* (circa 1725–26), an audacious example of self-advertisement.

I always find something different every time I look at this painting. Here are a few of my current thoughts:

1 The mushroom-shaped cork is clearly visible as is the string *ficelage* that held the cork in place as it sealed the bottle. This is the equivalent of the first photo of a champagne cork in flight!

2 This gentleman has just cut the string to release the cork using the knife held in his right hand. He has his thumb over the mouth of the bottle to prevent the champagne from gushing out. Note the typically 18th-century shape of the bottle with its distinct punt. Who is the producer? It can only be one of three: Ruinart (1729), Chanoine Frères (1730), Forest Fourneaux (Taittinger, 1734). Based on the way the present-day bottles look, then my money is on Ruinart.

3 Pouring from a height to increase the foam is an indication that, despite the cork flying high, the mousse was relatively weak in France in 1735. The glass is a regular wine glass, not a coupe or a flute. Note the way it is being held by both the diner and the server, clearly indicating this is the invention of modern-day wine geeks.

4 Again pouring from a height. The gentleman behind is obviously appreciating the mousse 'as it puns in the glass'.

5 None of the glasses in the painting are standing up; they are all either in hand or, as illustrated here, resting in bowls. The bowls are required for rinsing any glasses from sediment that would have still been in the bottle at this juncture.

6 More examples of geekily-held glasses.

7 Sealed bottles of champagne chilling in ice and water. The ice would come from the host's own ice house, which would be filled up every winter with tons of ice transported from frozen lakes (the ice destined for the great ice houses of Versailles came, for example, from Switzerland).

8 Jean François de Troy was an artist and draughtsman who was so renowned for his accuracy and detail that we can identify Calais as the source of the oysters being shucked from the size of the shells and colour of their flesh, yet the nobleman here – widely regarded by art historians as the host – is oddly proportioned. From the angle at which he is leaning, we can imagine where the top of the femur (thighbone) starts, which makes his upper leg seem improbably long. The humerus in his right arm is also suspiciously long, while his left arm is far from convincing in a way that has nothing to do with the cut of its sleeve, which is deliberately short to accommodate the ruffled cuffs. Were there originally two people sat here? Did one have to be cut and merged into one leaning figure to accommodate the knife hand of the bottle opener, which is so intrinsic to the composition? Or was the painting badly damaged and poorly repainted? After *Le Déjeuner d'Huîtres* was delivered to Versailles, highly skilled craftsmen carefully integrated it with the wall panelling, but it had to be removed in 1768, when the *petits appartements* were converted into offices and kitchens. According to the *Musée Condé*, the canvas had at one point been given a more regular shape and in 2000 it received a complete clean, which supposedly included the removal of repainted areas, yet the host of the lunch remains oddly proportioned. It seems to me that these clues are likely to lead to a more rational explanation of this mystery than the possibility of a meticulous draughtsman like de Troy painting such a malformed figure and being handsomely paid for it by the king of France.

This article by Tom Stevenson first appeared in *The World of Fine Wine* in 2020, and is reproduced here with kind permission of its editor, Neil Beckett, and the author.

> Henry Vizetelly (1882)
>
> # 4 THE BIRTH OF MOËT
>
> Early account-books from the house of Moët show how trade in the new sparkling wine was slow at first, but the period 1743–1833 saw a significant upturn. Writing in 1882, the London publisher and writer Henry Vizetelly takes up the story…

Those magnates of the champagne trade, Messrs Moët and Chandon, whose famous 'star' brand is familiar in every part of the civilized globe, and whose half-score miles of cellars contain as many million bottles of champagne as there are millions of inhabitants in most of the secondary European states, have their head-quarters at Epernay in a spacious château – in that street of châteaux named the Rue du Commerce, but commonly known as the Faubourg de la Folie which is approached through handsome iron gates, and has beautiful gardens in the rear extending in the direction of the river Marne. The existing firm dates from the year 1833, but the family of Moët – conjectured to have originally come from the Low Countries – had already been associated with the champagne wine trade for well-nigh a century previously.

If the Moëts came from Holland they must have established themselves in the Champagne at a very early date, for the annals of Reims record that in the 15th century Jean and Nicolas Moët were *échevins* [councillors] of the city. A Moët was present in that capacity at the coronation of Charles VII in 1429, when Joan of Arc stood erect by the principal altar of the cathedral with her sacred banner in her hand, and for having contributed to repulse an attempt on the part of the English to prevent the entrance of the Royal Party into the city, the Moëts were subsequently ennobled by the same monarch. A mural tablet in the church of St Remi records the death of D G Moët, Grand Prior, in 1554, and nine years later we find Nicol Moët claiming exemption at Epernay from the payment of *tailles* on the ground of his being a noble.

An old commercial book preserved in the family archives shows that in the year 1743 – at the epoch when the rashness of the Duc de Gramont saved

Jean-Rémy Moët, Maire d'Epernay (1758–1841). Pierre-Gabriel Chandon de Briailles (1778–1850).

the English army under George II from being cut to pieces at Dettingen – a descendant of the foregoing, one Claude Louis Nicolas Moët, who owned considerable vineyard property in the vicinity of Epernay, decided upon embarking in the wine trade. It is his son, however, Jean-Rémy Moët, born in 1758, who may be looked upon as the veritable founder of the present commerce in Champagne wines, which, thanks to his efforts, received a wonderful impulse, so that instead of the consumption of the vintages of the Marne being limited as heretofore to the privileged few, it spread all over the civilized world.

At Messrs Moët and Chandon's we had the opportunity of inspecting some of the old account-books of the firm, and more particularly those recording the transactions of Jean-Rémy Moët and his father. The first sales of sparkling wine, on May 23rd 1743, comprised 301 bottles of the vintage of 1741 to Pierre Joly, wine-merchant, *bon des douze chez le Roi*, whatever that may mean, at Paris; and a similar quantity to the Sieur Compoin, keeping the '*hotellerie ditte la pestitte Escurie*', Rue du Port Maillart, at Nantes in Brittany. The entry specifies that the wine for Nantes is to be left at Choisy-le-Roi, and taken by land to Orleans by the carters of that town, who are to be found at the

Ecu d'Orleans, Porte St Michel, Paris, the carriage as far as Choisy being 4 livres 10 deniers (about 4 francs) for the two half-baskets, and to Paris 3 livres 15 deniers for the basket.

Between 1750 and '60, parcels of wine were despatched to Warsaw, Vienna, Berlin, Konigsberg, Dantzig, Stettin, Brussels and Amsterdam; but one found no mention of any sales to England till the year 1788, when the customers of the firm included 'Milord' Farnham of London, and Messrs Felix Calvert and Sylvin, who had a couple of sample bottles sent to them, for which they were charged five shillings. In the same year Messrs Carbonnell, Moody and Walker (predecessors of the well-known existing firm of Carbonnell and Co) wrote in French for two baskets, of 10 dozens each, of *vin de champagne* 'of good body, not too charged with liqueur, but of excellent taste, and *not at all sparkling*!' while the Chevalier Colebrook, writing from Bath, requests that 72 bottles of champagne may be sent to his friend the Hon John Butler, Molesworth Street, Dublin, 'who if contented with the wine will become a good customer, he being rich, keeping a good house, and receiving many amateurs of *vin de champagne*.'

Shortly afterwards the chevalier himself receives 50 bottles of still wine, vintage 1783. In 1789, 120 bottles of champagne, vintage 1788, are supplied to 'Milord Findlater', of London – an ancestor, no doubt, of the wine-merchants of the same name carrying on business today, and whom the Moëts in their simplicity dubbed a 'Milord' – and in 1790 the customers of the house include Power and Michel, of 44 Lamb Street, London, and Manning, of the St Alban Tavern, the latter of whom is supplied on March 30th with 130 bottles of champagne at three livres, or two 'schillings' per bottle; while a month later Mr Lockart, banker, of 36 Pall Mall, is debited with 360 bottles, vintage 1788, at three shillings.

In this same year Monsieur Moët despatches a traveller to England named Jeanson, and his letters, some 200 in number, are all preserved in the archives of the house. On the 17th May 1790, he writes from London as follows: 'As yet I have only gone on preparatory and often useless errands. I have distributed samples of which I have no news. Patience is necessary, and I endeavour to provide myself with it. How the taste of this country has changed since 10 years ago! Almost everywhere they ask for dry wine, but at the same time require it so vinous and so strong that there is scarcely any other than the wine of Sillery which can satisfy them... Tomorrow I dine five miles from here, at Monsieur Macnamara's. We shall uncork four bottles of our wine, which will probably be all right.'

In May, 1792, Jean-Rémy Moët is married, and thenceforward assumes the full management of the house. On December 20th of the year following, when the Reign of Terror was fairly inaugurated, we find the accounts in the ledger opened to this or the other '*citoyen*'. The orthodox Republican formula, however, did not long continue, and '*sieur*' and '*monsieur*' resumed their accustomed places, showing that Jean-Rémy Moët had no sympathy with the Jacobin faction of the day.

In 1805 he became Mayor of Epernay, and between this time and the fall of the Empire received Napoleon several times at his residence, as well as the Empress Josephine and the King of Westphalia. The Emperor, after recapturing Reims from the Allies, came on to Epernay, on which occasion he presented Monsieur Moët with the cross of the Legion of Honour. In 1830 the latter was arbitrarily dismissed from his mayoralty by Charles X, but was speedily reinstated by Louis A Philippe, though he did not retain his office for long, his advanced age compelling him to retire from active life in the course of 1833. At this epoch the firm, which, since 1807 had been known as Moët and Co, was remodelled under the style Moët and Chandon, the two partners being Monsieur Victor Moët, son of the outgoing partner, and Monsieur P G Chandon, the descendant of an old ennobled family of the Mâconnais) who had married Monsieur Jean-Rémy Moët's eldest daughter.

The descendants of these gentlemen are today at the head of the business, the partners being on the one hand Monsieur Victor Moët-Romont and Monsieur C J V Auban Moët-Romont; and on the other, Messieurs Paul and Raoul Chandon de Briailles.

Extract from *A History of Champagne with notes on the other sparkling wines of France* by Henry Vizetelly, Vizetelly & Co (London) and Scribner & Welford (New York) 1882.

Henry Vizetelly (1882)

5 MOËT GETS INDUSTRIAL

A visit to Moët & Chandon's Epernay cellars in 1882 sees Henry Vizetelly highly impressed as he explores its endless hewn-chalk galleries and 'sufficiently mouldy' vaults. Making champagne on this grand scale proves not only to be complex and labour-intensive but, he finds, the processes involved can be fraught with danger too…

Facing Messrs Moët and Chandon's offices at Epernay is a range of comparatively new buildings, with their white façade ornamented with the well-known monogram M and C, surmounted by the familiar star. It is here that the business of blending and bottling the wine is carried on. Passing through the arched gateway access is obtained to a spacious courtyard, where carts laden with bottles are being expeditiously lightened of their fragile contents by the busy hands of numerous workmen. Another gateway on the left leads into the spacious bottle-washing room, which from the middle of May until the middle of July presents a scene of extraordinary animation. Bottle-washing apparatus, supplied by a steam-engine with 20,000 gallons of water per diem, are ranged in 15 rows down the entire length of this hall, and nearly 200 women strive to excel each other in diligence and celerity in their management, a practised hand washing from 900 to 1,000 bottles in the course of the day.

To the right of this *salle de rinçage*, as it is styled, bottles are stacked in their tens of thousands, and lads furnished with barrows, known as *diables*, hurry to and fro, conveying these to the washers, or removing the clean bottles to the adjacent courtyard, where they are allowed to drain, prior to being taken to the *salle de tirage* or bottling room.

The 'marrying'…

Before, however, the washing of bottles on this gigantic scale commences, le 'marrying' or blending of the wine is accomplished in a vast apartment, 250 feet in length and 100 feet broad, during the early spring. The casks of newly-vintaged wine which have been stowed away during the winter months, in the extensive range of cellars hewn out of the chalk underlying Epernay, where they have slowly fermented, are mixed together in due proportions in huge vats, each holding upwards of 12,000 gallons. Some of this wine is the growth of Messrs Moët and Chandon's own vineyards, of which they possess as many as 900 acres (giving constant employment to 800 labourers and vinedressers) at Aÿ, Avenay, Bouzy, Cramant, Champillon, Chouilly, Dizy, Epernay, Grauves, Hautvillers, Le Mesnil, Moussy, Pierry, Saran, St Martin, Verzy and Verzenay, and the average annual cost of cultivating which is about £40 per acre. At Aÿ the firm own 210 acres of vineyards; at Cramant and Chouilly, nearly 180 acres; at Verzy and Verzenay, 120 acres; at Pierry and Grauves, upwards of 100 acres; at Hautvillers, 90 acres; at Le Mesnil, 80 acres; at Epernay, nearly 60 acres; and at Bouzy, 55 acres. Messrs Moët and Chandon, moreover, possess *vendangeoirs*, or pressing-houses, at Aÿ, Bouzy, Cramant, Epernay, Hautvillers, Le Mesnil, Pierry, Saran and Verzenay, in which the large number of 40 presses are installed. At these *vendangeoirs* no less than 5,450 *pièces* of fine white wine, sufficient for 1,360,000 bottles of champagne, are annually made – that is, 1,200 *pièces* at Aÿ, 1,100 at Cramant and Saran, 800 at Verzy and Verzenay, and smaller quantities at the remaining establishments. All these establishments have their *celliers* and their cellars, together with cottages for the accommodation of the numerous vinedressers in the employment of the firm.

Extensive as are the vineyards owned by Messrs Moët and Chandon, the yield from them is utterly inadequate to the enormous demand which the great Epernay firm are annually called upon to supply, and large purchases have to be made by their agents from the growers throughout the Champagne. The wine thus secured, as well as that grown by the firm, is duly mixed together in such proportions as will ensure lightness with the requisite vinosity, and fragrance combined with effervescence, a thorough amalgamation being effected by stirring up the wine with long poles provided with fan-shaped ends. If the vintage be indifferent in quality the firm have scores of huge tuns filled with the yield of more favoured seasons to fall back upon to ensure any deficiencies of character and flavour being supplied.

The *méthode champenoise* brought to life in an engraving of the Moët & Chandon cellars in 1870. From the delivery of grapes to the resting, racking and riddling of the wine, the whole process then involved as many as 2,000 workers and produced 2.5 million bottles a year.

    The casks of wine to be blended are raised from the cellars, half a dozen at a time, by means of a lift provided with an endless chain, and worked by the steam-engine of which we have already spoken. They are emptied, through traps in the floor of the room above, into the huge vats which, standing upon a raised platform, reach almost to the ceiling. From these vats the fluid is allowed to flow through hose into rows of casks stationed below. Before being bottled the wine reposes for a certain time, is next duly racked and again blended, and is eventually conveyed through silver-plated pipes into oblong reservoirs, each fitted with a dozen syphon-taps, so arranged that directly the bottle slipped on to one of them becomes full the wine ceases to flow.

The bottling…

Upwards of 200 workpeople are employed in the *salle de tirage* at Messrs Moët and Chandon's, which, while the operation of bottling is going on, presents a scene of bewildering activity. Men and lads are gathered round the syphon-taps briskly removing the bottles as they become filled, and supplanting them by empty ones. Other lads hasten to transport the filled bottles on trucks to the corkers, whose so-called 'guillotine' machines send the corks home with a sudden thud. The corks being secured with agrafes the bottles are placed in large flat baskets called *manettes*, and wheeled away on tracks, the quarts being deposited in the cellars by means of lifts, while the pints slide down an inclined plane by the aid of an endless chain, which raises the trucks with the empty baskets at the same time the full ones make their descent into the cellars. What with the incessant thud of the corking machines, the continual rolling of iron-wheeled trucks over the concrete floor, the rattling and creaking of the machinery working the lifts, the occasional sharp report of a bursting bottle, and the loudly-shouted orders of the foremen, who display the national partiality for making a noise to perfection, the din becomes at times all but unbearable. The number of bottles filled in the course of the day naturally varies, still Messrs Moët and Chandon reckon that during the month of June a daily average of 100,000 are taken in the morning from the stacks in the *salle de rinçage*, washed, dried, filled, corked, wired, lowered into the cellars and carefully arranged in symmetrical order. This represents a total of two and a half million bottles during that month alone.

The bottles on being lowered into the cellars, either by means of the incline or the lifts, are placed in a horizontal position, and with their uppermost side daubed with white chalk, are stacked in layers from two to half-a-dozen bottles deep with narrow oak laths between. The stacks are usually about six or seven feet high and 100 feet and upwards in length. Whilst the wine is thus reposing in a temperature, of about 55° Fahrenheit [13°C], fermentation sets in, and the ensuing month is one of much anxiety. Thanks, however, to the care bestowed, Messrs Moët and Chandon's annual loss from bottles bursting rarely exceeds three percent, though 15 was once regarded as a respectable and satisfactory average. The broken glass is a perquisite of the workmen, the money arising from its sale, which at the last distribution amounted to no less than 20,000 francs, being divided amongst them every couple of years.

Deep in the cellars…

The usual entrance to Messrs Moët and Chandon's Epernay cellars – which, burrowed out in all directions, are of the aggregate length of nearly seven miles, and have usually between 11,000,000 and 12,000,000 bottles and 25,000 casks of wine stored therein – is through a wide and imposing portal, and down a long and broad flight of steps. It is, however, by the ancient and less imposing entrance – through which more than one crowned head has condescended to pass – that we set forth on our lengthened tour through these intricate underground galleries, this subterranean city with its miles of streets, crossroads, open spaces, tramways, and stations devoted solely to champagne.

A gilt inscription on a black marble tablet testifies that 'on the July 26th 1807, Napoleon the Great, Emperor of the French, King of Italy, and Protector of the Confederation of the Rhine, honoured commerce by visiting the cellars of Jean-Rémy Moët, Mayor of Epernay, President of the Canton and Member of the General Council of the Department', within three weeks of the signature of the treaty of Tilsit. Passing down the flight of steep, slippery steps traversed by the victor of Eylau and Jena, access is gained to the upper range of vaults, brilliantly illuminated by the glare of gas, or dimly lighted by the flickering flame of tallow-candles, upwards of 60,000lbs of which are annually consumed. Here group after group of the small army of 350 workmen employed in these subterranean galleries are encountered engaged in the process of transforming the *vin brut* into champagne.

The all-important operation of liqueuring the wine is effected by aid of machines of the latest construction, which regulate the quantity administered to the utmost nicety. The corks are branded by being pressed against steel dies heated by gas, by women who can turn out 3,000 per day apiece, the quantity of string used to secure them amounting to nearly 10 tons in the course of the year.

There is another and a lower depth of cellars to be explored to which access is gained by trap-holes in the floor – through which the barrels and baskets of wine are raised and lowered – and by flights of steps. From the foot of the latter there extends an endless vista of lofty and spacious passages hewn out of the chalk, the walls of which, smooth as finished masonry, are lined with thousands of casks of raw wine, varied at intervals by gigantic vats. Miles of long, dark-brown, dampish-looking galleries stretch away to the right and left, and though devoid of the picturesque festoons of fungi which decorate the London Dock vaults, exhibit a sufficient degree of mouldiness to give them an air of respectable

THE MADDENING MONOTONY OF RIDDLING

By the time fermentation is over, commencing from a few days after the bottling of the wine, a loose dark-brown sediment has been forming, which has now settled on the lower side of the bottle, and to get rid of which is a delicate and tedious task. As the time approaches for preparing the wine for shipment, the bottles are places *sur pointe*, as it is termed – that is to say, slantingly in racks with their necks downwards, the inclination being increased from time to time to one more abrupt. The object of this change in their position is to cause the sediment to leave the side of the bottle where it has gathered. Afterwards it becomes necessary to twist and turn it and coagulate it, as it were, until it forms a kind of muddy ball, and eventually to get it well down into the neck of the bottle, so that it may be finally expelled with a bang when the temporary cork is removed and the proper one adjusted. To accomplish this the bottles are sharply turned in one direction every day for at least a month or six weeks, the time being indefinitely extended until the sediment shows a disposition to settle near the cork. The younger the wine, the longer the period necessary for the bottles to be shaken, new wine often requiring as much as three months. Only a thoroughly practiced hand can give the right amount of revolution and the requisite degree of slope; and in some of the cellars men were pointed out to us who had acquired such dexterity as to be able at a pinch to shake with their two hands as many as 50,000 bottles in a single day, whilst 30,000 to 40,000 is by no means an uncommon performance.

Some of these men have spent 30 or 40 years of their lives engaged in this perpetual task. Fancy being entombed all alone day after day in vaults which are invariably dark and gloomy, and cold and dank, and being obliged to twist 60 to 70 of these bottle every minute throughout the day of 10 hours! Why, the treadmill and the crank, with their periodical respites, must be pastime compared to this maddeningly monotonous occupation, which combines labour, with the wrist, at any rate, with next to solitary confinement. One can understand these men becoming gloomy and taciturn, and affirming that they sometimes see devils hovering over the bottle-racks and frantically shaking the bottles beside them, or else grinning at them as they pursue their humdrum task.

antiquity. These multitudinous galleries, lit up by petroleum-lamps, are mostly lined with wine in bottles stacked in compact masses to a height of six or seven feet, only room enough for a single person to pass being left. Millions of bottles are thus arranged, the majority on their sides, in huge piles, with tablets hung up against each stack to note its age and quality; and the rest, which are undergoing daily evolutions at the hands of the twister, at various angles of inclination. In these cellars there are nearly 11,000 racks in which the bottles of *vin brut* rest *sur pointe*, as many as 600,000 bottles being commonly twisted daily.

Disgorgers at work…

We frequently come upon parties of workmen engaged in transforming the perfected *vin brut* into champagne. Viewed at a distance while occupied in their monotonous task, they present in the semi-obscurity a series of picturesque Rembrandt-like studies. One of the end figures in each group is engaged in the important process of *dégorgement*, which is performed when the deposit, of which we have already spoken, has satisfactorily settled in the neck of the bottle. Baskets full of bottles with their necks downwards are placed beside the operator, who stands before a cask set on end, and having a large oval opening in front. This nimble-fingered manipulator seizes a bottle, raises it for a moment before the light to test the clearness of the wine and the subsidence of the deposit; holds it horizontally in his left hand, with the neck directed towards the opening already mentioned; and with a jerk of the steel hook which he holds in his right hand loosens the agrafe securing the cork. Bang goes the latter, and with it flies out the sediment and a small glassful or so of wine, further flow being checked by the workman's finger, which also serves to remove any sediment yet remaining in the bottle's neck. Like many other clever tricks, this looks very easy when adroitly performed, though a novice would probably allow the bottle to empty itself by the time he discovered that the cork was out. Yet such is the dexterity acquired by practice that the average amount of wine, foam and deposit ejected by this operation does not exceed one-14th of the contents of the bottle. Occasionally a bottle bursts in the *dégorgeur*'s hand, and his face is sometimes scarred from such explosions. The sediment removed, the *dégorgeur* slips a temporary cork into the bottle, or places the latter in a machine provided with fixed gutta-percha corks and springs for securing the bottles firmly in their places. The wine is now ready for the important operation of the dosage, upon the nature and amount of which the character of perfected champagne, whether it be dry or sweet, light or strong, very much depends… Different manufacturers have different recipes for this composition of this syrup, all more or less complex in character, and varying with the quality of the wine and the country for which it is intended.

Storing, ageing, packing…

In these subterranean galleries, the way runs on between regiments of bottles of the same size and shape, save where at intervals pints take the place of quarts; and the visitor, gazing into the black depths of the transverse passages to the right and left, becomes conscious of a feeling that if his guide were suddenly to desert him he would feel as hopelessly lost as in the catacombs of Rome. There are two galleries, each 650 feet in length, containing about 650,000 bottles, and connected by 32 transverse galleries, with an aggregate length of 4,000 feet, in which nearly 1,500,000 bottles are stored. There are, further, eight galleries, each 500 feet in length, and proportionably stocked; also the extensive new vaults, excavated some five or six years back, in the rear of the then-existing cellarage, and a considerable number of smaller vaults. The different depths and varying degrees of moisture afford a choice of temperature of which the experienced owners know how to take advantage. The original vaults, wherein more than a century ago the first bottles of champagne made by the infant firm were stowed away, bear the name of Siberia, on account of their exceeding coldness. This section consists of several roughly-excavated low winding galleries, resembling natural caverns, and affording a striking contrast to the broad, lofty, and regular-shaped corridors of more recent date.

When the proper period arrives for the bottles to emerge once more into the upper air they are conveyed to the packing-room, a spacious hall 180 feet long and 60 feet broad. In front of its three large double doors wagons are drawn up ready to receive their loads. The 70 men and women employed here easily foil, label, wrap, and pack up some 10,000 bottles a day. Cases and baskets are stacked in different parts of this vast hall, at one end of which numerous trusses of straw used in the packing are piled. Seated at tables ranged along one side of the apartment women are busily occupied in pasting on labels or encasing the necks of bottles in gold or silver foil, whilst elsewhere men, seated on three-legged stools in front of smoking caldrons of molten sealing-wax of a deep green hue, are coating the necks of other bottles by plunging them into the boiling fluid. When labelled and decorated with either wax or foil the bottles pass on to other women, who swathe them in pink tissue-paper and set them aside for the packers, by whom, after being deftly wrapped round with straw, they are consigned to baskets or cases, to secure which last no less than 10,000lbs of nails are annually used. England and Russia are partial to gold foil, pink paper, and wooden cases holding a dozen or a couple of dozen bottles of the exhilarating fluid, whereas other nations prefer waxed necks, disdain pink paper, and insist on being supplied in wicker baskets containing 50 bottles each.

Power of the people…

Some idea of the complex character of so vast an establishment as that of Messrs Moët & Chandon may be gathered from a mere enumeration of their staff, which, in addition to 20 clerks and 350 cellarmen proper, includes numerous agrafe-makers and cork-cutters, packers and carters, wheelwrights and saddlers, carpenters, masons, slaters and tilers, tinmen, firemen, needlewomen, &c, while the inventory of objects used by this formidable array of workpeople comprises no fewer than 1,500 distinct heads. A medical man attached to the establishment gives gratuitous advice to all those employed, and a chemist dispenses drugs and medicines without charge. While suffering from illness the men receive half-pay, but should they be laid up by an accident met with in the course of their work full salary is invariably awarded to them. As may be supposed, so vast an establishment as this is not without a provision for those past work, and all the old hands receive liberal pensions from the firm upon retiring.

Every year Messrs Moët & Chandon give a banquet or a ball to the people in their employ – usually after the bottling of the wine is completed – in a hall handsomely decorated and illuminated with myriads of coloured lamps.

Messrs Moët & Chandon's wines are familiar to all drinkers of champagne. Their famous 'star' brand is known in all societies, figures equally at clubs and mess-tables, at garden parties and picnics, dinners and soirées, and on hotel cartes all over the world. One of the best proofs of the wine's universal popularity is found in the fact that as many as 1,000 visitors from all parts of the world come annually to make a tour of Messrs Moët and Chandon's spacious cellars.

Extract from *A History of Champagne with notes on the other sparkling wines of France* by Henry Vizetelly, Vizetelly & Co (London) and Scribner & Welford (New York) 1882.

Serena Sutcliffe MW (1988)

6 GOOD TIMES IN THE BELLE EPOQUE

From the 1880s, anyone who was anyone could be seen with a coupe of champagne in hand. Glinting in the glasses of the rich and famous from Paris to Pennsylvania, it embraced the dawn of the 20th century with gaiety and swagger. This was its Golden Age, 1880–1914. Serena Sutcliffe sets the scene.

The Belle Epoque started the century. It came after the Naughty Nineties, and social life was as coruscant as champagne itself – sparkling, witty and gloriously uninhibited. It was the era when people went out to be seen, to be entertained and to enjoy themselves. If you had it, you flaunted it. New money was being made, and old money still existed. And, somehow, they met over '*un verre de champagne*'.

It was an era of curves: vases, chair legs, there wasn't a straight line in sight. Of course, it began earlier; the scene was set in the Second Empire, in the pleasure-loving society of Napoleon III's France. Then, the rich, powerful, high-class *cocottes* held sway. The three great demi-mondaines of the 1890s were Liane de Pougy, la Belle Otéro and Cléo de Mérode. Heaven knows how much champagne drinking they inspired. The private rooms of Lapérouse were much in use.

Maxim's was the great meeting place. The 1900 Paris Exhibition fixed it firmly in the firmament of truly international haunts, and oysters and lobster were on the menu. The men lingered at the bar with their champagne, and the women (both respectable and less so) eyed each other with ill-concealed curiosity. The champagne, regrettably, tended to be sweet: it was its sole defense against its diabolical positioning in the meal, after the Sauternes and before the brandy. Only the British were well and truly launched on brut.

The French were consuming some seven million bottles of champagne and sparkling wines from the Marne a year at the turn of the century. But the

A period of vibrancy and optimism... Sipping champagne during the Belle Epoque was considered the height of respectability (even for those who weren't quite) and was encouraged by brightly coloured posters advertising 'the finest'.

Good Times in the Belle Epoch

pattern of drinking bore no comparison with that of today. No one bought a bottle on the way home and shared it in connubial bliss. One went out to the smart restaurants of the day, to the grand hotels, to the fashionable night spots, and was seen to be enjoying oneself. In Paris, this meant the Café de la Paix, Drouant of literary fame, the Ritz, the Grand Hotel, and Lucas at the Madeleine, with Majorelle's magnificent Ceylon lemonwood panelling. Somehow, this finds an echo in contemporary Champagne, where so many homes have a panelled room or two, well padded and substantial, the perfect setting for contemplating bubbles.

And what did all those mirrors of the era reflect? Colours, and flowers, and flamboyance. The Belle Epoque was not quiet: it was flashy. Everything was 'worked', nothing was left alone. It was art nouveau and Tiffany, encrustation and marquetry. It was colours that clashed and, it has to be admitted, ornate vulgarity. But it was fun. Against a social fabric that was far from stable, and a little malicious, everybody went out – '*on sortait*'. The most unlikely people mixed: the louche and the ladylike sat on the same banquette. It was the last fling of an age that was to end in the trenches. It was dying embers in Europe, but pioneering new money in America.

Mumm have some fascinating records of the booming champagne market in the United States. It sent 420,000 bottles across the Atlantic in 1877, and 1.5 million in 1902, its best year for that market. Veuve Clicquot's sales only caught up with the 1905–06 figures in 1973. In 1882, 36 million bottles of champagne were produced, a quarter for France and three-quarters for export. In 1900, Perrier-Jouët needed 200 people to ship one million bottles; now about 70 people handle three times as much. In Britain, in that first decade of the 1900s, André Simon was selling quantities of Pommery. In America, sales of champagne nearly quadrupled between 1900 and 1909.

North America, at that time as now, was the second-largest champagne market after Britain. Champagne was everywhere, but especially on the West Coast, where gold had made the hostelries of San Francisco magnets for both the hopeful and the hopeless. Genuine finds were celebrated with the best that money could buy, and that meant French champagne, just as one celebrates a stroke of good luck today. By 1900, it was the land barons who dominated the West and ordered the bubbly. Champagne was drunk with the same abandon in the steamy districts of New Orleans as in the altogether more tight-lipped ambience of New England. By 1909, it was well established in bars, certainly from the pictorial evidence of the time – although there is a degree of confusion as to what actually constituted 'champagne', especially when scrawled on a bar blackboard.

The two Paris World Fairs of 1889 and 1900 had done much to enhance the reputation of champagne. Here the houses did not exhibit as individuals but as members of the Association of Champagne Merchants. They had a Champagne Palace, designed by the Reims architect Kalas, where *remuage* and *dégorgement* were demonstrated and the public could buy glasses of champagne. This group presentation won the highest award at both Fairs.

Escoffier was the great chef of the Belle Epoque. In his autobiography, he recalls a gala dinner given by the Comte de Lagrange after his horse won the Grand Prix de Paris: Veuve Clicquot was sandwiched between Lafite 1846 and Yquem. He transformed London's Savoy Hotel, cooking for Edward VII, Emile Zola and Sarah Bernhardt. A Savoy wine list of 1901 shows a variety of champagnes and an even greater variety of 'dosages'. Not only could one choose one's vintage, but also the exact degree of dryness desired, with accompanying descriptions such as 'extra quality extra dry' (Bollinger), 'dry England' (Clicquot), 'extra-sec' (Deutz) and 'extra superior brut cuvée exceptionelle [sic] (Dagonet). The vintages ranged from 1884 to 1893.

In fact, the heyday for menus was the period between 1880 and 1914: they were often decorated by noted artists and have great value today. But not much can be gleaned from them with regard to how and when the champagnes were served. The very disparate list of wines could appear at the side of the food or grouped after it, but it was all very haphazard. What appeared to be a frightful mismatch (Louis Roederer Doux with roast duck) may not actually have been so: the printer may not always have lined up the food with any particular wine.

Gradually, other markets followed the British predilection for brut: in 1905 Mumm launched a drier version of Cordon Rouge in New York, although in France dry champagne only started to have any impact after 1910. Brand promotion began to be important: Mumm's accounts for 1907 show lists of gifts to the diplomatic corps, associations and restaurant personnel, as well as all sorts of objects which would have borne the name Mumm.

The artists of the era twirled and swirled with enthusiasm. The painters were Bonnard and Mucha, the designers and decorative architects Gaud, Guimard, de Feure, Majorelle, Vallin and André, the artists in glass Gallé, Daum and Tiffany, while sculpture was represented by Maillol. Some furniture, posters, jewellery and glass remain, but the wrought-iron fantasies are fast disappearing, none more so than the nostalgic entrances to the Paris Métro.

In London, at the height of Edwardian splendour, the great houses of the aristocracy on Park Lane (most of them now replaced by hotels) were the centre of the capital's social life. Parties were lavish, hospitality grand, and the champagne flowed. It is interesting to note that champagne never fell into either the exclusively male or female domain: men could order it without feeling effeminate, women could enjoy it without appearing brazen. There have been periods when red wine was thought to be a 'man's drink', while women sipped a little Hock, but champagne carefully treads between all the social pitfalls and has always been 'correct'.

The Edwardian gastronomic chronicler, Colonel Newnham-Davis, gives us a very clear picture of how champagne was served throughout a meal: this was the time, of course, when champagne was vintage and certainly weightier (more black grapes in many cases) than the cuvées we have now. It accompanied caviar, consommé, sole, tongue, salad, asparagus and ice cream (a tall order, even for this most noble of wines!), while a rosé was called to service for a meal consisting of caviar, clear soup, sole, lamb, foie gras, quails and ice cream. (Caviar, clear soup, sole and ice cream seem to have been consistent favourites to begin and end a meal.)

Little did the urban partygoers realize that in Champagne itself a battle was raging. Phylloxera, the dreaded predator of the vine, had taken its time in reaching the north of France, but its progress was inexorable. L'Abbé Dervin, in 1896, wrote the most illuminating book on the subject I know: *Six Semaines en Pays Phylloxérés*. It is the account of a marathon journey through all the viticultural regions of France in 1894 with the aim of giving advice to the vignerons of Champagne. Phylloxera had existed in France since the 1860s, when it was discovered in the Bouches-du-Rhône and in the Gironde: by the time this book was witten it was in the Marne. L'Abbé Dervin brought the Champenois encouragement that their vineyards could be rebuilt using phylloxera-resistant American rootstock, but there were many who did not share this draconian view, and the process of grafting all the vines in the Champagne region was not completed until after World War I.

From 'The Golden Ages', chapter II of *A Celebration of Champagne* by Serena Sutcliffe MW, Mitchell Beazley (London) 1988. Reproduced with kind permission of the author.

Tom Stevenson (1986)

7 WAR, RAGE, AND THE 'ROARING TWENTIES'

World War I put an end to the times of high living. Champagne's buoyant markets collapsed, and in-fighting over quality boundaries undermined any hope the region had of recovery. A series of plentiful harvests went unsold, until, as Tom Stevenson reports, the Champenois changed tack. Releasing their wines for sale on the home market proved to be a move that made all the difference…

World War I

In European warfare invading armies normally choose harvest to launch their attacks, and the year 1914 was no exception. On September 3rd Reims fell to the German forces at the end of their month-long advance; three days later Epernay too succumbed. But the power of the German sweep faltered and French forces were able to regroup and mount a counter-attack from the Paris region. There then followed, between September 7th and 9th, a most bitter clash of armies in the normally tranquil vineyards of Champagne: the Battle of the Marne.

Strategically, the Marne is important for the last line of defense it presents before the Seine. Once the Seine is crossed, Paris lies open to the invader. It was therefore vital for the French to retake the north bank and this they achieved amid vines heavily laden with fruit, reoccupying both Epernay and Reims by September 13th. Waged on the high ground in the Montagne de Reims, between Epernay and the Marne to the south and Reims to the north, there followed one of the most gruelling and protracted battles in human history, the line of trenches moving barely 100 metres throughout four long and bloody years.

Nobody who has ever taken the trouble to visit General Gouraud's observation post on a cold, dank winter's day could ever escape the hell-hole ambience of such a deathly place, which seems to reach out over the decades of time to shame and sicken the human race. My own memory is vivid: it was a bitterly cold morning, below −14°C, and the ground I trod, in which only days before I would have been up to my knees in mud, was as solid as rock. As I picked my way through the frozen woods towards the observation post which commands a unique view over the former battle-ground of the Marne, I wondered what it must have been like to be a soldier. It is a strenuous physical effort to scale on a good spring day, but in the pouring rain, amid hailing bullets, laden with uniform and the tools of war…

The north-facing slopes of the Montagne de Reims bore the brunt of the hostilities, yet the damage done to the vineyards during the Battle of the Marne was negligible compared with the inhuman slaughter and tragic loss of lives in the trenches. Work in the vineyards continued, with women and children dying while servicing the vines that the soldiers on both sides manipulated for their own strategic purposes. More than 20 children were killed bringing in that first wartime crop of 1914.

The collapse of world markets

In October 1917, while the attention of all France, particularly that of the people of Champagne, focused on the progress of the battles on the Western Front, Russia rose in revolution. This had considerable impact on the Champagne trade for, at a single stroke, 10 percent of its annual production, normally consumed in royal and aristocratic Russian circles, suddenly had no market. Quite predictably, the revolutionary government refused to pay any outstanding bills for their former masters' frivolous luxuries, a state of affairs which had disastrous consequences for Champagne houses, like Roederer, whose main market was Russian. Furthermore, after the Allied victory in 1918, Germany and the former Austro-Hungarian Empire were bankrupt and unable to make any significant purchases for a long time.

The bitterness and confusion over delimitation,[1] which had led to the drafting of a bill in 1911 outlining the two distinct districts, 'Champagne' and 'Champagne Deuxième Zone', was still unsolved and an amended law

---

1 In 1908, a law was passed restricting the use of the name Champagne to the wines of the Marne and Aisne, but excluding those of the Aube. The Aube's growers protested, causing the government to talk of abandoning geographical delimitations. This, in turn, angered the Marne growers, who rioted, destroying many cellars in Dizy, Damery and Aÿ. (Serena Sutcliffe MW)

was passed through the new government in 1919. This instigated for the first time the right of appellation in the form of the *Appellation d'Origine Contrôlée* (AOC) and regulations were imposed, including a cunning proviso which dumped the entire issue of the Aube wines and the controversial 'Champagne Deuxième Zone' firmly in the lap of the judiciary. After six years of litigation, the courts decided in favour of the Aube growers and, in 1927, a new law quashed the Deuxième designation once and for all, outlining a detailed list of communes eligible for the appellation Champagne, the broad outlines of which are still in existence today

Meanwhile, on January 20th 1920, the dwindling sales of champagne suffered yet another downward spiral, when the American Prohibition Bill was passed (although 'bootleggers' still managed to smuggle in substantial consignments). Prohibition was also imposed in various degrees in Scandinavian countries, another formerly prosperous market.

Traditionally, the British had been Champagne's most lucrative customers – after the drink had been popularized in society by the Marlboroughs and the Prince of Wales in the last half of the 19th century. Soldiers had since picked up the habit of wine-drinking in France during the war and upon returning to England had educated the middle classes, further increasing the popularity of champagne in the immediate post-war years. But when Britain went off the Gold Standard in 1931, the Champagne houses found themselves receiving just two-thirds of the price they had come to expect.

The disruption of world markets in the aftermath of the war, the waves of protectionism and concurrent fall in export sales inevitably affected the Champagne trade as it razed other industries; 1932 proved disastrous, with virtually no buyers for champagne. Despite a run of small harvests, the cellars in Reims and Epernay were brimming; it was estimated that had sales maintained their 1932 level, the Champagne houses possessed sufficient stock to tide over sales for the next 33 years. The last thing Champagne required was a plentiful harvest, but that was precisely what it got with the bumper crop of 1934.

Most houses simply refused to buy any grapes, even though the growers were practically giving them away. But little could be done to redress the situation since the houses were in just as bad a position as the growers. Some of the larger growers, however, began to make their own champagne instead of relying purely on the sale of grapes. It was a costly investment requiring several years to come to fruition and the vast majority of growers could not afford the necessary equipment. It was at this time that many growers began to group together to form the earliest co-operatives in Champagne.

Unresponsive export markets led many houses to turn their attention inwards and focus on long-neglected domestic sales. This they achieved with stunning success, building up a trade several times the size of their previous home market. In 1927 champagne sales on the French market accounted for eight million bottles; by 1935 it had passed 24 million. The French domestic market remains to this day far and away the largest consumer of champagne.

BRIGHTER TIMES IN THE JAZZ AGE

It is often thought that in the 1920s the cocktail usurped the position of almost every other drink. But from the number of times champagne appeared in diaries of the day, it is clear that its popularity continued. Nancy Cunard, that peripatetic lover of liberty and alcohol, describes her life in Paris: '…and then we would go and dance somewhere else in Monmartre. It was always champagne, and our heads were often swimming' (*Nancy Cunard* by Anne Chisholm, 1979). Evelyn Waugh's *Diaries* (1976) are chock-full of champagne; in June 1924, he took a train from Oxford to London: 'We found nothing to eat that seemed tolerable except bread and cheese but we drank some brown sherries, some champagne, many liqueurs and, smoking great cigars, got out at Paddington with the conviction that we had lunched well.' Champagne often confers this illusion upon the most meagre repast. A few months later, he gave 'a tiny dinner party with prodigious quantities of champagne at the Carlton Club…'

We know that copious amounts of champagne were drunk on the steamers that crossed the Atlantic. Joseph Wechsberg, who played the violin in a French ship's orchestra, describes how six bottles of Veuve Clicquot were kept in the cello of one of his colleagues. The Captain's Dinner, that obligatory social occasion, included an amazing array of dishes, but 'the stewards did not bother to show the wine card, simply asking the passengers if they preferred Mumm Cordon Rouge or the more expensive vintages of Charles Heidsieck, Reims…

Main text: extract from *Champagne* by Tom Stevenson, Sotheby's (London) 1986, reproduced with kind permission of the author. Boxed text: Serena Sutcliffe MW, *A Celebration of Champagne* (1988).

Don and Petie Kladstrup (2001)

8 ESCAPE FROM THE WEINFÜHRERS

Don and Petie Kladstrup recall the bravery of Robert Jean de Vogüé and his colleagues as they steered Champagne through the horrors of World War II, surviving hunger, oppression, concentration camps and Nazi greed…

No region suffered more pillaging of its wine than Champagne. Nearly two million bottles were grabbed by German soldiers during the first weeks of the occupation alone. It was, therefore, with immense relief that the Champenois learned that German authorities were sending in someone to oversee champagne purchases and, hopefully, end the looting and restore order. They were even more relieved when they found out who it would be: Otto Klaebisch of Matteüs-Müller, a winemaking and importing firm from Germany's Rhineland. 'We were so happy we got someone from the wine trade, and not a beer man,' Bernard de Nonancourt said. The de Nonancourts knew Klaebisch well because he had been the pre-war agent in Germany for a number of Champagne houses, including Lanson, which the family of Bernard's mother owned.

Brandy, however, was Klaebisch's original background. He was born in Cognac, where his parents had been brandy merchants before World War I. When France confiscated all enemy-owned property during the war, the Klaebisch family lost its business there and returned to Germany.

Otto, however, retained his taste for the finer things in life, especially great champagne. He pursued a career in the wine and spirits industry, putting his French background to good use.

That background made Klaebisch's appointment as weinführer of Champagne easier to take. 'If you were going to be shoved around, it was better to be shoved around by a winemaker than by some beer-drinking Nazi lout,' said one producer.

Klaebisch began his 'shoving' almost immediately. Unlike Heinz Bomers in Bordeaux, who had rented a small apartment, Klaebisch wanted to live somewhere more impressive. A château, for instance. He found what he wanted when he saw where Bertrand de Vogüé, head of Veuve Clicquot-Ponsardin, lived. After one look, Klaebisch issued orders for the château to be requisitioned. An angry de Vogüé and family were sent packing.

'Klaebisch was very happy to be here,' de Nonancourt remembered. 'He did not like combat and the last thing he wanted was to be sent to the Russian front.' Given his family connections and professional contacts, Klaebisch landed the soft assignment without difficulty. His brother-in-law was none other than Foreign Minister Ribbentrop, whose father-in-law, Henkel, was a good friend of Bordeaux's Louis Eschenauer.

Eschenauer, in turn, was a cousin of German port commander Ernst Kühnemann. Eschenauer was also part owner of Mumm champagne, another property that had been confiscated from German owners in World War I. He had hired Ribbentrop to represent that *marque* in Germany.

Only a wine genealogist could unravel the complicated family and professional tree that entangled winemakers and merchants throughout France and Germany. It went a long way to explain how Klaebisch became weinführer of Champagne.

Klaebisch, however, was different from the other weinführers. He enjoyed the trappings of military life and almost always wore his uniform. He was also impressed with titles. When he first met Count Robert-Jean de Vogüé, the man with whom he would be negotiating champagne purchases, he was deferential to the point of being obsequious, or, as one producer put it, 'too anxious to please'.

De Vogüé, head of Moët & Chandon, had a complicated family tree of his own. He was related to many of Europe's royal families as well as to many of France's leading wine producers. He even had connections with the Vatican. He also happened to be the brother of Veuve Clicquot's Bertrand de Vogüé, whom Klaebisch had just kicked out of his house.

Klaebisch ran into problems almost from the moment he moved in. The 1940 harvest was disastrous. The yield was 80 percent below average. Aware that Berlin expected him to supply a certain amount of champagne every month, Klaebisch visited the houses he had done business with before the war and asked them to make up the difference from their reserves. De Vogüé thought that was a bad idea. He feared that other houses would be angry and jealous. With

Many Nazi leaders during World War II had come directly from the wine trade. Like foreign minister Joachim von Ribbentrop, who had represented Champagne Pommery in Germany before the war, they felt officer status entitled them to the best.

international markets cut off and sales to French civilians prohibited, those firms might easily go out of business.

Even the houses Klaebisch wanted to do business with were unhappy. Yes, their market was 'guaranteed' but they also had to accept what the Germans were willing to pay, and it was not much. Producers feared that the huge quantities of champagne Klaebisch was demanding would soon deplete their stocks, leaving them stuck in the same economic morass they had been in during the 1930s. Those years, more than anything, defined the almost militant mood that still prevailed in Champagne when Klaebisch arrived. In 1932, Champagne houses had managed to sell only four and a half million bottles of the 150 million that were in their cellars. The mood among growers who sold their grapes to the houses was sour too. In 1933 and 1934, they were paid no more than one franc a kilo for their grapes. In 1931, they had been paid 11 francs, a loss of income that severely jeopardized their businesses. The picture improved in 1937 and 1938, but quickly turned bleak again when war was declared in 1939. In desperation, producers began walling up their champagne and shipping other stocks to the United States and Great Britain for safekeeping.

Escape from the Weinführers

Now they faced massive requisitioning. Pol Roger, the house that made prime minister Winston Churchill's favourite champagne, was ordered to send huge quantities of its 1928 vintage to Berlin each month. 'It was such a great vintage,' said Christian de Billy, president of Pol Roger, who was born in that year. 'We never had a lot and tried to hide what we could, but it was so wonderful and so well known, that it was impossible to keep it out of German hands. And Klaebisch knew it was there.'

As German demands for champagne escalated – at times Klaebisch was demanding half a million bottles a week – De Vogüé feared, more than ever, that houses like Pol Roger would not survive. On April 13th 1941, he called together producers and growers to set up an organization that would represent the interests of everyone in the champagne industry. 'We are all in this together,' de Vogüé told them. 'We will either suffer or survive but we will do so equally.' The organization they created was called the *Comité Interprofessionelle du Vin de Champagne*, or CIVC, which still represents the champagne industry today. At the time, the goal of the CIVC was to enable producers to present a united front and speak with a single voice. De Vogüé, it was decided, would be the point man. 'He had the courage and enough audacity to represent the interests of Champagne and to be the one and only delegate to the Germans,' said Claude Fourmon, who was de Vogüé's assistant. 'He never doubted the Allies would win the war, so his goal was to keep everything at an acceptable level. He wanted to make sure that everyone had something to start over with when the war ended.'

Klaebisch was unhappy about the CIVC and did not want to deal with it; he preferred to stick with his pre-war contacts. He knew that was how Heinz Bomers operated and he wanted to emulate the Bordeaux weinführer by taking complete control of the champagne business. Klaebisch summoned de Vogüé to his office in Reims.

There, he got right to the point. 'Here are the ground rules. You can sell to the Third Reich and its military, and also to German-controlled restaurants, hotels and nightclubs, and a few of our friends like the Italian ambassador to France and Marshal Pétain at Vichy. The Marshal, by the way, likes to have a good quantity for his own personal use.'

De Vogüé listened without interrupting as the weinführer outlined the conditions. 'Nobody gets any free samples, there are no discounts no matter how large the order, and no full bottles of champagne may be sold unless empty bottles are first turned in.' Then Klaebisch told de Vogüé how much champagne he wanted each month and what he was willing to pay for it. 'You can spread the order out any way you wish among the major houses just as long as I get my champagne,' he said.

De Vogüé was taken aback. 'There is no way we can meet those demands,' he said. 'Two million bottles a month? How do you expect us to do it?'

'Work Sundays!' Klaebisch shot back.

De Vogüé refused. To their credit, each man seemed to have an innate sense of how far they could push the other. After more heated exchanges, de Vogüé said champagne producers would work longer days to meet their quotas but only if the weinführer extended the number of hours they could have electricity. Klaebisch agreed.

De Vogüé, however, was not the only thorn in Klaebisch's side. In Berlin, Field Marshal Göring was demanding ever greater amounts of champagne for his Luftwaffe. The navy was also making huge demands. Buffeted from all sides, the weinführer went back to de Vogüé. This time, he was more conciliatory. 'We've had our disagreements,' he said, 'but I've got a problem with Berlin and I hope you will see fit to help me.' Klaebisch described how Göring was pressuring him to supply more champagne. He then proposed that if the CIVC would keep the champagne coming, he would make sure producers had all the supplies they needed such as sugar for their dosages, fertilizer for their vineyards, even hay for their horses.

De Vogüé said it was a deal.

It was an especially good deal for Pol Roger. Not long afterwards, a spokesman from Pol Roger contacted the weinführer's office to say they were doing some repair work in their cellars and needed cement. Klaebisch arranged for its immediate delivery. Pol Roger used the cement to wall up and hide some of its best champagne from the Germans.

'The Champagne houses did their best to perform a little sleight of hand,' admitted Claude Taittinger, head of Taittinger Champagne. 'Most tried to preserve their best wines and palm off the inferior blends on the enemy.' They knew, for instance, that bottles whose labels were stamped 'Reserved for the Wehrmacht' and often had a red bar running across them were unlikely to fall into the hands of their regular customers. As a result, most of the houses did not hesitate to use them for their worst cuvées. 'What they forgot,' said Taittinger, 'was that Klaebisch was a connoisseur and capable of cracking the whip now and then to show he was not always fooled by our tricks.'

One day at lunchtime, Klaebisch called up Roger Hodez, secretary of the *Syndicat des Grandes Marques de Champagne*, an association representing the major Champagne houses, and invited him for an apéritif. 'We've never had a drink together,' the weinführer said: 'Why don't you drop by my office and we'll have one.' Hodez felt he could not refuse.

When he arrived, Klaebisch invited him to sit down and poured him a glass of champagne. Then he poured one for himself. The weinführer seemed to be in a good mood and Hodez began to relax. Then, suddenly, Hodez's nose wrinkled as a ghastly odour rose from his glass. Bravely, he took a sip. The taste was only slightly better than the smell. There was no sign Klaebisch had noticed Hodez's discomfort. 'What do you think?' he asked affably.

Before Hodez could reply, the weinführer suddenly leaned across his desk and put his face inches away from Hodez's. 'Let me tell you what I think,' he snarled, his voice rising in crescendo. 'It smells like shit! And this is what you want me to give the Wehrmacht to drink? I want the house that made this crap struck from the list of firms supplying champagne to Germany. I wouldn't dare send their stuff to Berlin!'

Hodez shrank back in his chair, fumbling for words as he tried to pacify Klaebisch. 'I'm sure it was only an accident,' he stammered, 'a case of dirty bottles perhaps, or maybe…' Before Hodez could say anything else, however, he was excused from Klaebisch's office.

The shaken trade representative went straight to de Vogüé and told him what had happened. De Vogüé immediately contacted the champagne house and warned officials of what Klaebisch had said. The head of the firm shrugged, saying he did not care. 'We're not making much money from the Germans anyway. We'll be better off selling a little of our champagne on the black market and holding the rest until after the war.'

De Vogüé shook his head. 'That's not the point,' he said. 'We're all in this together and you have to provide your fair share.' He instructed the firm to send its portion of champagne to several other houses, which agreed to bottle it under their own labels.

Klaebisch, however, was more suspicious than ever that champagne producers were trying to trick him. He began conducting spot checks of champagne bound for Germany, pulling out bottles, popping their corks, sniffing their contents and then tasting them. That is how François Taittinger ended up in jail.

François was 20 years old when he was brought in to help run the family firm after his uncle had become totally deaf. Like others, he underestimated Klaebisch's knowledge of champagne and thought he could outfox the weinführer by sending him champagne that was distinctly inferior in quality. When Klaebisch discovered it, he ordered François to his office.

'How dare you send us fizzy ditch water!' he yelled.

François, known for his quick temper, shot back: 'Who cares? It's not as if it's going to be drunk by people who know anything about champagne!'

Klaebisch threw François into jail. In the same cell were a number of other champagne producers who had also tried to pass off bad wine.

A few days later, the eldest of the Taittinger brothers went to Klaebisch's office to plead François' case. Guy Taittinger was a former cavalry officer and a born diplomat. He regaled the weinführer with stories about his days in the French army. He described how he once had to 'drink a bottle of champagne that had been decapitated with a saber and poured into a backplate of armour.' Klaebisch was amused, so much so that finally he shook his head, put up his hand and said, 'Okay, you win. Your brother can go.'

Most people in Champagne saw Klaebisch not as a Nazi diehard but more as an arbitrator between the French wine community and Berlin. Never was that more evident than when Vichy launched a forced labour programme, *Service du Travail Obligatoire*, or STO, to supply Germany with workers for its factories and industries. In one week alone, Pol Roger had 10 of its workers hauled off to Germany; the next week, 17 more.

'There's no way we can continue like this,' de Vogüé warned Klaebisch. 'We don't have enough people for our regular work, let alone for the harvest. If you do not get some of our workers back, you will have no champagne next year.' The CIVC itself tried to keep the houses functioning by rotating experienced workers from one champagne maker to another. Still, the companies were falling far short of their imposed quotas.

The weinführer, who prided himself on his efficiency, quickly contacted authorities in Berlin. Faced with a choice between less champagne or less labour in their factories, the Germans chose the latter and allowed some of the more experienced and older workers to return to their cellars.

Each concession from Klaebisch, however, seemed to generate another edict. From now on, he said, a German officer must accompany every worker going into the *caves*. Producers thought it was ridiculous and completely impractical. When the weinführer backed off, there was a huge sigh of relief, for the chalk cellars, the *crayères* of Champagne, were being used by the Resistance, both as a place of refuge and as a place to stockpile arms and supplies.

In fact, the Resistance was doing a great deal more. It had picked up on the fact that champagne shipments were providing significant military intelligence. Through them, they could tell where the Germans were preparing a major military offensive. They first became aware of this when the Germans, in 1940, ordered tens of thousands of bottles to be sent to Romania, where, officially, there was only a small German mission. Within a few days, Romania was invaded by the German army. Afterwards, bottles of bubbly were distributed to all the troops, a way of saying to the soldiers that 'the Führer thinks of his men first'.

From that time on, the Resistance, with help from the major Champagne houses, kept meticulous track of where large shipments of champagne were going. Alarm bells went off towards the end of 1941 when the Germans placed a huge order and asked that the bottles be specially corked and packed so that they would be ready for transport to 'a very hot country'. That country turned out to be Egypt, where Rommel was about to begin his North African campaign, pushing into Libya, Morocco, Algeria and Tunisia. The information was relayed back to British intelligence in London.

As the war continued, relations between Klaebisch and de Vogüé deteriorated. Klaebisch felt more and more as though he were being taken advantage of and 'sandbagged' by de Vogüé. He was annoyed that de Vogüé always referred to him as Klaebisch, never Herr Klaebisch or Monsieur Klaebisch or even Captain Klaebisch, just Klaebisch.

But that was a mere irritation. Far more serious was that Klaebisch and other German authorities were becoming more and more convinced that de Vogüé and his colleagues at Moët & Chandon were actively helping the Resistance. Their suspicions were correct.

In the early days of the occupation, Moët & Chandon had been pillaged more than any other Champagne house. The Chandon château on the grounds of Dom Pérignon's abbey had been burned down and many other buildings belonging to Moët were taken over to house German troops. To add insult to injury, the company had also been ordered to supply the Third Reich with 50,000 bottles of champagne a week, or about one-tenth of all the champagne the Germans were requisitioning.

'Under those conditions, I and others at Moët, the entire top echelon, couldn't help but resist,' said Moët's commercial director, Claude Fourmon.

De Vogüé himself headed the political wing of the Resistance in the eastern region of France. In the early stages of the war, he had argued against an armed resistance that could endanger innocent lives. As the war ground on, however, his feelings began to change and he welcomed the Resistance into Moët's 24 kilometres of cellars. 'At the very least,' said his son Ghislain, 'my father turned a blind eye to sabotage and subterfuge, and to tampering with champagne and its shipment.'

On November 24th 1943, Robert-Jean de Vogüé asked his cousin René Sabbe to serve as translator for a meeting he and Claude Fourmon were scheduled to have with Klaebisch. Because the recently completed harvest had been so small – and so good – they were hoping to persuade Klaebisch to reduce the amount of champagne he was planning to requisition.

Shortly after they arrived, the telephone rang in an office next to Klaebisch's. A young officer interrupted the meeting to tell the weinführer that the call was for him. Klaebisch excused himself. Within minutes he was back and sat down at his desk, crossing his arms over his potbelly.

'Gentlemen,' he said, 'that was the Gestapo. You are all under arrest.' On cue, several officers with pistols drawn burst through the door and took the three men into custody.

'We were completely stupefied,' Fourmon later recalled. De Vogüé had just persuaded Klaebisch to let houses sell more champagne to French civilians. I don't know exactly what triggered the call but I think the Gestapo wanted to take de Vogüé out of the line of command.'

De Vogüé's first reaction was: 'Let Fourmon go; he knows nothing.' He also pleaded for the release of Sabbe, saying he was there only to translate. De Vogüé's appeals were to no avail.

All three were charged with obstructing the trade demands of the Germans and imprisoned. Sabbe was released a few days later because of his age, but Fourmon was sent to Bergen-Belsen, a concentration camp in Germany.

De Vogüé was sentenced to death.

The sentence sent shock waves through Champagne. For the first time in history, the entire industry – growers and producers, labour and management – went on strike. Klaebisch was stunned and, at first, did not know what to do. He branded the strike an 'act of terrorism' and warned that force would be used against the perpetrators unless it ended immediately. The Champenois ignored him and stepped up their protest.

In the face of such unprecedented action, Klaebisch seemed paralyzed. Calling out troops, he feared, could result in even greater unrest and force the Germans to take over the production of champagne, something he knew they were ill prepared to do.

There was something else Klaebisch feared as well: the spotlight. The last thing he wanted to do was to call attention to himself, especially now when everything seemed to be falling apart. To make matters worse, his brother-in-law and mentor, Joachim von Ribbentrop, had fallen out of favour, and Klaebisch could all too easily picture himself suddenly freezing with other German soldiers on the Russian front.

After more fruitless appeals to the Champenois to end their protest, Klaebisch and the Germans gave in. They agreed to 'suspend' de Vogüé's sentence but said they were only doing so because he had five children. Instead, he was put in prison.

Despite his clashes with de Vogüé, this was not what Klaebisch had expected or wanted. 'I can well imagine Klaebisch was uncomfortable with my father's arrest,' Ghislain de Vogüé said. 'I suspect he was just obeying orders he had been given.'

But punishment of the champagne industry had only just begun. Champagne houses that had supported the strike were hauled before a military tribunal and given a choice. They could pay a heavy fine, 600,000 francs (about one and a half million francs in today's currency), or the head of each house could spend 40 days in prison. Nearly all paid the fine.

Moët & Chandon suffered the worst. 'They decapitated Moët,' Claude Fourmon later said. Nearly all of the top management was sent to prison or concentration camps.

Hoping to discourage further disobedience and justify their crackdown against Moët, Klaebisch and other German authorities produced a propaganda film. It showed faked cases of Moët & Chandon champagne being seized and opened, all of them filled with rifles and other weapons. The film was distributed to movie theatres throughout France and Germany. The Germans also forced French newspapers to run an article saying de Vogüé had been helping 'terrorists'.

Within a few months, the German Occupation Authority had completely taken over the running of Moët. The man they put in charge was Otto Klaebisch.

IN MANY WAYS, the weinführers accomplished exactly what the Third Reich wanted. They helped stop the pillaging, restored order and supplied Germany with an extremely lucrative product. More than two and a half million hectolitres of wine, the equivalent of 320 million bottles, were shipped to Germany each year.

More important, the weinführers mitigated a situation that could have resulted in far worse consequences for France. They served as a buffer for a battle that raged within the German leadership over how to deal with France, between Nazis like Göring who wanted to 'smash and grab' and treat France like a conquered country and those who favoured a less ruthless approach, incorporating France into a German-dominated new Europe and 'providing it with a little fodder', so it could be milked for all it was worth.

Above all, the weinführers recognized the economic and symbolic importance of France's wine industry and did all in their power to make sure it survived. It was for their benefit too, for they realized that when the war ended and they returned home to their businesses, it was essential to have someone – namely, the French – to do business with again.

While the war continued, however, and especially as it began turning against Germany, most people in France became convinced that the best guarantee of survival was to rely on themselves, not on the weinführers and certainly not on Pétain's Vichy government which was becoming more fascist by the day. That meant finding unconventional methods and having the courage to bend or break established rules.

As Janet Flanner (journalist and writer for *The New Yorker*) predicted when the war first began: 'Owing to the Germans' mania for systematic looting – for collecting and carting away French bed linen, machinery, Gobelin tapestries, surgical instruments, milk, mutton, sweet champagne – the French will have to become a race of liars and cheats in order to survive physically.'

IN JULY 1944, OTTO KLAEBISCH, the weinführer of Champagne, placed a large order for champagne for the German military with the CIVC. Three weeks later he abruptly cancelled it and fled back to Germany.

With Patton's Third Army rapidly advancing towards Champagne, the Germans had to leave quickly; so quickly, in fact, that they did not even have time to set off all the explosives they had planted under bridges.

Nor did they destroy Champagne's vast cellars as Himmler had threatened.

Nevertheless, the German occupation had left companies and personal lives in tatters. There were millions of francs' worth of unpaid bills for champagne the Nazis had shipped to Germany. Champagne houses, notably Moët & Chandon, were in disarray after their executives had been imprisoned and the houses themselves had been placed under direct German control.

The Champenois were relieved when they heard that Robert-Jean de Vogüé, who had headed both Moët and the CIVC, was still alive after a year and a half in a slave-labour camp. They were horrified, however, when they saw his condition.

De Vogüé was not supposed to have survived. The Nazis had put the letters NN against his name – *Nacht und Nebel* (Night and Fog) – which meant work him to death and dump him into an unmarked grave. Just after he arrived at the camp, a sadistic guard told him: 'You know what they say about Ziegenhain, don't you? Those who come to Ziegenhain come here to die.'

De Vogüé almost did.

One morning he awoke to discover that an infection in the little finger of his right hand had become much worse. As he examined it more closely, he realized that gangrene had set in. When he asked for a doctor, the authorities ignored him. De Vogüé knew he would die unless he did what was necessary himself. He found a piece of glass and sharpened it as best he could. Then he began to cut. With no anaesthetic, the pain was unbearable but de Vogüé continued to cut until he had removed his entire finger. Using the rags of his concentration camp clothes, he finally stopped the bleeding. The crude operation saved his life, but it was almost for naught.

When his camp was liberated, de Vogüé began walking. He had gone only a few kilometres before he collapsed. As he lay unconscious on the road, a British officer passed by and stopped. He was a man with whom de Vogüé had once worked in Champagne. The Englishman jumped out of his jeep and picked up de Vogüé; then he notified de Vogüé's family that he was bringing him home.

For de Vogüé's five children, it was an exciting moment. They had no idea of their father's condition and had decorated the living room with signs of 'Welcome Home, Papa'.

When de Vogüé arrived, all the joy vanished. No one recognized the frail, stick-like figure who could no longer stand on his own. He bore no resemblance to the elegant, dynamic man who had run the Moët & Chandon Champagne house and who had faced down Otto Klaebisch.

Now he hung between the shoulders of the British officer and his brother-in-law. His greeting was so faint the children were not even sure he had spoken. Their mother began to cry as she ushered the men into the bedroom to help put her husband to bed. For days, there was doubt he would recover.

De Vogüé's assistant, Claude Fourmon, who was arrested with him in Klaebisch's office, arrived back in Champagne in even worse shape. Fourmon had been sent to Bergen-Belsen where each day was a test of survival. He would fix a date to live and then, when that date passed, he would pick another one. 'If I can just make it until January 13th,' he would tell himself, 'then I can make it.' When January 13th arrived, he picked another date.

Those dates stretched on through the winter of 1943–44. The cold was unbearable. 'I sang,' Fourmon said. 'I sang against the cold. I sang hymns, children's songs, anything. Songs seemed to be the only thing that helped.'

When he finally returned home, Fourmon, like de Vogüé, was barely alive. He had been tortured and was no longer the ebullient young man whom the Gestapo had arrested in Reims two year earlier. 'I came back not young anymore,' Fourmon said. He was 30 years old.

Extract from *Wine & War, The French, The Nazis and France's Greatest Treasure* by Don & Petie Kladstrup, Hodder & Stoughton (London) 2001. Reproduced here with kind permission of the authors and publisher.

Evelyn Waugh (1964)

9 FIZZ, BUBBLY, POP IN THE SWINGING SIXTIES

The 1960s saw a return to prosperity for Champagne. Writing in 1964, Evelyn Waugh finds both favour and fault with this 'most modern of wines', it being more convenient than a cocktail and fundamentally suitable for 'frequent occasional use'…

Some years ago I had the happy experience of joining a miscellaneous company of English politicians, peers, novelists and journalists on a tour of Champagne. We had been invited to Reims by the vintners for the blessing of a stained-glass window they had presented to the cathedral. The ceremony was stripped of most of its dignity by the irreverence of the French press-photographers but the days of hospitality were memorable. We perambulated the huge archaic cellars of Pommery and the formal gardens of Moët; the elaborate processes of the *vendange* (harvesting of the grapes) and vintage were demonstrated. We were entertained in the houses and offices of many local magnates whose names had hitherto been abstractions on the labels of their wines.

They are an outstandingly handsome set, the champagne barons and baronesses, mostly the descendants of the nobility of other provinces who, a hundred years ago, migrated to this bleak region and married the heiresses of the original simple farmers of the land and then, not content, as most fortune hunters would be, to live at ease, took charge of their wives' dowries, learned the business and enormously increased its value.

Everywhere we were regaled with bottles, some of dignified age, some in turbulent youth. We had a thundering good time. It must therefore seem ungrateful to say that it was several weeks before I again drank champagne. An illusion of adolescence had been dissipated. Until that lavish beano I had held that champagne was the ideal beverage for any hour of the day and night and for every physical condition. Now I am obliged to admit that the French know better and that it is a wine for (frequent) occasional use.

Champagne is in a sense the most modern of wines. It claims a monastic origin but, in fact, it was little known outside its own district until the Russian invasion at the fall of Napoleon. The history of the Widow Clicquot, which has been charmingly written by Mme de Caraman-Chimay, wife of the present head of the firm, is typical of the great Champagne houses. Mme Clicquot, *née* Ponsardin, was a bourgeoise of Reims. Born 12 years before the Revolution, widowed before Austerlitz, she inherited a property in which viticulture was a minor concern. Her father was a Jacobin; she the ancestress of three dukes. Throughout her long widowhood she devoted herself to perfecting the processes of manufacture and to selling her wine abroad. Her rivals were also prospering.

Early in the 19th century champagne became the symbol of prosperity and gaiety and so it has remained in the darker and duller succeeding century.

It is a manufactured wine owing less to nature and more to human skill than any wine in France. It is inimitable. Gruesome attempts have been made in New Jersey to produce an equivalent. It is almost indestructible and will stand changes of temperature and physical agitations that would ruin a Bordeaux or a burgundy; still more a port. Champagnes of the same brand and year are identical in Epernay, Hollywood and Tokyo. In the early years of the export trade horrible things appeared in the bottles – *veux de crapaud* and *couleuvres* – and the correspondence of the rival agents is full of anxiety about the condition of the delayed cargoes. Patient scientific investigation has cured all that. Today one can be completely confident of finding every bottle clean to the last drop. I do not remember ever finding a bad cork. In extreme age the wine loses its fizz, and sometimes darkens in colour and takes on a flavour of Madeira. There are those who relish it in this condition. During the war it was discovered that one of the London railway hotels still had a bin of flat, brown, 60-year-old champagne still priced as it had been in its youth. There, in the mornings, through the ravages of bombs, a little group of coeval gourmets used to meet and sip in great content.

By its nature champagne can be produced only on a large scale. The hereditary skills of the various workers have to be fertilized by great capital investment. In the course of the last 150 years Reims, once the sacring place of the kings of France, has become the centre of one of its most important export industries. A handful of families own and manage the entire business. Each has its own trade secrets and each produces a wine of its own character. When you find a genuine champagne bearing a label that is not of one of the great houses you can (I think) be sure that it is the product of one of them which they are reluctant to sell under their own names; sometimes merely a surplus part of their regular production. Many London wine merchants have a wine bottled for them in Reims or Epernay which they sell under names of their own at a lower price than the famous brands. These they recommend for use at balls and weddings but they are worth the experiments of serious drinkers who may sometimes be surprised by finding a vintage of high quality under an unfamiliar title.

The champagne vintners, like those of the Douro, can blend their wines to satisfy the tastes of their customers. In the years before 1917 the Russians were the most important and they liked it sweet. Sugar was added before fermentation. In many parts of Europe a wine only slightly less sweet than the Russian is still preferred but in this century the words 'sweet champagne' have acquired a pejorative sense suggestive of the bordello, while 'dry' fatuously suggests sparkling wit. English and Americans are guilty of the modern flight from sweetness which is driving into neglect the finest Sauternes, hock and even port. I have seen a ghastly (I hope false) report that the incomparable Château d'Yquem is now making a dry wine for New Yorkers who are proud of the name but cannot enjoy its riches. Pink champagne also has a louche reputation – ballet shoes and *cabinets particuliers*. Sometimes I believe it is ordinary wine with some tasteless colouring matter added. Veuve Clicquot Rosé on the other hand is a rare, splendid and quite distinct wine.

Most of the wines of Champagne are made from a mixture of black and white grapes. There are, however, the delicious *blancs de blanc*s, the best of which are very slightly sweet and *crémant* instead of *mousseux*. These have the great advantage that they can be tossed down in bumpers without the impediment which the fizz causes in the normal gullet. There are also, of course, the still white wines of the district, *champagne nature*, delicate and refreshing, which I have very rarely met outside France.

But for most of the world champagne means 'Fizz', 'Bubbly' or 'Pop', the international symbol of high living. I began this essay by stating that it should be a matter of frequent, occasional use, sometimes as the last of many wines at a formal banquet but best 'discussed' – to use an antiquated term – in privacy.

For two intimates, lovers or comrades, to spend a quiet evening with a magnum, drinking no apéritif before, nothing but a glass of cognac after – that is the ideal. At midnight with a light supper, then too it is excellent. There are those – I am no longer one of them – who find a pint sustaining in mid-morning drunk in solitude after one's letters are answered before facing the social trials of the day. The worst time is that dictated by convention, in a crowd, in the early afternoon, at a wedding reception.

Since the austere '40s people in England have realized that champagne is relatively inexpensive. It has the great advantage to the host that the hard-drinking young do not much like it. They look for whisky. If they find it, they are irremovable and after an hour or two become boisterous or even truculent. When only champagne is offered them, honour has been satisfied and they soon slink off disappointed.

Champagne parties, I am told, are now taking the place of cocktail parties. No skilled barman is needed. The wine, when spilled, does little damage. Neat devices are on the market with which half-empty bottles can be sealed for future use. But, however convenient and inexpensive these assemblies, they have a disadvantage that should be noted; they smell. Many things that are very good in the mouth, such as Camembert cheese, can be offensive to the nose. Champagne is one of them and like cheese should be taken on a full stomach. To enter a house at seven, when it is full of people who have eaten nothing for some hours, who have drunk champagne and are obliged by the noise and press to shout into one another's faces, makes one long for the wholesome, gross reek of rum grog.

But this is not the note on which to end an act of homage to one of the great man-made goods that have not only survived into our day but actually thrived and become refined there. Lament the modern age as we will. Declare with justice that we can no longer build or paint; that we have made all but the most remote corners of our country uninhabitable and destroyed the charms of travel. But in one thing we have it better than our great-great grandfathers – the copious bounty of the harvest on those chilly battlefields of Champagne and of the invention and industry in the dank chalk caves where miles of bottles lie maturing for our delight.

First published as 'Fizz, Bubbly, Pop' in *Wine & Food*, No 123, 'Autumn Number' 1964 (priced five shillings); editor in chief: André L Simon; editor: Hugh Johnson. Reproduced here by permission of The Wylie Agency (UK) Ltd.

Joe Fattorini (2022)

10 CHAMPAGNE, OUR SOCIAL SIGNIFIER

Joe Fattorini looks at champagne from a Millennial perspective, and insists that Champagne Socialism – once a symbol of hypocrisy and pretence, a comical oxymoron – has turned a corner. Now the pundits are right: everyone should drink it!

To be fair, Gary Neville, the former captain of Manchester United Football Club, doesn't have much in common with Stalin. One led a diabolical red army on a devastatingly successful campaign through Europe. The other ruled Russia from 1922 to 1953. But they do have one thing in common. Both are rare defenders of 'Champagne Socialism'.

'Champagne Socialism' must be among the smaller hills worth (metaphorically) dying on. A two-word epithet, flung like a barb by those who see hypocrisy, cant and humbug from opponents on the political left. Or even within the political left. A comical oxymoron up there with 'military intelligence', 'affordable caviar' and 'Microsoft Works'. Two words squished together that would normally spring apart like magnets repulsed by their mutual polarity. So why would Stalin and the man Sir Alex Ferguson once called 'the best English right back of his generation' defend it?

And can Champagne Socialism tell us something about Champagne? And Socialism? Is it really the case that socialists shouldn't drink champagne?

Gary Neville captained Manchester United at the height of its success in the noughties. Like all professional footballers at the peak of their game he earned a small fortune. Today he is estimated to be worth over £20 million. Gary enjoys the high life. A nice home. Smart car. A string of property investments and a successful hotel and restaurant business. He enjoys champagne. I know. I once shared a couple of glasses with him as we chatted at the opening of one of his restaurants, Café Football.

Gary Neville is also a socialist. More than that. He's a socialist of the 'Champagne' sort. As he said in 2021: 'People quite often call me [a Champagne Socialist] and I say, "Yeah, you're right, I am". People should be entitled to drink champagne if they want to drink it... Let's get standard class up to first class.'

For Gary, the problem is not with champagne. Or with what it is. Or what it costs. The problem is with a society where champagne is only affordable to an elite. An elite he belongs to. But Gary doesn't want to be the only one drinking champagne. He'd like everyone to drink it.

In this – if nothing else – Gary Neville shares his views with Joseph Stalin. There are mixed reports about Stalin's opinions on soccer. Some say he loved it. Some that he had no interest in it. But he certainly threatened Soviet players with dire consequences if they didn't beat foreign teams. Like Sir Alex Ferguson but with a big moustache. In 1936 Stalin had a special soccer tournament played out in Red Square. A huge surface was laid out, and players played the game for the glory of the Soviet Union.

That same year – 1936 – football wasn't the only thing on Stalin's mind. 1936 was the year Stalin demanded a huge increase in the production of Soviet 'Champagne'. It wasn't actually champagne. It wasn't even anything like champagne. But importantly it was called 'Champagne'. Sort of. 'Sovetskoye Shampanskoye' or 'Сове́тское шампа́нское'. Sovetskoye Shampanskoye was made in a different way from real champagne. In bulk and from different grapes. It was important that this proud, Soviet product carried the same name as the luxury beverage from the degenerate West. It tasted different too, sickly sweet to westerners. And it came from different parts of the world, Crimea, Hungary, Belarus, and in the south in Moldova.

Stalin's edict had huge consequences. Moldova became – per head and per hectare – the world's biggest wine producer. The Soviet Union created a vast rail network with sprawling sidings dedicated to moving millions of bottles north to cities like Moscow. The world's biggest cellars (Milestii Mici) and second biggest (Cricova) were dug out to house winery equipment and maturing bottles.

As the bottles poured into the Soviet Union, Stalin declared this 'Champagne' was 'an important sign of well-being. Of the good life'. Like Gary Neville, Stalin believed the proletariat should be entitled to drink Shampanskoye, or 'Champagne', if they wanted to. Ultimately he was successful. Under the Soviet Union, the average factory worker could afford a bottle of Sovetskoye Shampanskoye for regular celebrations and parties. Something that couldn't be said of an average factory worker in the UK or US. Then – or despite the efforts of Gary Neville – now.[1]

This is perhaps unfair on poor Gary Neville. Gary would like everyone to be wealthy enough to enjoy real champagne. Stalin did the opposite. He created a facsimile of champagne, a bastardized replica, that gave the impression that everyone was wealthy enough to drink champagne. Even if they weren't.[2] But Stalin knew that the name was more important than the thing. The 'writer is the engineer of the human soul'. It's the name that carried the symbolism, not the wine itself. He had called it champagne, 'Shampanskoye', to take the meaning and symbolism of champagne and inserted it into his own ersatz Soviet replica.

So how had champagne itself acquired a meaning beyond 'quality sparkling wine'? Fortunately, several champagne Socialists have sought to explain.

The historian and social theorist Eric Hobsbawm was more often described as a Champagne Communist. Hobsbawm was an unapologetic admirer of the Soviet Union and regular drinker of Champagne.[3] Hobsbawm was also one of the influences behind the notion of 'invented tradition', a comical oxymoron a bit like Champagne Socialism itself. Invented tradition is the notion that ideas in culture that we think of as traditional and emerging from the distant past are, in reality, quite recent. That they can be and are invented. Champagne fits his mould.

The Champagne Bureau talks about champagne's celebrated and glittering past. An icon of Frenchness, stretching to the Baptism of Clovis I, the first king to unite the Frankish tribes in the sixth century. But this story forgets to mention that champagne didn't even have bubbles until twelve hundred years later. Kolleen M Guy argues in *When Champagne Became French: Wine and the Making of a National Identity* (2003) that champagne didn't truly become central to French identity until the 19th century, in the period between the

---

[1] Ironically, Stalin himself wasn't a noted drinker of the stuff. He had a penchant for the sweet red wines of his homeland Georgia. But preferred to sip at a glass of water, pretending it was vodka, while his politburo grew drunk and loosened their tongues, revealing insights he could later turn against them, or their colleagues.

[2] This is an early example of what the writer Alexei Yurchak termed 'HyperNormalisation'. This described the feeling among people in the late-period Soviet Union where everyone knew Soviet society wasn't working, and what people were told was a lie. And the people telling the lies knew the people hearing them knew they were lying. But that because nobody could envision an alternative everyone just accepted the fakeness as normal.

[3] In a famous interview with Michael Ignatieff, Eric Hobsbawm was asked if the deaths inflicted by Stalin on the Soviet Union could be justified. Hobsbawm replied: 'Probably not… because it turns out that the Soviet Union was not the beginning of the world revolution. Had it been, I'm not sure.' Ignatieff pressed him by asking: 'Had the radiant tomorrow actually been created, the loss of 15, 20 million people might have been justified?' Hobsbawm answered: 'Yes.'

beginning of the Franco-Prussian War and the beginning of World War I. Citing Eric Hobsbawm, Kolleen Guy writes: 'During this time champagne became an object of mass culture, a centrepiece of bourgeois society both in France and abroad. Historians have noted that this was an era of rapid transformation when social groups and their milieu underwent dramatic change, resulting in a search for new ways to mark social status and to structure social relations. Champagne became part of this repertoire of symbolic devices used to delineate social boundaries, supplying a common denominator for those claiming membership of certain social groups'.[4][5]

Looked at this way, champagne starts to become problematic for the committed socialist. How can someone committed to equality and the liberation of the proletariat from bourgeois codes and capitalist hegemony truly enjoy a 'symbolic device used to delineate social boundaries'? How can they relax drinking a symbolic artefact used to 'mark status and structure social relations'?

The relationship between champagne and emerging bourgeois social relationships worked two ways. Champagne became what the Harvard and Oxford marketing professor Douglas Holt calls an 'ideological parasite'. Champagne's images and values of luxury, celebration and the good life didn't only come from good marketing. Things like advertisements and PR. But more subtle cultural strategies where champagne latches onto ideologies and cultural myths like a parasite. For instance, by nestling in the guts of films where it takes on the values of the heroes. The James Bond films. *Breakfast at Tiffany's*. *The Great Gatsby*. Alfred Hitchcock's *Champagne*. And the 1936 film (an important year) *Champagne Charlie* featuring 'Champagne Charlie' Courtland, a smooth, sophisticated but unethical gambler making his money among the rich and famous. The very antithesis of socialist values.

Not only films, as champagne's symbolism also feeds off television programmes like *Absolutely Fabulous*. Or crawls under the skin of sports like Formula One. Holt argues[6] that as well as inserting brands like champagne into film, ideological parasites construct the articulation between the brand and the myth through 'journalistic packaging', 'subculture affiliation' and 'status competition'. Every one of them anathema to the true socialist.

4 Guy, Kolleen M, 'Wine, Work and Wealth: Class Relations and Modernization in the Champagne Wine Industry, 1870–1914', Department of History, University of Texas at San Antonio (1997).
5 As it happens, the French don't use the term 'Champagne Socialist'. They use the equally derisive term '*gauche caviar*'.
6 Holt, Douglas B, 'Jack Daniel's America: Iconic brands as ideological parasites and proselytizers', Journal of Consumer Culture (2006).

Ironically, it's 'journalistic packaging' that has helped to create not only the Champagne brand, but also the Champagne Socialist brand. Turning those two words into a media heuristic for hypocrisy, cant and humbug.

There are easy targets. Perhaps too easy. Like Muammar Gaddafi, the 'Brotherly Leader' of the Great Socialist People's Libyan Arab Jamahiriya. Commentators let it be known that after a hard day crafting his Third International Theory, Gaddafi liked nothing more than a relaxing glass of Laurent-Perrier Rosé. Or Nicolae Ceaușescu, President of the Socialist Republic of Romania. After he and his wife Elena were executed by firing squad in 1989, Romanians discovered a personal cellar filled with champagne. And highlighted it when they auctioned off the contents for charity. It's easy to see why this hit home. I happened to travel to Romania soon after the Ceaușescus were executed. There were still bullet holes in the buses in Timișoara. While the Ceaușescus enjoyed champagne, the population were drinking a brutal local grappa distilled in lead stills that was gradually poisoning everyone.

Or Robert Mugabe, the former President of Zimbabwe and leader of ZANU-PF. Mugabe was an avowed Marxist-Leninist whose political party was a member of the Socialist International (SI) throughout his time as leader. Once a hero of the western Left, there was no better way to highlight his fall from leftist favour than point out that Mugabe celebrated his 85th birthday with two thousand bottles of champagne, including 1961 Bollinger and Moët & Chandon. The birthday party took place only a few months after Zimbabwe's annualized inflation rate had reached 89.7 sextillion percent.[7]

But these are easy targets. And, some might argue, not true 'socialists' at all. Rather, corrupted dictators who clung to the ideology as part of their fig-leaf of authority. What about socialists who aren't dictators?

Like Friedrich Engels. Marx's best friend, closest ally and co-author of 'The Communist Manifesto'. Engels was one of the authors of Socialism as a doctrine. Yet he was known by his son-in-law as 'the great beheader of champagne bottles'. A biography of Engels by Tristram Hunt titled *The Frock-Coated Communist* (2009) underlines the point with the subtitle 'The Life and Times of the Original Champagne Socialist'.

I used to walk past Engels' house in Primrose Hill in north London when I worked at Bibendum wine merchants. If I had to stay the night, I'd book in at

---

7 That's 89,700,000,000,000,000,000,000%.

a hotel on the Finchley Road, just off Frognal. As it happens, Frognal was where Ramsay Macdonald, Labour's first prime minister, had a seven-bedroom house. It was said that some of his Labour colleagues disapproved of the size of the house. Not to mention Macdonald's habits.

While Engels is retrospectively seen as the first Champagne Socialist, Macdonald was perhaps the first to have the term applied to him in his lifetime. Macdonald was unquestionably working class, the illegitimate son of a farm labourer and a housemaid. Yet as his status as a politician grew, so did his tastes. He ate and drank well. Not least champagne. As party leader he would enter the opulent eve-of-Parliament dinners given by the Marchioness of Londonderry alongside his hostess, with whom he was said to be obsessed. They would enter under Londonderry House's famed Rococo chandelier, walking down the grandest staircase in London and into the ballroom, which was larger even than the Waterloo Chamber at Apsley House, home to the Duke of Wellington.

Among the Labour movement, this cavorting was deemed to have corrupted Macdonald. To have softened him. And to eventually lead him to sell out the party to the National Government of 1931. He became the first for whom Champagne Socialism was a critique. More among his own party than the opposition. Churchill could hardly throw the charge at him… Churchill was reckoned to have drunk 42,000 bottles of champagne in his lifetime. But that's where the power and sting of 'Champagne Socialist' kicks in. Who is really surprised that the son of a Lord, grandson of the Viceroy of India, a descendant of the Duke of Marlborough who was born in a palace… might quite like to drink a lot of champagne?

Macdonald might have been the first, but he was far from the last. New Labour was the creation – in part – of 'Champagne Socialist' Peter Mandelson who bought his house with an ill-advised loan from 'Champagne Socialist' Geoffrey Robinson. The party was supported by donations from celebrities like 'Champagne Socialist' writer JK Rowling. And today high-profile supporters of the modern left include 'Champagne Socialist' actors like Emma Thompson, Martin Freeman and Richard Wilson, 'Champagne Socialist' singers like Lily Allen and Charlotte Church, and 'Champagne Socialist' comedians like Shappi Khorsandi, David Baddiel, Eddie Izzard and Frank Skinner. Although Frank Skinner doesn't drink so 'you can't call me that. I'm a Fizzy Water Socialist'.

Champagne is two things. It's a drink. A delicious one. A unique one. 'You can always identify champagne by its mouth-filling perfume,' said Michael

Schuster when I was studying for the Master of Wine. It's also a symbol. A signifier. A drinkable locum for privilege, prestige and power. Is it possible for the Socialist to divorce one from the other?

'Pleasure without champagne is purely artificial.' So wrote the author of *The Soul of Man Under Socialism* (1891). He argued that '[w]ith the abolition of private property, then, we shall have true, beautiful, healthy Individualism. Nobody will waste his life in accumulating things, and the symbols for things. One will live. To live is the rarest thing in the world. Most people exist, that is all.'

The author was perhaps the greatest Champagne Socialist of them all, Oscar Wilde. In 1997, the writer John Mortimer gave an address at the Birthday Dinner of the Oscar Wilde Society. 'I am frequently called a Champagne Socialist,' said Mortimer. 'And when I'm not being called a Champagne Socialist, I'm being called a Bollinger Bolshevik. Now I don't think there's anything about Socialism that requires you to wear a bobble hat, and an anorak, eat muesli for breakfast and read *The Guardian*. I do think that Oscar Wilde who wore astrakhan collars and velvet suits, and drank a good deal of champagne, was just as much entitled to be a Socialist as Ken Livingstone, or me, or Dennis Skinner or anyone else.'

Champagne drinkers of the world… unite.

The rapper and record executive Jay Z, with his wife Beyonce Knowles, at the 'Armand de Brignac' champagne party in Cannes (2008). Jay Z used music to make his way out of Marcy Projects, one of Brooklyn's most violent neighbourhoods. Today, as one of America's most successful hip-hop artists and businessmen, he is co-owner (with LVMH) of the Armand de Brignac brand, also known as 'Ace of Spades'.

Robert Walters (2022)

11 THE PLATINUM ERA

Robert Walters argues that champagne is now entering a new era, where terroir-specific wines are valued at least as much as blends, and where the connection between vineyard practice and quality is no longer up for meaningful debate.

Can we still believe in miracles? If not, then we might be surprised to learn that in recent decades, this is precisely what has occurred in Champagne. Of course, I'm not talking about the religious kind of miracle. No loaves and fishes here, no lepers cured, no corpses raised from the dead. There is, in fact, no need for such supernatural phenomena; the etymology of the term 'miracle' comes to us from the Latin *miraculum*, simply meaning something that inspires wonder or astonishment. In this context, the rise of the great growers of Champagne can be fairly described as miraculous. For it's a story so fantastic that no one would have believed it possible, had it not actually happened.

For as long as sparkling wines have been produced in Champagne, it's been the Houses or *grandes marques* of the region that have dominated production. And for the best part of 200 years, these large Houses have enjoyed an unchallenged reputation as the producers of their region's (and therefore the world's) finest *mousseux*, or sparkling wine.

For all of this time, the Houses have repeatedly explained to us that their success could be attributed to two factors: the climate and soil of their region, and their savoir-faire in sparkling wine production. In terms of the savoir-faire, pretty much all of the emphasis was placed on the cellar work. In fact, until recent years, I don't ever recall attending a wine tasting with a *grande marque* where the practice in the vineyard was spontaneously mentioned at all – the magic happened was in the cellar and in the bottle.

Questions about vineyard practice – perhaps something on Champagne's surprisingly high yields or conventional viticulture – would quickly be batted away. 'Trust us,' we were told: 'We know what we're doing,' 'Champagne is different,' 'Can you not see that we make the best sparkling wines in the world?', 'Is that not enough?'

How could anyone argue with this? Champagne did, after all, consistently produce the world's most celebrated sparkling wines, and the very best of these, until the early 2000s, were exclusively made by the Houses under their *cuvée de prestige* labels. This truth seemed to put the Champenois beyond critique.

But then, in the 1980s, the ground started to shift ever so slightly. A pair of small grower-producers (wine producers who owned their own vines and made wine from their own fruit), Anselme Selosse and Francis Egly, started radically diverging from the viticultural and winemaking norms of their region. The wines of these growers changed accordingly, and for the better. In the years that followed, Selosse and Egly gained themselves a growing band of followers and the praise of several critics, most notably the French writer Michel Bettane.

A new approach to viticulture

By the late 1990s a number of other Champagne growers had started to make similar progress. These included Pascal Agrapart (who had actually begun his journey in the 1980s), Pierre and Sophie Larmandier of Larmandier-Bernier and Jérôme Prévost of La Closerie. By the 2000s, the movement was gaining genuine traction and names like Cédric Bouchard and Vouette et Sorbée were quickly developing cult-like followings. Of course, the list today is far longer and would certainly include the stunning wines of Ulysse Collin, Chartogne-Taillet, Bérêche, Suenen, and any number of others.

The modus operandi of all these 'great growers' (to distinguish them from those growers who have not changed their approach) followed a system that was in direct contrast to the typical practice of their region. They eschewed herbicides and chemical fertilizers (ubiquitous in the Champagne region throughout this period and still the norm), they worked with far lower, more balanced yields (Champagne is far and away the highest-yielding premium wine region in France), and they harvested considerably riper fruit with riper acidity.

The logic behind these changes, and many more, was simple enough; these growers had been bitten by the terroir bug and they had come to realize, mostly thanks to their interactions with the great growers of other regions, that making great wines which spoke clearly of the vineyard (rather than simply the cellar) required a fundamentally different approach to the one that had come to dominate their region. This new approach led to much more vinous wines that seemed to speak a completely different language. They were deeper, more characterful, more fruit-driven and more robust, and this latter attribute, in turn, allowed them to be aged longer before bottling. It also meant that fewer interventions were needed in the cellar – less filtration, less inoculation, fewer dosage additions. The final wines were also more versatile: equally at home served on their own or at the table with food.

The idea catches on…

The elephant was now well and truly in the room. How was it possible that such a radically different approach was capable of producing such compelling wines? Hadn't we been told by the '*ancien régime*' that their way of working was the best, if not the only way? How then were we to reconcile the two narratives and the two very different wine styles now offered by Champagne?

At first the Houses argued (with some irony) that the new-found appreciation of the best grower wines was largely the result of marketing and fashion – two factors that had been key to the success of the *grandes marques* themselves. Sometimes the language that the Houses used was openly bitter, but a door had opened that could not be closed. It was now clear that vineyard practice mattered as much in Champagne as it did for quality wines in Burgundy, Alsace, Saumur, etc. This revelation not only had profound implications for Champagne, but it also raised questions for every sparkling wine producer anywhere in the world who followed the interventionist, cellar-first model.

Today, things have come full circle. The wild success of Champagne's top growers has had a significant influence on the practice and communications of the Houses themselves. These great brands can now be heard talking openly about the changes they are making in the vineyards. They are even willing to acknowledge that these changes are improving their wines.

Getting site-specific

All of this would have been miraculous enough, but there is another postscript to the story that is arguably even more incredible. In line with their 'terroir-first' approach, the best growers have tended to release wines from specific villages, vineyards or terroirs. As the number of these wines has grown – from the south of the region to the very north – a totally new vision of Champagne has emerged. Instead of a vast area, the size of a small country, where the wines are typically blended from many vineyards to produce a 'house style', today we can buy and taste any number of properly farmed, properly ripe, 'single terroir' champagnes, each with their own distinct personality and interest.

Who had heard of the villages (let alone tasted the wines) of Congy, Montgueux, Ludes, Gueux, Vrigny, Merfy and Saint Thierry – or even Oiry and Vertus – before this revolution? Some of these villages were not even marked on regional maps. Yet today they produce some of the Champagne's most thrilling wines. Who had heard of the single-vineyard sites that now adorn so many of the best growers' labels? Even when some of these places were well-known, and occasionally bottled separately, the wines of the best growers typically revealed these terroirs in a completely new and more potent way. Who, for example, could have imagined that the vineyards of Ambonnay or Avize were capable of the depth and power that we find today in the wines of Egly, Selosse and Agrapart?

Blending can produce great wines in Champagne, as it can anywhere, but we now know that there are countless terroirs across the region capable of producing greatness on their own. Today we no longer have simply 'house-styles' to choose from. Today, thanks to the diversity of terroirs that the best growers farm and the quality of their work, we can discuss, and taste unblended, many of the myriad sub-areas, villages and vineyards of the region, and we can celebrate each of their unique attributes. Today, we can embrace Champagne as a region that's as complex, varied and rewarding as any still wine area, including Burgundy.

And if all that isn't a miracle, then I don't know what is.

TANGOING WITH TERROIR

5

Grandes marques vs grand growers… Some take sides, but not everyone has to. Every vineyard is unique and its contribution is as important to a multi-vintage blend as it is to a single-site champagne.

SMALL STEPS BACK TO BURGUNDY
William Kelley (2019)

THESE CHARISMATIC HILLS
Peter Liem (2022)

GET SET, GO!
Robert Walters (2016)

THE GREENING OF CHAMPAGNE
Tyson Stelzer (2019)

BUBBLE, BUBBLE, TOIL AND TROUBLE
Tyson Stelzer (2019)

William Kelley (2019)

SMALL STEPS BACK TO BURGUNDY

The strength of its brands and the passion of its artisan growers both give cause for celebration in Champagne. And while these two versions of fizz appear to have the region travelling fast in two different directions, William Kelley explains that far from tearing Champagne in half, both can reveal the beauty of this region's terroir. He introduces three inspirational growers at the centre of the game…

To understand Champagne, it's necessary to understand its history. From the seventh to the 18th century, Champagne followed a similar path to that of Burgundy: wine growing and winemaking were overseen by the Benedictine monks, who divided the land into small parcels and farmed it accordingly. But in the aftermath of the confiscation of monastic lands that followed the French Revolution, Champagne and Burgundy took divergent paths. While Burgundy remained wedded more or less faithfully to the concept of terroir, the worldly merchants and négociants of Reims and Epernay capitalized on the fashion for sparkling wine among Europe's elites to create modern champagne over the course of the 19th century. Blended from wines sourced all over the region and frequently containing as much as 300 grams per litre of sweetening sugar, this unctuous and expensive beverage soon became a symbol of luxury – and a considerable commercial success. And if the concept of terroir had its origins in Roman Catholic monasticism, 19th-century champagne was to a considerable extent the creation of frequently protestant engineers and tradesmen from German-speaking northern Europe, a patrimony reflected in the names of many Champagne houses today.

Since sparkling champagne was created by merchants rather than wine growers, it's unsurprising that it should have been first and foremost a brand from the very beginning. Blending in pursuit of a consistent and characterful house style, Champagne's important houses emphasized the *marque* – or 'brand' – above their wines' origins on their labels and in their marketing. Naturally, a product so easy to understand triumphed in domestic and export markets alike, eclipsing all other sparkling wine regions in the consciousness of consumers. Until recently, in other words, the history of Champagne was the history of its brands. And while Champagne has long been home to small producers, bottling some of their own wine, it was not the small producers but the big brands that enjoyed the greatest prestige.

The grower revolution and the pursuit of terroir

For most of Champagne's 19th- and 20th-century history, brand trumped terroir. Of course, there were exceptions: Eugène-Aimé Salon's eponymous champagne has derived from a single vintage and a single village – Mesnil – since its inception in the 1910s; Philipponnat has bottled the wine from its celebrated Clos des Goisses since 1935; and with the 1979 vintage, Krug began producing a single-vineyard vintage *blanc de blancs* that attained immediate celebrity. But the fact remains that to this day, many of the *chefs de caves* who preside over Champagne's *marques* employ the term terroir, if at all, in reference to the shared regional characteristics that unite Champagne's wines: a cool climate and generally chalky soils. All of Champagne's 34,300 hectares are accommodated in only one single appellation – whereas Burgundy, by contrast, divides its 29,375 hectares into full 84 different *appellations d'origine contrôlées* (AOC). Champagne's classification system of Premier and Grand Crus applies not to single vineyards but to entire villages. And what's more, the majority of the region's most successful brands continue to be blends derived from vineyards located all over the Champagne AOC.

If the rediscovery of terroir in Champagne can be credited to the grower movement, it's important to note that the grower movement antedates the Champenois rediscovery of terroir. Grower-bottling – designated by the letters RM standing for *Récoltant-Manipulant* on the label – has been around for some time. After all, the Special Club group (the *Club Trésors du Champagne*) that unites some of the region's best growers was founded back in 1971, and several of its members had been bottling their own wine since the 1920s. But the reintroduction of the Burgundian concept of terroir, that had left Champagne with the monks, began more recently. In the beginning was Anselme Selosse, who worked in Burgundy and returned to his family estate in Avize in the 1970s, intent on working the soils, reducing yields and fermenting his wines in wooden barrels. Not long after, influenced by French wine critic Michel Bettane, Ambonnay's Francis Egly moved in a similar direction, bottling a single-vineyard *blanc de noirs* from his Les Crayères vineyard for the first time with the 1989 vintage. And Pierre and Sophie Larmandier in Vertus began to farm organically and then to vinify their wines in wood in the 1990s. Coalescing into a movement – with Selosse, by force of personality, emerging as its *de facto* philosopher and public face – what might be called Champagne's Burgundian turn gathered steam. Today, growers who fall more or less under this mantle can take considerable credit for the upswing in interest in fine champagne among wine lovers in France and all over the world.

Doing justice to Champagne's two faces

The contrast between Champagne's big houses and small growers invites simple polarities that present the choice between (in one influential importer's words) 'farmer fizz and factory fizz' as a zero-sum game. Wine lovers often form strong allegiances to one or the other, either remaining fiercely loyal to the *grandes marques* or entirely eschewing them. In reality, this is a false choice, but appreciating Champagne's 'two faces' for their respective merits certainly does present a cognitive challenge. In many respects, the world of the *grandes marques* exhibits closer parallels with that of the Médoc's *crus classés* than it does with the growers of the Côte d'Or: both share a sense of terroir that is more monolithic than kaleidoscopic; both emphasize consistency and blend for complexity rather than isolating small cuvées; and both, at their best, produce wines of incredible class and longevity. What's more, the acclaim bestowed on the leading growers has clearly motivated the *grandes marques* to evolve: fully half of Louis Roederer's 230 hectares, for example, is now certified organic. There's more work to do but the *grandes marques*' best *tête de cuvée* bottlings are very fine indeed. At their best, the *grandes marques* represent a different and long-established vision of what champagne can be, not an inferior one. And many of the growers recognize what the *grandes marques* have done to cultivate the region's international renown, as well as envying them their advantages – such as, in some cases, large stocks of ancient reserve wines kept for blending.

There's no doubt, however, that Champagne's finest small growers have inspired and refreshed the region. Even though grower champagne still accounts for only a tiny fraction of the region's exports, wines from the likes of Anselme Selosse, Cédric Bouchard, Jérôme Prévost, Olivier Collin and Emmanuel Lassaigne generate excitement in the marketplace that very few of the *grandes marques* can match. Vinous, concentrated and intensely characterful, the best grower champagnes offer the same kind of excitement that wine lovers derive from the highly differentiated wines of the Côte d'Or. With a myriad cuvées, *lieux-dits* names and disgorgements, they can be just as complex to comprehend. The idiosyncratic styles that some of the leading growers have developed can be disconcerting, even divisive, the most sought-after sold on strict allocation. I certainly don't believe that their wines should be subjected to any kind of glass ceiling that reserves the highest scores and plaudits for the *grandes marques*.

Here are three of my favourite growers, and why…

Cédric Bouchard: Champagne's reclusive revolutionary

Bouchard was born into a wine-growing family, but he only discovered a passion for his *métier* while working as a *caviste* – or wine merchant – in Paris. Returning to his hometown in the late 1990s, he began his tiny domaine when his father gifted him just under one hectare of Pinot Noir vines in the *lieu-dit* Les Ursules (in the Côte des Bar). 'I was delighted at the time, but Les Ursules is north-facing and it really isn't easy to ripen grapes, so in retrospect it was something of a poisoned chalice,' he laughs.

The 2000 vintage was Bouchard's first, and, from the beginning, his approach has challenged almost all the precepts of conventional champagne. In a region dominated by blends, all his wines derive from a single vineyard, a single grape variety and a single vintage. While most of Champagne's *vins clairs* are produced from grapes picked – to put it charitably – on the cusp of ripeness, their asperity tempered only by chaptalization and dosage, Bouchard picks late and adds neither. And if Champagne remains France's highest-yielding *appellation d'origine contrôlée*, Bouchard's yields of between 20 and 30 hectolitres per hectare would be considered low even by the best domaines of

Burgundy's Côte de Nuits. He even calls champagne's very identity – its bubbles – into question, by bottling at just over four bars of pressure rather than the conventional six.

Only the most immaculate of grapes are flattered by such uncompromising methods. Farming organically, Bouchard works his soils, prunes short and debuds hard. During the harvest, he employs fully 40 pickers for his tiny domaine – less than four hectares in surface area – and the atmosphere is more military than carnivalesque: 'Don't bother visiting me around harvest time,' he assures me, 'I'm too serious.'

With yields as low as Bouchard's, grapes ripen all the more rapidly, so timing is critical: 'We can lose acidity in just 24 hours.' It takes his team only an hour-and-a-half to bring in his 0.12-hectare parcel in *lieu-dit* Haut Lemblée, and the whole domaine is picked out in just three days. There's no sorting, because Bouchard is adamant about leaving any grapes that aren't perfect on the vine for the birds. 'I can't make wine from grapes with botrytis, from grapes with unripe stems, from frosted grapes – if the grapes don't give me the right feeling, even if I can't explain why, I won't make wine,' he explains. Once any fruit meeting such stringent criteria arrives at the winery, Bouchard retains only the first juice, discarding the rest, and it ferments in tank, abortive experiments with oak having convinced him that stainless steel offers the purest expression of his terroirs. Intervention is minimal: ambient microflora are responsible for both alcoholic and malolactic fermentation (there are no added yeasts), and Bouchard has only racked a wine twice in his career. When the wines are bottled, Bouchard adds less sugar than most producers, resulting in lower pressure inside the bottle, and encourages a leisurely *prise de mousse* of some three months.

These exacting methods produce – in an average year – some 14,000 bottles that number among Champagne's most singular. Vinous and textural, their freshness comes from neither carbonation nor the refrigerator, for they're as beautifully balanced at room temperature after an hour in the glass as they are immediately after the cork is popped and the bottle removed from the cool of the cellar. Despite Cédric's eschewal of dosage, there's nothing austere about these wines, young or old, though there is invariably plenty of tension, and a chalky grip on the finish that has nothing in common with the brittle, tartaric edge of so much poor-quality champagne. In fact, in shape and scale there isn't really anything like the wines of Roses de Jeanne – the label under which, since 2014, all of Cédric's wines are now released – in the region. Perhaps that's partly because the Kimmeridgian marl topped by Portlandian limestone that characterizes the Côte des Bar has more in common with Chablis than it does with the rest of Champagne. But I suspect more than equal credit is owed to Bouchard's unique approach to making wine.

Olivier Collin: The artist of Congy

Olivier Collin is frequently portrayed as a Champagne-newcomer, yet while this estate's latest incarnation dates back less than two decades, its antecedents reach back far further. The Collins have been wine growers in Congy for generations. Written records date back to 1812, when Jean-Bapriste Collin, vigneron, purchased a parcel of vines in the village, so it's likely the family have been established here for longer still. By the early 20th century, the Collins had begun bottling their own wines, and George Collin, Olivier's great-grandfather, won a prestigious prize in the *Concours Général Agricole de Paris* in 1935. By the 1970s, the Collins were among the founding members of the *Club de Viticultures Champenois*, today known as the *Club Trésors du Champagne* or Special Club. Olivier's father, however, didn't especially enjoy the precarious existence of a small Champagne producer in a seldom-visited area; so he stopped bottling his wines, leasing the family's vineyards to Pommery. The Collin family's winemaking patrimony thus fell into abeyance.

In the 1990s, Olivier Collin became a wine lover and began to contemplate taking over the family's vineyards. But breaking a contract with a large négociant isn't a simple matter. Collin studied for a law degree and also undertook a BTS technology diploma in viticulture and oenology to prepare himself for the battle to come. And in 2001, he spent two months working for Anselme Selosse in Avize as a *stagiaire* (intern). In due course, Olivier was able to negotiate the release of some 8.7 hectares of his family's holdings in time for the 2003 vintage; but their crop was promptly devastated by frost. It was only in 2004, therefore, that he began to produce wine of his own.

Collin's first step on taking back his family vineyards was to purchase a tractor and begin ploughing the soils. Living soils, he believes, are a prerequisite for terroir expression, and from the beginning he has aspired to produce terroir-driven wines. Chemical fertilizers and herbicides were accordingly replaced with organic compost and laborious working of the soil; but while he had witnessed biodynamics first-hand *chez* Selosse, Collin's concerns about the effects of copper accumulation in the soils have precluded his following suit. While he employs sulphur against oidium, he prefers to use a relatively benign and above all biodegradable synthetic product to battle mildew rather than employing the traditional (and approved organic) copper sulphate.

Collin has fermented his wines in used burgundy barrels from the beginning, but his techniques have evolved. An old hydraulic Coquard press has been replaced by a new, state-of-the-art version from the same firm. Reserve wines entered the equation in 2009, and today an ever-increasing array of large oak *foudres* now supplement 225-litre *pièces* for their storage. And at the same time, Collin began topping up his *vins clairs* during their maturation, eliminating the oxidative, biologically-aged characteristics that characterized some of his early releases and which suggested analogies between his style and Selosse's. 'I came to believe that if a wine is going to age gracefully, it has to start out life young,' he explains. Though dosage remains well below three grams per litre, some cuvées today see a touch more than they did in the past, rendering them a little less severe – 'less elitist', as Olivier puts it, crediting his wife Sandra's influence in tempering his tendency to be uncompromising.

Today, Collin is investing all his resources in building up his stocks of reserve wines and extending the time his cuvées see *sur lattes* before disgorgement. With each new release seemingly more impressive than the last, Champagne Ulysse Collin today ranks as one of the most exciting producers in the entire region.

Anselme Selosse: Leader of Champagne's artisanal revolution

Anselme Selosse may have officially retired in 2018, but his influence will continue to shape Champagne for many years to come. 'My first harvest,' he recalls, 'was the 1974 vintage, and I sold it in November 1978 for the equivalent of 3.70 Euros per bottle. It wasn't easy to sell!' Today, by contrast, a thirsty world clamours for Selosse's bottles, and he's rightly credited with a leading role in transforming contemporary champagne. Indeed, Selosse looms so large in the region that he sometimes casts a shadow over other producers. Phrases such as 'worked with Selosse' or 'inspired by Selosse' are used routinely by the trade, but they hardly do justice to the originality of the diverse diaspora of growers touched by his influence.

Selosse was the first grower in Champagne explicitly to draw inspiration from Burgundy, where he studied at the Beaune oenology faculty between 1969 and 1973. 'In Champagne at that time the idea of quality production in the vineyard simply did not exist,' he explained in a 2018 *Decanter* magazine interview with Robin Lee. 'In Burgundy, I witnessed a different relationship between those who produced and those who sold the wine, and it made a big impression. In Champagne it was simply the more you produced, the more you got paid. In Burgundy, even in those days, the wine was assessed for its quality and valued accordingly.' In Champagne, Selosse also observed, the market placed a premium on vintage, whereas in Burgundy it was the wine's origin that had the biggest impact on its price. And it is in his career-long emphasis on quality over quantity and site over vintage that Selosse's time in Burgundy has most consistently manifested itself.

Believing that phytosanitary treatments, fertilizers and productive rootstocks and clones had artificially augmented yields at the expense of concentration and character, Selosse sought modest yields from balanced vines growing in living soils. In the 1930s, yields in Champagne averaged 24 hectolitres (hl) per hectare; by the 1950s, that had risen to 33; in the 1960s, to over 50; and by the 1970s and '80s, to over 60hl per hectare. Just as importantly, during the same period, the average weight of a grape cluster in Champagne more than doubled. Selosse was the first to reverse this tendency, and he was soon followed by others.

At vintage time, Selosse was also an outlier, harvesting later than most other producers in Champagne in pursuit of fully mature fruit that would not require supplemental sugar from chaptalization. And in the cellar, winemaking was, from the beginning, Burgundian, with fermentation mainly in 228-litre *pièces* from the Tonnellerie de Mercurey and François Frères, some 20 percent of which are renewed each year. Selosse is a partisan of indigenous yeasts, and isolated his own proprietary selections from his cellar for the second fermentation in bottle – something that's usually only achieved with commercial selections. The ensuing wines were always vinous and concentrated, and it was their 'Burgundian' style that made the biggest impression on visitors to his cellars in the 1980s.

Over the years, however, Selosse increasingly came to focus on what he describes as the 'one gram of mineral substance in a litre of grape juice, not the 250 grams of organic matter.' 'Scientists say,' he explained when we last tasted together, 'that the vines don't take up minerals from the soil, but no one has ever been able to spell out for me where that one gram of mineral salts comes from.' From this perspective, biological ageing (on the lees) and controlled oxidation become ways to 'burn away' the organic matter, effacing the ephemeral influence of vintage and leaving behind only the terroir-derived mineral residue that interests him. These techniques draw not on Burgundy but instead from Selosse's fascination with the wines of Spain – especially the biological maturation of Jerez and the long *élevage* of Rioja. Precisely because he is interested in the mineral and not the organic, he privileges texture over aroma. 'In the old days of the *tastevin*' [the small silver saucers used for tasting in the cellar] 'texture was all-important; with the advent of the ISO tasting glass' [which amplifies aroma yet distracts from texture] 'the way we make wine changed.'

What does this mean at a technical level? Selosse leaves eight to 10 litres headspace in his barrels and tops them up little by little as fermentation subsides. At the end of November or early in December, they're fully topped up and thenceforth left alone. Since his cellar, thanks to fans, remains cooler than the outside environment but warms and cools following its fluctuations, a layer of flor (the white film of yeast so important to fino sherry) develops in spring as the cellar warms. Thereafter, Selosse and his team smell the barrels: any that are oxidative are stirred, reintroducing the heavy lees into suspension to return the wine to a more reductive state; and any that are reduced, Selosse agitates with the same *dodine* (mixer) to expel dissolved carbon dioxide. Throughout their *élevage*, the barrels' bungs are only loosely closed, as Selosse says he wants the wines to breathe. Reserve wines are stored in a so-called perpetual reserve, offering an average of vintage variation; whereas his cuvée Substance is drawn from a true solera established in 1986, intended to efface vintage variation entirely. (*See* pages 234–243 for a full description of these reserve wines.)

Champagnes produced from *vins clairs* such as these display a unique aromatic range and intensely sapid aromas. 'I'm interested in making small quantities of very specific wines for certain drinkers and certain occasions,'

Selosse told me in Avize, adding that while he admires the prosperity and plenty that Atlantic capitalism has created, he regrets its tendency to globalize away strong regional identities and tastes. 'I have no interest in making champagne that appeals to everyone,' he readily admits, and his intensely characterful wines do indeed divide opinion. Foremost among Selosse's critics is wine writer Tom Stevenson, who questions whether Selosse's 'oxidative' approach is even 'a legitimate style'. Of course, even Stevenson acknowledges Selosse's pervasive influence in Champagne, for it is Selosse's very willingness to break with the region's tired conventions and follow his own ideas that inspires and liberates other producers. As Adrien Dhondt, a young grower in the Côte des Blancs, explains: 'Anselme has influenced me a lot, because he succeeded in realizing his own conception of wine: whether one likes or dislikes them, his wines are unique in the world. He showed me the path I was looking for.'

Selosse may have retired in 2018, but thousands of bottles he crafted during his career's 45 vintages await disgorgement in his cellars in Avize: his influence will be enduring.

First published in *The Wine Advocate* in 2019. Reproduced with kind permission of the author.

Peter Liem (2022)

THESE CHARISMATIC HILLS

The most compelling attribute of a wine is its ability to tell us something about the place it comes from. Champagne is no exception, but because it is blended, it is tempting to think the importance of terroir is diminished. Peter Liem explains that terroir is as fundamental to champagne as it is to any other fine wine – he outlines the distinctive flavours and characters we can expect from each of its many villages.

In the late-20th-century paradigm that set the stage for our understanding of Champagne today, terroir was largely acknowledged only in a region-wide sense: the Champagne region was differentiated from other sparkling wine regions of the world by its chalky soils and northerly climate. At best, different *crus* were mentioned, recognizing one Grand or Premier Cru as distinct from another and vinifying them separately, but emphasis was firmly placed on the champagne-making process as the primary factor in creating a wine's character.

Today the prevailing attitude among Champagne's top producers has returned to a recognition of place as a determining influence, even more so than grape variety – Pinot Noir from Cumières and Pinot Noir from Verzenay, for example, have significantly different personalities, and winemakers will use them accordingly. Contemporary producers are increasingly preferring to work with as large a palette as possible, vinifying smaller parcels separately to preserve the characters of individual terroirs and create a greater assortment of possibilities, and as they seek to explore their terroirs with greater precision, they are in turn gaining a more detailed and sophisticated understanding of individual sites and what they can bring to a blend.

From this perspective, the expression of terroir is equally as vital to a blended wine as it is to a single-origin one, yet here it plays a different role: rather than being showcased on its own, it lends its character to a larger whole, much like an individual instrument in an orchestra or an ingredient in a dish. This doesn't diminish its impact, but instead allows individual components to

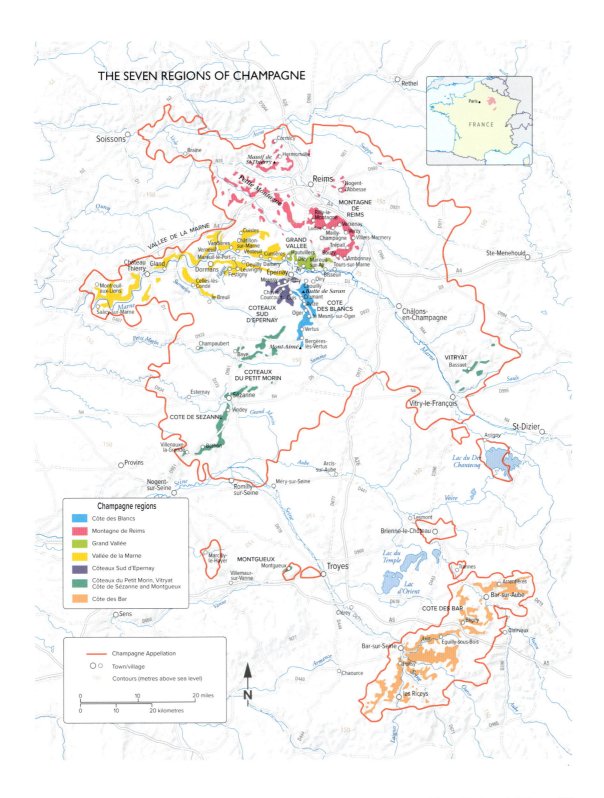

These Charismatic Hills   183

contribute to a greater completeness and complexity. When a house like Krug blends 146 different wines in its Grande Cuvée 169ème Edition, or vinifies 25 separate wines from Le Mesnil alone in a single harvest, this demonstrates a belief that greater precision and diversity of character in individual components results in higher quality in the final blend.

Champagne sub-regions

Champagne covers a large area, and naturally there are variations in the characters of the wines produced across the appellation, as the geology, climate and geography can change significantly. The paradigm dominant in the 20th century divided Champagne into three major sub-regions – four, if you count the Côte des Bar, which until 20 years ago was often overlooked. Yet considering the diversity of the Champagne region, this seems inadequate. The Comité Champagne, Champagne's governing body, has a complex schema that outlines no fewer than 20 different sub-regions in the Champagne appellation, yet this is perhaps a little too granular for the layperson. In my 2017 book *Champagne* I proposed seven broad sub-regions, which may still be unsatisfactory but provides a starting point for further discussion:

1 Côte des Blancs

The Côte des Blancs is aptly named, no matter whether it refers to the fact that over 97 percent of the region's vineyard area is planted with Chardonnay, Champagne's predominant white grape, or whether it describes the region's soil, which is the most uninhibitedly chalky in Champagne, sometimes with just 20 or 30 centimetres of topsoil above a bedrock of pure Cretaceous chalk. Chardonnay thrives in this calcareous environment, more so than Pinot Noir, which is often suited to slightly deeper soils.

In addition, conventional wisdom in Champagne states that Chardonnay prefers an east-facing exposure to receive the gentle morning sun, whereas Pinot Noir benefits from south-facing slopes as it requires as much warmth as possible throughout the day.

The Côte des Blancs fulfills these criteria of soil and slope perfectly, lying on a 20-kilometre-long, east-facing escarpment that runs south of the city of Epernay. At its north is the Butte de Saran, a large formation around which lie the vineyards of Chouilly, Cramant, Oiry and Cuis. As is the case in much of the heart of Champagne, the soils are clay-heavy at the top of the slope and chalkier on the plain below: Oiry, on the plain, has the least amount of topsoil, resulting in racy, linear wines, while the vineyards of Chouilly and Cramant have varying degrees of chalk and clay depending on where they lie. In general, Chouilly's wines are broad and generous, with those of the *lieu-dit* Mont Aigu showing the most complexity and refinement; Cramant, on the southern side of the Butte, tends to be firmer and more structured, but again it depends on where the vines are located.

Moving south, Avize is again a story of chalk and clay, with parcels predominant in one or the other – this typically relates to elevation more than to location within the village. Selosse blends the two soil types in his iconic Substance bottling, to offer a complete picture of Avize; Agrapart, in contrast, separates the plots into different cuvées – the amply expansive Avizoises is from clay vineyards, while the racier, more savoury Vénus comes from chalk sites (as does Minéral).

Between Avize and Oger, the character of the chalk changes, at least organoleptically. The vineyards of Oger form a large, warm amphitheatre that encourages high ripeness, yet this is underlined in the wines by a bright, saline chalkiness that contrasts with the darker, graphite-like minerality of Avize and Cramant. This same chalkiness continues south into Le Mesnil-sur-Oger, where the topsoils become even more meagre, and the wines more nakedly mineral-driven.

Due to this fierce chalk character, Le Mesnil has a reputation for making austere wines, yet this is a misconception fuelled by the underripeness of the late 20th century, and the best wines of the village, such as Selosse's Les Carelles, Krug's Clos du Mesnil, Pierre Péters' Les Chétillons, or Salon, are in fact markedly rich in body and presence, even if they are driven by their incisive minerality.

Across the border in Vertus, the northern portion of the village is much like Le Mesnil, with little topsoil over the chalk; south of the village, however, the slope gradually shifts to the southeast and even south, with areas of deeper clay, and there remains a little Pinot Noir grown here, a testament to the village's history. South of Vertus, the Côte des Blancs terminates in Bergères-les-Vertus and Mont-Aimé, where a high proportion of silex, or flint, gives a characteristic smokiness to the wines.

2 Montagne de Reims

The Montagne de Reims covers a large area, and could feasibly be divided into several sub-regions. The Montagne itself (at 280 metres, calling it a 'mountain' is generous) is a large, horseshoe-shaped plateau open to the west, around which vines are planted on three flanks – this is the most famous sector of the Montagne de Reims, and indeed one of the most renowned in Champagne, often called the Grande Montagne to differentiate it from the Petite Montagne to the west.

A major distinction – not one of quality, but of character – can be made in the Grande Montagne between the south-facing Grand Cru villages and the north-facing ones. On the southern side, Bouzy and Ambonnay are both renowned for producing charismatic and long-lived Pinot Noir, with Bouzy's wines generally appearing more generous and expansive, and Ambonnay's darker and more structured, due in part to the slope's slight turn to the southeast there. Many of the best producers, such as Benoît Lahaye and Pierre Paillard in Bouzy or Egly-Ouriet, Marguet and Eric Rodez in Ambonnay, are making site-specific champagnes within these villages, giving us a greater understanding of the nuances of their terroirs.

In contrast, the northern *crus* typically produce wines that are cooler and more discreet in tone, marked by firm acidic structures and a dark, almost metallic minerality. Despite facing predominantly north, these slopes are relatively gentle, allowing for plenty of sunshine to aid ripening, although this often takes longer than on the southern side. Verzy, Verzenay and Mailly-Champagne are the principal villages here, each with its own character but each also reflecting its northerly location, and there are a number of outstanding producers expressing these terroirs, including Mouzon-Leroux, Adrien Renoir, Hugues Godmé, Pehu-Simonet and Mailly Grand Cru.

Between the northern and southern *crus*, the contour of the Montagne causes a portion of the vineyard area to face east, and in an anomaly for this Pinot-dominated region, there are two east-facing villages that are primarily planted with Chardonnay. Trépail, bordering Ambonnay, has notably chalky soils with little topsoil, and David Léclapart makes the best wines here, which are racy and tense. In neighboring Villers-Marmery the clay topsoils grow slightly deeper, and the wines tend to be rounder and richer, with a characteristic waxiness: Arnaud Margaine is the top grower.

Further west of Mailly-Champagne, the Grande Montagne continues through several distinguished Premier Cru villages, where the soils gradually shift: while the base of the slope remains relatively chalky, the other portions create opportunities for all three major varieties to thrive. In Ludes, both Bérêche and Huré Frères create superbly expressive wines, as does Vilmart in Rilly-la-Montagne.

Moving west beyond the D951, the principal north-south road connecting the cities of Reims and Epernay, the soils become more varied still, with the influence of younger, Paleogenic topsoils becoming much more prominent in many places. This area is often referred to as the Petite Montagne due to its lower elevation, although some refrain from using the term as it can sound pejorative. It's home to excellent terroirs, growers and wines, and it's a significant source of Meunier grapes, which thrive in the gravel and limestone here. Jérôme Prévost is undoubtedly the most sought-after producer, but there are plenty of others worth seeking out, from Emmanuel Brochet and Frédéric Savart to Roger Coulon, Lelarge-Pugeot, Perseval-Farge and Thomas Perseval.

Finally, in the very north of both the Montagne de Reims and the Champagne appellation, the Massif de St-Thierry includes 17 villages that mostly lie on predominantly sandy terroirs, which impart a distinctive tension and freshness of fruit. Chartogne-Taillet and Francis Boulard are long-established growers here, with more steadily emerging.

3 Grande Vallée

Historically, the area referred to as the Vallée de la Marne begins at Tours-sur-Marne and runs west along the Marne River all the way until the appellation ends at Saâcy-sur-Marne in the Seine-et-Marne department, about 70 kilometres in a straight line but much further if you either travel by road or follow the winding path of the river itself.

When speaking with people in Champagne, however, mentions of the Vallée de la Marne tend to reference those villages in the river valley west of Cumières, while the area between Cumières and Tours-sur-Marne is often called the Grande Vallée, or Grande Vallée de la Marne. This may seem like a semantic detail, yet there are compelling reasons as to why these two regions should be differentiated.

To begin with, the geography of the two is very different: while the valley to the west is largely sheltered between hillsides on both banks of the river, the Grande Vallée is a predominantly south-facing slope facing a plain on the opposite side, and it essentially constitutes the southern flank of the Montagne de Reims, with which, geologically speaking, it has much more in common. In this sector the bedrock of chalk remains highly influential, perhaps most nakedly in Bisseuil, with its racy, saline Chardonnay, but also throughout the vineyards of Aÿ and Mareuil-sur-Aÿ, especially in the magnificent Clos des Goisses hillside, owned by Philipponnat.

Much of the vineyard surface area in these villages contains a thin layer of topsoil above the chalk, composed largely of calcareous clays and marls, and together with the south-facing exposure this creates an ideal home for Pinot Noir, which accounts for nearly two-thirds of all the plantings in the Grande Vallée – this contrasts with the Meunier-dominated Vallée de la Marne to the west.

Aÿ is rightfully regarded as one of the great Pinot Noir terroirs of Champagne, and the only village in the Grande Vallée classified as Grand Cru. Renowned for the quality of its wines since the Middle Ages, Aÿ can be delicately perfumed and elegantly complex, as demonstrated by the chalky parcels that Louis Roederer uses to create Cristal Rosé, or it can be rich and bold, like Bollinger's Vieilles Vignes Françaises or Selosse's La Côte Faron. Mareuil-sur-Aÿ, just next door, can offer a similar profile depending on location, but often feels more lifted, less brooding: Marc Hébrart makes cuvées from each village that illustrate this well.

Dizy and Hautvillers are top-quality Premier Cru villages, forming the backbone of blends such as Gaston Chiquet's Special Club, but Cumières features more often on its own, renowned as one of the warmest terroirs in the Marne. Its south-facing slopes produce fragrant, richly flavoured champagnes, such as those made by Georges Laval or René Geoffroy.

4 Vallée de la Marne

West of Cumières, the river valley begins in earnest, with slopes on both banks suitable for vine-growing, and as the river flows west towards the centre of the Paris Basin, the bedrock of Cretaceous chalk gradually descends further below the surface. From Cumières to the far west of the appellation is still a significant distance, roughly 35 kilometres as the crow flies, and the terrain in between is far from homogeneous, showing considerable variations in the soil, slope and microclimate.

Between Cumières and the town of Dormans the area can be divided, much like Paris, into the Rive Droite and Rive Gauche – Right Bank and Left Bank – which refer to the northern and southern banks of the river, respectively. On the Rive Droite, chalk lies at the base of the hillsides along the river between Damery and Châtillon-sur-Marne, with increasingly younger clays, sands and limestones as one progresses up the slope. While Meunier reigns supreme throughout the Vallée de la Marne, this sector is home to all three major varieties, with Venteuil having notably almost as much Pinot Noir planted as Meunier.

Beyond Châtillon, the southern exposures continue in Vandières and Verneuil, yet the chalk is sufficiently below the surface at this point that those younger Paleogenic limestones and clays become the primary influence, creating wines of fresh fruit and lively structure: Nowack and Cazé-Thibaut are leading the vanguard in revealing the potential of this sector. There are two primary transverse valleys in this area, however, that run roughly north-south, and one of the particularities of these is the presence of a green clay called illite; this is rare in Champagne but prominent in the wines of Moussé Fils and André Heucq in Cuisles.

On the Left Bank, the chalk continues west of Epernay as far as Oeuilly, where Tarlant makes the magisterial Cuvée Louis, although much of the slope is composed largely of various limestones, marls, clays and sands from the Paleocene and Eocene epochs, including a characteristic sandy clay known as Sparnacian that's common in several areas of Champagne. Cretaceous chalk ceases to have an influential presence west of Oeuilly, yet the soils remain highly calcareous. Near the village of Mareuil-le-Port, around which Dehours makes excellent single-vineyard champagnes, a transverse valley is carved out by the Flagot, a tributary of the Marne, which winds between the renowned Meunier terroirs of Leuvrigny and Festigny: Christophe Mignon and Apollonis are good sources here.

Beyond Dormans the soils grow progressively younger still, with Eocene limestones, clays and marls predominating. Around the town of Celles-lès Condé there is some hard limestone on steep slopes: Tarlant's vibrant La Vigne Royale, made of Pinot Noir, comes from this area. The appellation continues past the town of Château-Thierry, and here, at the far western end, there are several growers bringing this area into the spotlight, such as Françoise Bedel, Bourgeois-Diaz and Christophe Baron.

5 Coteaux Sud d'Epernay

Another area that is historically included in the Vallée de la Marne is the sector around the village of Pierry, just southwest of Epernay. There are 11 villages here that banded together in 1996 to create an association called *Les Coteaux Sud d'Epernay*, and collectively they demonstrate a terroir that's distinctly different from the Vallée de la Marne proper, to the north and west, and from the Côte des Blancs to the east. In some ways it's a transition between the two, containing more chalk than the former and more clay than the latter, although the soils are remarkably diverse, changing frequently even within a single village. Pierry is the only Premier Cru here, containing limestone, clay and Sparnacian soils, and it's home to growers such as J-M Sélèque and Bruno Michel, as well as to Taittinger's Château de la Marquetterie. Its neighbour Moussy also produces excellent wines, most notably those of José Michel, while on the opposite side of the valley in Chavot-Courcourt, Laherte Frères is the Coteaux Sud's finest producer.

6 Coteaux du Petit Morin, Sézannais, Vitryat, Montgueux

These areas do not constitute a region on their own, but they can be related to each other in several ways. Historically they have been grouped together with the Côte des Blancs largely by default, but this is potentially confusing because nobody in Champagne actually thinks of these areas as being in the Côte des Blancs, least of all the producers themselves. An ideal approach would probably be to treat all of these separately, as they each have a distinct identity.

The Coteaux du Petit Morin or Val du Petit Morin, named for a small river that originates here and flows into the Marne, extends southwest from the tip of the Côte des Blancs almost to the town of Sézanne. A portion of it is a continuation of chalk, set on rolling hills rather than the rigid slopes of the Côte des Blancs, but as the terrain moves west it turns more varied, with sands, clays and Sparnacian soils all in the mix. This creates opportunities for all three major varieties, with Chardonnay accounting for slightly more than half the plantings and Meunier another 37 percent. Ulysse Collin is undoubtedly the finest grower in this sector, focusing on Chardonnay in chalky soils.

Continuing south, the soils continue to be mixed in the Sézannais or Côte de Sézanne, with large areas of chalk among younger limestones and clays. Vines have been growing here since at least the 12th century, yet like much of Champagne they were lost to phylloxera in the late 19th century, and most of the region was not replanted until the 1960s or 1970s. Today, Chardonnay is predominant here, covering three-quarters of the vineyard area, and compared to the Côte des Blancs the wines are typically lighter in body and higher in tone, with fresh, citrusy flavours. Much of the wine produced here still goes to house blends; some Côte des Blancs growers such as Pierre Moncuit or Guy Charlemagne own vineyards that they bottle separately from their other cuvées, and some internationally known growers in the Sézanne itself include Barrat-Masson, Marie Copinet and Thierry Triolet.

Around the town of Vitry-le-François, 63 kilometres east of Sézanne and 58 kilometres southeast of Epernay, a wine-growing area of 15 villages has been steadily growing in prominence, often referred to as the Vitryat, Perthois or Coteaux de Vitry. While this was an important viticultural region in medieval times, it nearly disappeared after phylloxera, and it wasn't until 1989 that the modern appellation boundaries there took shape. Plantings have increased significantly in the past couple of decades, virtually all of them Chardonnay (97.5 percent), which thrives in the Turonian chalk of the region. About 10 to 20 million years older than the Campanian chalk of the Côte des Blancs, these soils are mixed with marl and clay, producing fresh, floral Chardonnay that tends to be forward and light-bodied. Today it's increasingly sought after in blends, although Pascal Doquet's Horizon comes entirely from this sector, and other growers are emerging.

Further to the south, Montgueux is an island of vines just west of the city of Troyes, built on a predominantly south-facing hillside of chalk. While it's often grouped with the Côte des Bar since it's in the Aube department, it's entirely unrelated to that region, as Montgueux lies not on Kimmeridgian but rather on Turonian chalk, like the Vitryat. It wasn't planted in earnest until the 1960s by pioneers such as Jacques Lassaigne, whose son Emmanuel makes the village's top wines today, but it's now become an important source of Chardonnay, with a distinctive, almost tropical-fruit ripeness from its warm southern exposure.

7 Côte des Bar

In the south of Champagne, a sizeable area is unsuitable for vine production, yet southeast of the city of Troyes the appellation resumes in the Côte des Bar, in the department of the Aube. Here the soils are not based on chalk as in the

Marne, but rather on Kimmeridgian marl, identical to that of its southern neighbour, Chablis. Unlike in Chablis, the primary grape variety in the Côte des Bar is Pinot Noir, which accounts for over 80 percent of the plantings in this region.

The Côte des Bar is separated into two areas: the Barséquanais, around the town of Bar-sur-Seine, and the Bar-sur-Aubois, named for the town of Bar-sur-Aube. Together they account for almost 23 percent of the entire Champagne appellation, and it's difficult to articulate significant differences between the two: both lie on pure Kimmeridgian, with younger Portlandian soils located in fringe areas on the upper slopes. Unlike the contiguous, vine-covered slopes of the Marne, the vineyards in the Côte des Bar are scattered in pockets on rolling hillsides, and their southerly location results in a slightly warmer climate, producing distinctly round, voluptuously fragrant Pinot Noir. This is valued by houses for blending with the cooler wines of the north, yet there have historically been some important producers based here as well, such as Drappier, Fleury and Pierre Gerbais.

In addition, a remarkable array of new growers has emerged from this region over the past couple of decades, embodying the ideals of a new generation and bringing a previously marginalized terroir into the spotlight. In many ways this development of the Côte des Bar is reflective of the Champagne appellation and culture as a whole as it progresses into the 21st century, with both growers and consumers treating champagne first and foremost as a wine like any other. This includes asking the same questions of champagne as they would of any other wine: questions of identity and meaning, of viticulture and sustainability, of terroir and expression of place. In their explorations of these ideas, producers are in turn creating a more varied diversity of wines, from traditional blends to single-vineyard champagnes, vintage-dated cuvées to perpetual reserves, brut to non-*dosé*. There is no style that is intrinsically better than another, but a greater diversity of wines in Champagne offers more opportunities for different expressions, and the appellation is richer for it, as are we as champagne consumers.

> Robert Walters (2016)
>
> # GET SET, GO!
>
> Robert Walters tells the story of the Aube 'underdog' who gave up growing grapes for the *grande marques* so that he could gain his commune the recognition it rightfully deserved. From Champagne outsider to Montgueux hero…

If you drive from Troyes in the Aube for only a few kilometres west, along the D660, direction Auxerre, you will soon see a small, isolated, vine-covered hill appear in the landscape a little way off to your right. Perched on this hill, overlooking Troyes and the Vallée de la Seine, is the tiny township of Montgueux. On the slopes here, we will find the vineyard of a small yet significant grower by the name of Emmanuel Lassaigne, who produces wine under the label Jacques Lassaigne – his father's name.[1]

Montgueux is possibly the only Champagne village or terroir that sits completely on its own – a hilly outcrop of vines in a vast agricultural plain. All the other villages of Champagne seem to form part of a sub-region or a continuous collection of vineyard settlements, such as the Côte des Blancs, Côte de Sézanne, Montagne de Reims, Côte des Bar, Vallée de la Marne, Vallée de la Vesle, Vallée de l'Ardre and Coteaux Sud d'Epernay. Montgueux may be a part of the Aube department, but this is an artificial, bureaucratic classification: the village is isolated, on the other side of Troyes from the Côte des Bar (home to the rest of the Aube growers), and has a completely different geology.

As Emmanuel Lassaigne tells it, the soils of Montgueux are, in fact, closer to those of the Côte des Blancs than to those of the rest of the Aube. 'Montgueux is the geological continuation of the Côte des Blancs,' he says. 'The same soil, chalk, but 15 million years older. In fact, it's the bottom part of the chalk, and this creates some differences that are important. We don't have the same fossils, and we have a little bit of *silex* [flint] in the chalk, which does not

---

[1] Make sure you get the right Lassaigne – it's an old name in this village, and there are perhaps six growers who carry it on their label.

occur in the Côte des Blancs except in a small area near Vertus called Le Mont Aimé, at the very edge of the Côte des Blancs.'

Montgueux's unique isolation (in terms of both location and geology) has been important in its history, its late development and its lack of recognition. Even today, and even with a well-respected grower located here, some maps of Champagne do not show Montgueux, and many historical articles on Champagne – even articles on the Aube – did not refer to it.

Although Montgueux has always been a part of the AOC of Champagne as it was formalized in 1936, it did not truly emerge as a wine-growing area until the 1950s and 1960s when négocants started to look for grapes outside their traditional sourcing zones and encouraged the growers of the village to plant vines.[2] Prior to this era, very few vineyards were located here. It may be hard to imagine today, but before World War II, Champagne was for the most part a poor region (certainly for those on the land), and grape growers generally struggled. So it was only in the late 1950s and early 1960s that enough incentive arose to plant vines in Montgueux, and Jacques Lassaigne and his brother, along with one other family, the Beaugrands, were the first to do so.

The kick that was needed...

Initially, the new vignerons were farming only to sell grapes to the négociants, but in the 1970s Jacques Lassaigne began to make some wine to sell directly to market. The family managed to survive with this structure, selling both fruit and bottles of wine, until the late 1990s, when it suffered financial difficulties and began to contemplate selling out. The potential demise of his family's estate was one of the key factors that brought Emmanuel Lassaigne home to help his parents. This was no easy decision; he had already forged a successful career outside the wine industry, with an international manufacturing firm. Yet, the idea of his parents losing the farm they had worked so hard to establish disturbed him. And there were other motivations. Foremost: Lassaigne felt deeply frustrated by the lack of recognition that Montgueux received in the Champagne region.

To understand this lack of acknowledgement and Montgueux's lowly position in Champagne's pecking order, we need to look over our shoulder.

[2] There were previous laws and decrees, most famously the 1908 legislation that included only the Marne and Aisne and excluded the Aube completely, but since AOC Champagne was officially passed into law in 1936, the Aube, including Montgueux, has been part of the Champagne region.

Rebel/hero, Emmanuel Lessaigne

For as long as sparkling wine has been made in Champagne (in fact, even longer), there has been a strong tradition of viewing the Aube as a poor cousin, an area that does not really belong in the AOC. Although it is difficult to justify such bias today, many in the Aube feel as if they're still looked down upon by the more famous villages to the north. And if the Aube has struggled against such bias, imagine what a little outpost like Montgueux has had to contend with. At least the vineyards of the Côte des Bar can point to centuries of vine-growing tradition. Montgueux cannot.

Large houses have denied sourcing wines from Montgueux even when they have begrudgingly acknowledged that they sourced some from the Aube, and the few local growers who sold bottled wine did not put the name of the village on their labels, because they felt that the poor reputation (or lack of recognition) of the area would discourage sales. For an intelligent, educated and keenly sensitive local like Emmanuel Lassaigne, this was a source of disquiet.

One incident in particular crystallized Lassaigne's sense of injustice and finally motivated him to do something about the situation. Around the time that his parents started to consider selling their vineyards, Lassaigne found himself on a tour of the Veuve Clicquot facilities. He was not visiting as a wine grower; rather, he was there in his previous career capacity, chaperoning a group of Heineken executives who were interested in viewing Clicquot's bottling technology. One of the senior men at Heineken knew Lassaigne well and so asked the Clicquot people: 'Do you work with grapes from Montgueux?'

The response was short and sharp. 'Montgueux? Oh, no! We only work with the grapes of the Marne!'

In fact, during that period, Veuve Clicquot was the largest purchaser of the grapes of Montgueux, buying the fruit of 40 out of a total of 200 hectares. 'At the time, I said nothing,' Lassaigne told me. 'I was there with another job. But it was not right. You can say you don't like our fruit. You can decide not to buy our fruit. But to buy so much of it and then deny it? This is not right. This is not fair. So, I thought, we must put Montgueux on our bottles and say that we are proud of our terroir. Our terroir is not better, it is not worse, but there is a typicity here, and I wanted to show it. That was the beginning for me.

'I was born here. If people say that where you were born is shit and you disagree, well, you are motivated to do something about it.'

Embracing the 'Meursette' personality…

Not everyone in the north was reluctant to acknowledge Montgueux. In the 1980s, one of the main buyers of its grapes was Charles Heidsieck. The *chef de cave* there at the time was the renowned Daniel Thibault, who was quoted as saying: 'If there is a Montrachet in Champagne, it is in Montgueux that we will find it!' He was referring to the richness of the Chardonnay wines that can be grown on the southeast or southwestern slopes of this village. This statement must have been viewed with scepticism and surprise in an era when most négociants denied they sourced wine from the Aube at all. (Some still do deny it.) Yet, Thibault was onto something. Locals today talk of their wines as having a '*Meursette*' personality (Meursault-like) with age, a characteristic that is evident even in wines raised only in stainless steel.

So Lassaigne quit his job and returned to the family firm in 1999. His first priority was to save the business, and soon he was making radical changes that involved a great deal of risk. The estate used to sell all of the wines it made at the domaine, directly to the visiting public, but Lassaigne stopped this and decided to sell his wines only to the best retailers and restaurants. 'By the end of 2002, I only had two customers! So it was not very easy.' In a policy that is very rare in Champagne, you still can't buy a bottle at Lassaigne's cellar.

Lassaigne quickly began to make changes in the management of his family's vines; then he updated the way the wines were made and packaged. Not everything happened at once, of course. Many changes were small and were implemented along the journey, as Lassaigne gained experience. His goal was (and is) to constantly strive for improvements in quality and in revealing the Montgueux terroir. As Lassaigne puts it: 'Each step is a detail. One detail doesn't change anything. But all the details together make a big difference.'

Great grower behaviour

Today, the Lassaigne methodology reads like a model for great grower behaviour. In the vineyards, he works organically, cultivating only between the vines and rolling the grass flat inter-row. No fertilizers, herbicides or pesticides are used, even those allowed under organic regulations. 'I have never understood organic pesticides: you kill, but you do it kindly,' he laughs. Crop levels are regulated via pruning and the absence of fertilizer, and the fruit is picked ripe. In the winery, he ferments according to the parcels that he will bottle together (a sort of blending at the press) and he makes two plot-specific cuvées: Le Cotet and Clos Sainte-Sophie. He avoids sulphur, adding only a little at the press and none during the *élevage* or at bottling. He doesn't fine or filter, disgorges by hand and does not add any dosage after disgorgement; he doesn't feel he needs to. In the hands of a genuine grower like Lassaigne, the southern slopes of Montgueux can produce opulent, layered champagnes that have ample fruit and texture.

One significant point of difference between Lassaigne and many of the other great growers of Champagne is that Lassaigne is officially classed as a '*négociant-manipulant*' because he buys some fruit from a few small growers in Montgueux. Lassaigne makes these purchases following very strict criteria: his source vineyards are only in Montgueux and must be old vines – between 45 and 60-plus years of age. Then, they must have very chalky soils and enjoy a south or south-eastern exposition. Finally, they must be managed by good growers who work well. Also, he buys only grapes, not juice or wine, and he presses the fruit himself. These purchases add another 40 percent to his production.

Lassaigne purchases fruit in order to give his estate access to the other significant terroirs of Montgueux that he does not own, at least for the moment – his estate is tiny, at just 3.8 hectares in two *lieux dits*, the Le Cotet and Bouilleratte. 'The point of me being a négociant is not to make more wine. It's to have additional terroirs to work with so that I can make true Montgueux,' he says.

Although Lassaigne initially worked only with stainless steel, today he ferments and ages his wines in both steel tanks and barrels. He explains it this way: 'I do both; I like both. Diversity is always interesting, but I would say this: each barrel is different, each tank is the same. And also, it is possible to make a good wine from a bad terroir in wood, with the makeup that the wood brings. In tank, you cannot. In tank, you need a great terroir to make a great wine. That is why we put the Millésimé only in tank. The oenologist will say that you should only raise a basic cuvée in tank. I am the opposite. Well, not the opposite, as I also raise my basic cuvée in tank, but I am different, as I do both my basic cuvée and my Millésimé in tank.'

It is fascinating, in a cellar like this, to be able to taste the same cuvée from both vessels. It is clear that by the passing of time in oak, elements are both lost (something of the precision and clarity) and gained (another kind of expression, more textural and more complex). Lassaigne enjoys the different expressions, and admits: 'The only goal here is to catch and keep the aromas of the terroir. That's the only focus. I don't know if we succeed, but my focus is this. That's why we don't add [much] sulphur, why we don't do filtration and things like this.'

Lassaigne used to pay workers to come in once a year and clear his soil of *gadoues*, the city waste once used as fertilizer in the region. There wasn't much used at Montgueux, but Lassaigne was determined to rid his soils of whatever was there. Now this work is finished but it remains a marker of the kind of attention to detail that he has brought to his estate.

Anything's possible!

Lassaigne's story is a remarkable one that in many ways shows what is possible in our modern world. Here is a grower from a village that is still so poorly known that it often does not appear on regional maps; a village where hardly anyone expected high-quality wines of place to be grown. Here is a grower who took many risks, strived for greatness, refused to compromise and today is very successful. And he achieved this success in just over a decade. The lesson for Champagne growers seems to be this: as long as you have a terroir that can produce high-quality wines with personality, as long as you strive for excellence in your vineyard work and winemaking, and as long as you know what you are doing, there is a market waiting for you.

Lassaigne is grateful for his success and talks freely of his debt to those who came before. 'We are here because of two reasons. The first is the *Grande Maisons* [*grande marques*] – Moët, Veuve Clicquot, Laurent-Perrier, etcetera – that created the market. We have to say thank you to these people. We are not competitors. Rather, it is because of them that we are able to be champagne makers. The second reason is Anselme Selosse, because he pushed the smaller vignerons to be at the same level as the *Grande Maisons*. I know him a little bit, and when I see him I say: "Thank you for what you did over the last 30 years." Today, it's very easy for us because of these two things.'

Part XVI of *Bursting Bubbles: A Secret History of Champagne and the Rise of the Great Growers* by Robert Walters, Quiller (Shrewsbury) 2016. Reproduced with kind permission of the author.

Tyson Stelzer (2019)

THE GREENING OF CHAMPAGNE

For decades, Champagne has been the laughing stock of responsible growers everywhere, notoriously piling on herbicides, fungicides, pesticides, fertilizers and even Parisian rubbish to shamelessly bolster its poor vines to ludicrous yields. But the slow march to change is now gathering momentum, and, in the past few years, has intensified like never before. Tyson Stelzer charts Champagne's quickening stride to sustainability…

In the silent dormancy of winter, the skeletons of naked vines reveal the stark disparity of soil treatments, even from afar. From the upstairs terrace of his home above his Larmandier-Bernier cellars at the southern end of the Côte des Blancs, Pierre Larmandier showed me a panoramic view of the hillside of Vertus. 'Ten years ago, we could look out and it was only *our* vineyards that appeared green in December, thanks to grasses cultivated in the mid-rows, but now there are more and more,' he points out excitedly.

It's a spectacular visual manifestation of a slow yet steady transformation in the mindset of Champagne growers. Just 17 years ago, Larmandier and Anselme Selosse (at Jacques Selosse) expressed interest in purchasing a vineyard in Vertus, and the agent was surprised that both showed such concern for the way the vines had been tended, without the use of herbicides, having never seen buyers pay this sort of attention before.

Selosse and Larmandier were instrumental among a small band of like-minded growers, the radical pioneers who inspired a generation of Champenois to embrace responsible viticulture. Their story is now familiar, and rightfully celebrated. A new chapter is unfolding, with an unexpected and dramatic twist.

Later on, the same day, I found myself bumping through the hallowed ground of Le Mesnil-sur-Oger on the edge of Vertus in the big truck of

Larmandier's neighbour, organic leader Pascal Doquet. A stark and surprising reality begins to emerge as he points out the green vineyards: 'Louis Roederer, Taittinger, Moët & Chandon. The large houses are planting grasses in the mid-rows, ploughing and taking better care of the vines than the small growers,' he reveals.

The romanticized aura of growers as the heroes who are saving Champagne from the industrialized menace of the houses has long been the rhetoric of the wine world. Not only is this a fundamentally flawed and simplistic misconception, the truth today is that precisely the opposite is playing out between the vines.

Nobody understands this better than Doquet, president of Champagne's organic body, the *Association des Champagnes Biologiques*. It was a sign of the evolution of the mindset of the region that Doquet was elected a board member of the *Syndicat Général des Vignerons* in 2018. 'It was significant for them to have an organic grower in this position!' he exclaims.

'The big houses are in contact with the customers and have to show a better and greener technique in response to public expectation,' he points out. 'Growers who are selling their grapes don't have to show customers what they are doing in the vineyards.'

The truth in Champagne today is that the leaders in sustainability in the vines and the wines, those whose vineyards set the pace in thwarting chemical intervention and who inspire, encourage, cajole and incentivize their partners to take up the challenge and step into a new millennium of responsibility are, with a small number of notably famous exceptions, not by and large the growers themselves, but the houses and cooperatives, even and most notably some of the biggest players of all. Louis Roederer and Veuve Clicquot have forged forward as the new leaders of Champagne's eco-revolution. 'The change in the vineyards in the last decade has been unbelievable!' enthuses Dominique Demarville (Veuve Clicquot). 'The growers were the pioneers, and now the big houses have done great things in our own vineyards.'

The big dilemma of yields

While it took famous growers to lead the charge towards more environmentally friendly practices, if this were to ever gain widespread traction, it had to be the big houses who took it up. For Champagne, sustainability is more than just doing the right thing for the vineyards, the workers, the planet and the customers: an eco-friendly approach shakes the very core of the fabric of the Champagne model, not only in how the grapes are grown but, tellingly and crucially, in how the growers are paid.

Champagne's antiquated and grossly simplistic classification system has long dictated that growers are remunerated on nothing more than volume and *cru*, with a blatant disregard for quality. No wonder yields have spiralled in recent decades, reaching an average of nearly 100 hectolitres (hl) per hectare in the first decade of the new millennium, from less than 60hl over the 30 years prior. In the enormous 2018 vintage, there were reports of as much as 250hl per hectare on the southern Côte des Blancs.

'The problem with Champagne is that every grower considers the maximum yield permitted by the appellation to be an economic minimum,' Jean-Hervé Chiquet (Jacquesson) admits. About 90 percent of growers harvest the maximum permitted by the appellation, plus whatever remains on the vines.'

In 2018 the maximum permitted yield was 10.8 tonnes per hectare, plus an additional 4.7 tonnes for reserves, hence 15.5 tonnes in total. This equates to a maximum pressing of 98,800 litres per hectare, or 98.8hl, which breaks down to just under 80hl of cuvée and 19hl of *tailles*. Across the entire appellation, Champagne is currently averaging around 75hl per hectare. 'In Vertus, you are considered a bad grower if you do not produce 100 hectolitres per hectare,' reveals Larmandier, who limits his yields to 60–70hl. 'People produce too much in the Côte des Blancs, and the big houses just buy everything.'

This creates a dilemma around sustainability, because herbicides, fungicides and chemical fertilizers bolster yields, while grasses cultivated in mid-rows create competition and diminish yields. 'You lose in quantity but you win in quality,' explains Jean-Baptiste Lécaillon, who manages Champagne's biggest biodynamic vineyard at Louis Roederer. 'It's all about the discussion between quality and quantity. This has been the debate for 300 years.'

The wake-up call of 2017

With no incentive to boost quality at the expense of quantity (and hence return), it was going to take a dramatic wake-up call for growers and houses to get off the downward spiral of chemical warfare that has ravaged the landscape of Champagne vineyards since the 1970s. That wake-up call came in 2017.

Chardonnay vines edged by red roses in a Taittinger vineyard. Roses share the same soil, sun and water requirements as grape vines (in fact, they are fussier), so will act as an early warning system: the grower will know when treating for mildew is necessary.

'I was worse than stressed, I was disorientated by the harvest of 2017,' discloses Herve Dantan (at Lanson). 'It was the most complicated harvest I have ever faced. What happened at the end of August was terrible – a deluge of rain followed by very warm days, accelerating the onset of botrytis. We lost an enormous amount of fruit. It was a revelation that we have to change something in the vineyards. We saw it in 2005 and 2011, but we did nothing. Now we must respond. With global warming, we will have to face harvests like 2017 again. We always have rain here, but the difference is that 30 years ago, it came during harvest in October, when it was too cold for botrytis; now it's warmer so botrytis takes off. We need to change our viticulture in order to be ready.'

The big lesson of 2017 came in the startling disparity between traditional and sustainable viticulture. In a vintage that unleashed botrytis and mildew the like of which Champagne has never seen, it was the vineyards that survived unscathed that were the surprise exceptions.

'In 2017 the estate vineyards of Veuve Clicquot and Louis Roederer had zero botrytis – zero,' reveals Demarville. The same phenomenon was observed in sustainable vineyards across the region. There are four factors at play here. An absence of herbicides and competition from grasses in the mid-rows not only builds resilience in the vines to resist botrytis, but also lowers susceptibility by decreasing vigour and yields. Further, grasses in the mid-rows push the roots deeper into the chalk, crucial for heightening mineral expression in the wines, and also for diminishing uptake of water during downpours. Finally, the grasses absorb the water before it reaches the roots of the vines.

Moët & Chandon is introducing electric straddle tractors to tend its vines: their lower noise levels and daily fuel savings of over 90% help towards reducing the company's carbon footprint. Moët recycles 99% of its waste and uses 100% green elecricty.

Houses take the lead

Dantan noted that all of his sustainable growers had better results than those practising chemical viticulture in 2017. He immediately took action, establishing a new department within Lanson, under which growers can obtain sustainable certification, and committing to paying a higher price for their grapes. 'We are working very hard to engage our growers in sustainable viticulture,' he says. 'As a big brand, we have a role to work alongside our growers and demonstrate that the future of Champagne is about being more ecological.' Still in its early days, the programme has had a good response, and he hopes he might have all growers signed up within five years. The harsh economic truth is that when sustainability might save their yields, growers are interested.

'In quality and sustainability, the Champagne region is changing very, very fast,' observes Olivier Krug. But the difficulty is still those growers who supply grapes and don't produce their own wines. If you inherited half a hectare from your grandmother and you are working in a car factory, you just want your vineyard for revenue, so it is very challenging for me to ask you to change the way you work.'

In response, Krug has joined Lanson and many of Champagne's top houses in handling the paperwork, audits and costs of sustainable certification for its growers. 'We do the administrative stuff, so they can concentrate on their field,' explains Krug senior winemaker Julie Cavil, who works closely alongside growers and already has 20 percent certified. At Veuve Clicquot, Demarville has appointed a team of three dedicated exclusively to helping their growers with sustainability, but admits it might take a decade to get everyone on board. 'The Champagne region is on the move, and all the serious houses are doing this: Bollinger, Louis Roederer, Moët, Laurent-Perrier, Nicolas Feuillatte, Mailly Grand Cru,' he says. 'When I studied winemaking in Avize 30 years ago, viticulture was all about chemicals, but now they are explaining to the next generation that you must protect biodiversity and be careful with the planet, so I am very confident for the future of this region.'

Certifiable

Despite the region's best efforts, Champagne's erratic climate makes practising a fully certified biodynamic or even organic regime a nail-biting pursuit. The biggest menace in this wet and humid place is disease, a challenge to manage organically or biodynamically, without the fall-back of systematic fungicide sprays. Like many houses and growers, Billecart-Salmon adopts organic and biodynamic practices without seeking certification, so as to uphold the flexibility to intervene when rot sets in. 'A lot of biodynamic vineyards yielded zero in 2016 and 2017,' points out Antoine Roland-Billecart. Anselme Selosse is Champagne's champion of intuitive wine growing, rigorously biodynamic, yet emphatically non-prescriptive, so as to respond to save his crop when he needs to. 'A production system which does not allow you to produce is not a production system at all,' he proposes.

Of Champagne's 33,868 hectares, just over two percent (700 hectares) are certified organic, of which one-fifth are owned by Louis Roederer. 'There is a big fight on in organics,' says Lécaillon. 'Consumers want organic but growers don't. You need a high level of technical attention to be organic, and it's not possible for everybody, especially on a large scale. It's demanding and costly, and without the knowledge or the money, you are better to be inorganic.' For this reason, the region established sustainable certification as an option to go 'halfway to organics', as Lécaillon puts it. In 2001, the French Ministry of Agriculture developed *Haute Valuer Environmentale* (HVE), and in 2014 the Comité Champagne launched *Viticulture Durable en Champagne* (VDC). Both certifications are roughly similar and require minimum standards in chemical inputs and biodiversity less rigorous than organics. Eradication of herbicides is widely agreed to be the most important first step in vineyard improvement, yet VDC still permits full use of herbicides on up to half of the vineyard area.

Meanwhile, all of Champagne's top houses and growers have already fully eradicated herbicides in their own vineyards. Nonetheless, HVE and VDC are a good interim step, though far from sufficiently rigorous to be an adequate end point in themselves.

The Comité Champagne aspires to completely eradicate herbicides by 2025, and has already made some progress towards this goal. Twenty percent of Champagne vineyards have been certified HVE or VDC, with a goal of 100 percent by 2030. The region halved its use of nitrogen fertilizers in the first 15 years of this century. Pests rank third after disease and weeds among the woes afflicting Champagne vineyards, and pesticides have now been almost completely eradicated, thanks to pheromone sexual confusion techniques.

The copper sulphate crisis

Disease is Champagne's most deadly menace, and its most elusive. 'We need to have products that are very efficient with mildew,' emphasizes Demarville, 'or we can lose the crop in 24 hours.' Without chemical intervention, he estimates that he would have lost 50–70 percent of his crop to the rains in May 2018.

Copper sulphate is currently the only alternative to chemical fungicides to control mildew permitted under organic and biodynamic certification, yet itself remains controversial, as debate continues over whether there is a cumulative effect of toxicity in the soil. And it has just become more controversial still.

In January 2019, the European Commission lowered the limit for copper sulphate application under organics from its current cap of 6kg per hectare per year over a five-year average to just 4kg per hectare per year spread over seven years.

'There is a concern that this regulation will lead some organic growers to give up their certification,' says Doquet, who has gone in on behalf of the growers to 'fight' with the Commission. Between 2012 and 2017, almost two-thirds of organic growers in Champagne used more than 4kg per hectare per year.

In the village of Mareuil-sur-Ay, Laurent Bénard (at Bénard Pitois) used 6kg in the challenging 2012 and 2016 seasons. 'With the change of climate the storms damage the fruit, the temperature is high and it's humid, so we are in danger!' he exclaims. 'And it is even worse in the Aube and the Vallée de la Marne, where it rains more!' Even those who use less are unhappy. 'We have been using 3–4kg of copper in our vineyards for 100 years and there is no toxicity, so it is a nasty decision to kick us!' says Lécaillon.

There are murmurs that the EU is ultimately planning to forbid use of copper sulphate in vineyards altogether. 'If we are not allowed to use copper sulphate, we cannot be organic in Champagne,' says Jean-Hervé Chiquet (at Jacquesson), who has organic certification for one-third of his vineyards.

Intensive research is currently underway to develop a new organic product to replace copper sulphate, or even new grape varieties resistant to mildew. Demarville hopes that within 10 years Champagne will be able to eradicate chemical treatment of not only mildew, but also oïdium and botrytis. For now, fighting disease without resorting to chemical fungicides is a dilemma with no simple solution.

Back to the old way

Champagne's march back to a more sustainable way promises the possibility of great improvements in quality, as the deep history of the region attests.

'Champagne was organic for three centuries,' Lécaillon reminds us. 'Champagne in the 1950s was made by peasants who were proud of their work and doing their best for the soils that they were giving to their children. It has only had chemicals since the 1960s. A century ago, the yields were very low and the wines were very concentrated. We developed our biodynamic conversion to go back to the levels of balance we used to have in the 1950s and 1960s. The best champagnes ever produced were made between 1945 and 1970. And my target in 20 years is to come back to this. Biodynamics and organics are not a goal in themselves, but a tool to take us back to the golden age of champagne!'

Extract from *The Champagne Guide 2020–21* by Tyson Stelzer, Wine Press (Brisbane, Australia) 2019. Reproduced with kind permission of the author.

Tyson Stelzer (2019)

BUBBLE, BUBBLE, TOIL AND TROUBLE

Does global warming spell certain doom for the region that has built a wine style around its cold climate? Things have hotted up in Champagne in a climactic drama that has played out over the past 30 years. As the fight against climate change intensifies, Tyson Stelzer finds the region responding in force…

The weather in Champagne has become dramatically more extreme and unpredictable over the past three decades, and this is a bigger concern for the region's vineyards than an increase in temperature of close to 1.2°C. The 2016 season brought catastrophic frost, hail and rain, inflicting the most widespread devastation in history, only then to be outdone by the toughest season in living memory the very next year, with Champagne decimated by the worst rot the growers had ever seen.

There was rejoicing in the streets when 2018 brought record yields of clean fruit of unprecedented ripeness, but enthusiasm waned when the emergent *vins clairs* lacked acidity and endurance. The 2019 crop suffered further extremes when an all-time record late July heatwave of 42°C shrivelled the grapes to raisins.

'How can we manage and anticipate these spectacularly chaotic climatic events?' Charles Heidsieck *chef de cave*, Cyril Brun, commented to me in dismay mid-way through the harrowing 2017 harvest.

In a region that has devoted centuries to refining its viticulture and winemaking to build ripeness and generosity – not to mention a wine style conceived in answer to cold seasons – there is much that is being done. The Champenois have rallied and launched a concerted response that encompasses everything from where, how and which grapes are grown, to the methods of vinification and even the fundamental style of the wine itself.

Pick earlier

'We started harvest in August in 2003, 2007, 2011, 2015, 2017 and 2018,' observes Ruinart *chef de cave*, Frédéric Panaïotis. 'There were only two August harvests in the last century and already six this century, so if this isn't a sign of global warming, what is?!'

In the past 30 years, Champagne harvest dates have moved forward by a fortnight. 'When I arrived in Champagne 25 years ago, the harvest was at the end of September, and now it is mid-September, and one year in three it is at the end of August,' observes Veuve Clicquot *chef de cave*, Dominique Demarville.

Accelerated ripening during August has introduced a new challenge in determining the optimum date of harvest. 'This is the new issue: waiting for flavour and phenolic maturity while the sugar level continues to rise,' reveals Rodolphe Péters, who took a risk against rising rot by holding off harvesting his Pierre Péters Chardonnay in Le Mesnil-sur-Oger until it achieved flavour ripeness at a high sugar level of 11.5 degrees potential in 2017.

Harvest faster

Harvesting during the warmer weeks of August means that ripeness is moving faster, as is the risk of the onset of rot. Péters picked his entire 2017 crop in one week rather than two.

'It's not enough just to decide when you want to harvest, you need to have the resources to do it!' points out Cyril Brun.

In the village of Vertus, brothers Charles-Henry and Emmanuel Fourny invested in a second press in 2018 to keep up with the new pace of harvest.

Send in the robots

A faster response calls for both infrastructure and a workforce, and Champagne is facing a new crisis of manual labour. 'The challenge for us is to find the workers in the vineyard, because the young generation would rather work in an office,' says Demarville. This is exacerbated in August, when most of Europe would prefer to be sunning itself on a faraway beach.

'I think we will have robots harvesting sooner than expected, because it's too hard to get pickers today,' predicts Sophie Déthune at Paul Déthune in Ambonnay. 'It's hard to imagine that 20 years ago we had to get an answering machine because everyone was calling and offering to pick for us! Now we don't get a single call.'

Demarville believes robots will be very important for the future of Champagne. 'We introduced robots in the wineries and the cellars 20 years ago, and now the next step is to use them in the vineyards,' he suggests. Numerous trials are currently underway in the region, but not everyone is convinced. 'I fight against the robots, because the more you go in that direction, the more you lose contact,' says Louis Roederer *chef de cave*, Jean-Baptiste Lécaillon. 'The story of wine is about going into my terroir, not with satellites and robots, but staying in touch with the soils and the vines and the wines.'

Pick at night

With increasingly warm and early harvests, it's not uncommon for afternoon temperatures to reach 30–35°C. Warm grapes oxidize much faster than cold grapes, so Demarville is negotiating with his vineyard teams to pick during the cooler hours of the day, in contrast to the traditional French work day. 'We can have people picking from 5am to 1pm,' he proposes. 'And we must learn how to pick at night.'

Some have attempted night picking with head-mounted mining lamps, but this has proven challenging and, inevitably, increases the cost of the grapes. Robots may be the better answer.

Chill the grapes

In 2019, Billecart-Salmon was the first in Champagne to build a cold room to chill the grapes, with capacity to chill 40–45 tonnes to five degrees overnight. The afternoon's harvest is ready for cold pressing at 5am the following morning. 'Instead of chilling the musts, we chill the grapes!' exclaims Antoine Roland-Billecart. 'We have done trials, and overnight chilling makes a big difference in acid retention in the grapes.'

Others in the region are contemplating the same, from growers as small as Veuve Fourny to houses as large as Dom Pérignon itself. 'But we can't chill prior to pressing like they do elsewhere, because we have such a huge volume harvested in such a short time,' worries Dom Pérignon *chef de cave*, Vincent Chaperon. 'And it is also a question of energy.'

More precise viticulture

'To keep sufficient acidity and freshness, we must change how we cultivate the vineyards and ensure the roots go deeper and deeper,' Demarville emphasizes. This necessitates a much more eco-friendly approach with the vines. The extremes of recent seasons have prompted an imperative for sustainable viticulture across Champagne like never before (see pages 199–206).

Péters suggests that even Champagne's low, closely spaced vineyard rows might need to be reconsidered. 'It's very hard to grow low vines close together without fungicides and herbicides,' he points out. 'We will have to change our method of cultivation and find ways to enlarge the rows and train higher canopies.'

Brun suggests a detailed, individualized approach to each vineyard site. 'I feel we are going to enter into an era of viticultural precision,' he says, 'by treating groups of plots in particular ways and working more precisely. Different sites, different clones and different varieties respond differently.'

Plant new varieties

Champagne's warming climate has spurred a renewed interest in the region's 'old' varieties of Pinot Gris, Pinot Blanc and, most of all, Petit Meslier and Arbane. In the very warm 2018 vintage, Bollinger harvested Petit Meslier and Arbane at a full ripeness of 12.5 degrees potential and fantastic acidity of seven grams per litre. 'The old varieties are interesting for us in the wake of global warming,' says *chef de cave*, Gilles Descôtes. 'We don't need them now, but we might in 20 years!'

The Comité Champagne has a project underway to create hybrid varieties that will mature slower, hold their acidity longer and exhibit greater resistance to disease in warmer seasons. Such extreme measures are more than controversial. 'I'm not sure they are true to the Champagne tradition,' worries Charles Philipponnat, president of Philipponnat. 'Personally I think we should maintain the best of what we have.'

Lécaillon agrees. 'It is completely crazy to suggest we should change the varieties in Champagne!' he exclaims. 'I make sparkling wine from Chardonnay and Pinot in California and I have done so in Tasmania, and you can adapt the way you grow and make wines to suit the climate. I think to change the varieties would be the biggest mistake; we would lose all that we have built in history. We don't have Pinot, Chardonnay and Meunier here because someone decided it would be good, but because these grapes are suited to the soils and to the place.'

Create new clones

A more sensible response is to play with clones rather than varieties. Lécaillon shares a nursery with other like-minded estates, including Péters, to cultivate a wide selection of clones. 'Some clones are better suited to warm weather than others,' points out Péters, who evolves his clonal selection according to changes in climate, pressure of disease and even evolving popular tastes.

Meanwhile, the freshening influence of Chardonnay has never been in higher demand in champagne blends, and many are replanting Meunier and Pinot to Chardonnay. 'In the future, we will need more Chardonnay, less Meunier, and Pinot Noir with more freshness,' says Brun.

Plant new areas

The push to expand the Champagne appellation has been on hold for a decade, ever since the global financial crisis put a dampener on sales growth, but the opportunity for the region to reconsider sites better suited to warmer temperatures is compelling.

'Maybe there are some current lands that are no longer suitable?' postulates Brun. 'And maybe there are some areas that we need to plant? We are moving further north.'

Block malolactic

Of all the strategies to counter warmer seasons in the winery, blocking malolactic fermentation is the one that many houses and growers are increasingly trialling. 'To maintain energy, balance and finesse, if we need to increase the malic acidity, we will,' reveals Alice Paillard of Champagne Bruno Paillard. 'Everything needs to change for everything to stay the same!'

Many houses that have traditionally always carried out malolactic fermentation are blocking it in more and more parcels. 'With malolactic and with oak, it does not have to be everything or nothing, it could be in between,' suggests Brun. 'We need to be globally more flexible in everything we do. To be able to do a lot of work in a short time, and to deal quickly with emergencies. We have to be quite pragmatic and ready to learn from our mistakes. The Champenoise can be perceived to be quite arrogant. But we need to keep our feet on the ground and to redefine what is champagne.'

Use fresher reserves

For the little house of AR Lenoble in Damery, climate change has fundamentally turned the role of reserve wines on its head. 'In the past, reserves were about adding complexity and depth to a blend,' says head of the house, Antoine Malassagne, 'but after four of the earliest harvests in history this century, acidity levels are much lower than they used to be, and we are now talking about how we can use reserves to enhance freshness.'

Such progressive change of thinking applies not only to the small players. 'For me, the new challenge in Champagne is selecting the reserves,' reveals Moët & Chandon *chef de cave*, Benoît Gouez.

Play with phenolics

A warmer climate threatens to challenge even the fundamentals of what defines the champagne style and its ageing potential. 'We are probably at the end of a cycle where we had only to rely on the acidities for longevity,' Brun suggested disconcertingly as we tasted his 2018 *vins clairs*, showing half the malic acidity of a normal year.

Chaperon has been contemplating this since 2003, the vintage that recorded the lowest acidity on record. 'Freshness, vibrancy and tension are more important to Dom Pérignon than acidity,' he discloses. 'And we have more levers to achieve this than acidity – we have minerality, phenolics, bitterness and aromatics. In particularly ripe seasons like 2009, we have to play with other dimensions like phenolics to maintain freshness.'

Release vintages earlier

Many houses made the astute decision to release the fast-maturing 2009 vintage before the enduring 2008, and such dexterity is increasingly important as Champagne's vintage extremes become ever more pronounced.

This is exacerbated by the recent decline in sales of vintage champagne, now, surprisingly, the poorest performing category of all. 'We have a problem in Champagne, a big problem,' declares Duval-Leroy *chef de cave*, Sandrine Logette-Jardin. 'Because of climate change, we have the ability to make more and more vintage cuvées, but we don't have the ability to sell all of them.' In response, Duval-Leroy has made the bold and unexpected decision to market its vintage cuvées and prestige Femme de Champagne as non-vintage in all but the very finest years. Pierre Péters has done the same with its Millésime L'Esprit and Blanc de Blancs Extra Brut NV.

Declining sales push vintage releases out, a great virtue for enduring seasons blessed by extended lees age, but a pitfall for vintages that need drinking sooner, without the stamina to go the distance. 'Most of the Champenois think the 2018 vintage will be popular, but I don't expect that it will age at all well, and if they release it in order, it will be too late,' Brun warns. 'But it would be daring to release 2018 before 2014!'

Make Coteaux Champenois

I have recently made two sojourns to Burgundy, the place that provides more context and perspective for the future of Champagne than any other. Not only in warming climates and trends in viticulture, vinification and single-site bottlings, but also in the production of Chardonnay and Pinot Noir as still wines.

Coteaux Champenois still wines have long been an interesting curio, largely constrained to smaller players and little production volumes, but recent warmer vintages have enticed many houses to come out to play. The 2015 and especially 2018 harvests marked a turning point, and I have seen sneak previews of stunning new Côteaux Champenois in development for the first time at Louis Roederer, Veuve Clicquot, Charles Heidsieck and André Clouet.

'Coteaux Champenois is innovating backwards,' proposes Lécaillon, 'because whenever they had lunches here in the 1950s they had a glass of champagne, a glass of Coteaux Champenois *blanc* and a glass of Coteaux Champenois *rouge*. And in 20 years' time we might make super white wines or red wines! Champagne's handicap until now has been ripeness, so we created sparking wine because we didn't have the climate to make still wine, and if we no longer have that handicap, then we will do something different. Climate is changing, and it has always changed, and it is the ultimate job of farmers to adapt to the changes. Let's not complain about it, but embrace it and find the tricks and the wine styles that can make the best possible wines in this place at this time. Before 1850, there was more still wine than sparkling wine produced in Champagne. And maybe history will reinvent itself and we will go back to that? Maybe in years to come we won't make sparkling wine anymore. That wouldn't be a problem.'

Such radical suggestions would change the game for the Champagne. But don't fear, the bubbles are here to stay, and Coteaux Champenois will remain in their shadow for at least the foreseeable future, if for no other reason than economic necessity – great Côteaux Champenois commands half the price of champagne, and the region can't afford this *en masse* just yet.

Warming to climate change

Climate change to date has been a blessing for Champagne. 'For now, the weather in Champagne is for the better,' says Francis Egly, Champagne's finest grower at Egly-Ouriet in Ambonnay. 'Twenty or 30 years ago, we sometimes had very difficult years in which it was very hard to achieve good ripeness, but now this is easier.'

'One day it might be for the worst if it goes too far,' foresees Jean-Hervé Chiquet at Jacquesson, 'but for now we are eliminating the worst vintages of the past, like 1972, 1977 and 1984.'

Even on the warmest site in all of Champagne, Charles Philipponnat agrees. 'It is true that on average grapes are riper, but so far this has been a good thing for Champagne,' he says. 'Clos des Goisses is a good case study because technically it is too warm by Champagne standards, but it hasn't been a problem yet. I believe the soil and the slope and the regime are more important than the temperature. Our wines today are grown in warmer conditions than 20 years ago and we have gained precision, so what is the problem?'

In spite of the challenges facing Champagne today, the ultimate measure must always come down to the quality of the wine in the bottle. For Champagne's top houses, who rigorously uphold fanatical attention to the finest detail with their vines and their wines, while maintaining an adaptable dexterity in the wake of the frenzy of changes around them, that quality has never been higher than it is today.

'It's time to move further,' invites Chaperon. 'To stay true to what champagne is, but to move beyond. Not to be a prisoner to our own rules and our strict appellation, but to change and reinvent. What will be the champagne of 2050? This is the question.'

Extract from *The Champagne Guide 2020–21* by Tyson Stelzer, Wine Press (Brisbane, Australia) 2019. Reproduced with kind permission of the author

6

BLAME IT ON THE FIZZICS

Feared for the uncertainty and danger it brought to the winemaking process, the champagne bubble was initially the bane of the cellarmaster. But, once conquered, loved forever. Champagne physicist Gérard Liger-Belair charts the life of this tiny transformer and explains its power to elevate.

Gérard Liger-Belair (2004)
BLAME IT ON THE FIZZICS

University of Reims physics professor Gérard Liger-Belair charts the life and times of the champagne bubble. The celebrated bottle-fermentation process means that there will be over a million in every glass we pour – and each will contribute, in its own microscopic way, to the experience we have of this wine. Gérard explains how…

I'm a physicist. What's a physicist doing writing about champagne? Well, the story begins on a summer afternoon when I was a student in the midst of finals and thought it would be a good plan before getting on with studying to stop somewhere on the way home to have a beer...

Now keep in mind that this is a physics student stopping somewhere to have a beer, and besides, I had a predilection for fluid dynamics and, on the side, photography. The sunlight, the hot day, the alcohol, my studies, and the thought of actually trying to study more later on all helped to focus my attention on the golden bubbles rising up through the beer and along the sides of the glass in front of me... I sat, mesmerized. I thought: 'Effervescence really belongs to that category of daily phenomena that naturally engage the imagination; I could just as well be watching the clouds in the sky, flames popping in a fireplace or waves breaking on a beach.' I suppose that I could have just left it at that, but I wanted to know more. I wanted to see closer, get my camera. I suddenly realized, in a flash of free association (and slight intoxication), that I wanted to study carbonated beverages.

A year later I had a master's degree in fundamental physics and was still a bubbles addict. I bought a secondhand macrophotographic lens and, over the holidays, started taking photographs of bubbles rising in a glass filled with soda. I spent whole nights developing film and enlarging pictures in my bathroom, which – to my girlfriend's chagrin – I had transformed into a makeshift darkroom. Six months and many sleepless nights later, I mailed some of my best shots to the research department of Champagne Moët & Chandon, along with some initial scientific observations describing what was occurring in the photographs.

My grand plan was this: champagne makers such as Moët & Chandon sold 262.6 million bottles in 2001 – the equivalent of about $3 billion in sales. For an industry that banks so much on bubbles, finding ways to better understand the bubbling process and eventually to improve the beverage's hallmark fizz seemed like a smart idea. Department head Bruno Duteurtre asked me to come to Moët & Chandon's headquarters in Epernay (the capital of champagne wines) to lay out my photographs, thoughts and research plans. The people I met with were captivated by the idea of this research, and, a few weeks later, I moved from Paris to Reims to begin my dissertation in the Laboratory of Oenology at the University of Reims. With colleagues from both the university and Moët & Chandon, I started my official investigation into the physical chemistry of champagne bubbles…

Gérard Liger-Belair (*left*) and fellow physicist Guillaume Polidori at their optical workbench, using laser tomography to capture the flow patterns of champagne bubbles in a flute.

Blame it on the Fizzics

Champagne Cork Popping Revisited

We all associate champagne with ice buckets but how does the temperature of a bottle of champagne affect the way in which a cork pops out of it? We decided to investigate by examining champagne corks popping out of champagne bottles of various temperatures. During the first 30 centimetres of the cork's trajectory after exiting the bottle, which corresponds to the field of view covered by the objective of our high-speed video camera, we measured the average velocity reached by the popping cork. Though there is some natural variability, it clearly appeared that the velocity of the cork increases as the wine's temperature rises.

Above It is far safer when a bottle of champagne comes uncorked with a subdued sigh, but most of us would admit to having popped open a champagne bottle with the kind of dramatic bang that is so wonderfully captured here…

Left As the cork pops, escaping gas reaches a glacial −90°C in a surprisingly blue haze of frozen CO_2.

The driving force exerted on the cork by gases under pressure in the bottleneck increases with temperature for two reasons. First because, generally, gases expand as temperature rises; however, since the volume of the champagne bottleneck remains constant, the pressure of the gas expanding within this constant volume causes increased pressure there. The second reason is that the ability of champagne to retain dissolved CO_2 decreases as temperature increases. This is because, according to the laws of physics, the solubility of gases (their ability to remain dissolved in the champagne liquid) decreases with increasing temperature. Therefore, the dissolved CO_2 progressively escapes from the champagne as the wine gets warmer, invades the space in the bottleneck beneath the cork, and contributes to increasing the explosive pressure under the cork.

What Is the Best Way to Pour Champagne?

Have you ever wondered how best to pour champagne into a flute to preserve the precious fizz? Is the traditional method of pouring into an upright glass the best, or is it better to pour into a glass held at a slant? How can we ensure that the bubbles are shown off to their best effect and remain in the glass for the optimal amount of time?

The concentration of dissolved CO_2 in champagne and sparkling wines is the real key to the production of bubbles. But the act of pouring champagne into a glass is far from inconsequential. We investigated the effects of two different pouring methods on dissolved CO_2 concentration. One method involved pouring champagne straight down the middle of a vertically oriented flute. The other involved pouring champagne down the side of a tilted flute. The latter 'beer-like' way of serving champagne was found to have significantly less impact on the concentration of dissolved CO_2 than the former method. This is because the beer-like way of pouring is gentle. The champagne flows softly along the glass wall to progressively fill the flute. Pouring champagne straight down the middle of a vertically oriented glass produces turbulence and also traps air bubbles in the liquid, both of which force dissolved CO_2 to escape more rapidly.

Temperature, again, plays a part. We discovered that the higher the champagne's temperature, the more dissolved CO_2 is lost during the pouring process – thus we found the first analytical proof that low temperatures help champagne retain its effervescence during pouring. The reason for this is that

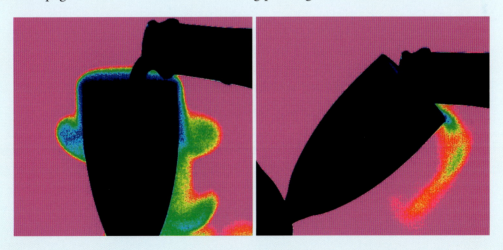

Caught by an infrared video camera, the loss of CO_2 (seen here in blue/green), and therefore of potential bubbles, decreases if champagne is poured like beer, on the side of a tilted flute.

the viscosity of a liquid (in everyday terms, how 'thick' or 'thin' it is) normally decreases (that is, the liquid grows 'thinner') as its temperature increases. Think of how honey becomes thinner and flows more easily when heated, thereby decreasing in viscosity; in just the same way, increasing the temperature of champagne decreases its viscosity. In turn, low champagne viscosity promotes more turbulence and agitation in the liquid during the pouring process, thus forcing dissolved CO_2 to escape more rapidly from the champagne.

These findings were corroborated when we employed a new dynamic tracking technique that uses infrared imaging to make visible the cloud of gaseous CO_2 that escapes during the pouring process (*see* the two images on page 219). Our conclusion? It is quite simple: we should treat champagne a little more like beer at least, when it comes to serving it.

HOW MANY BUBBLES IN YOUR GLASS?

The issue about how many bubbles are likely to form in a glass of champagne is of concern for sommeliers, wine journalists, experienced tasters, and anyone wondering about complex phenomena at play in a glass of bubbly. We have recently attempted to provide an accurate scientific answer. If we assume a classic flute contains 0.1 litres of champagne, we estimate that 0.7 litres of gaseous carbon dioxide must escape in order for equilibrium to be reached. If each bubble is about 500 micrometres in diameter, that leaves 11 million bubbles needing to escape – more than the population of New York City! But not all the gas is released in bubble form. Some escapes direct from the surface of the wine. Closer inspection of glasses poured with champagne revealed that bubble trains rising elegantly towards the champagne surface originate from tiny dust particles attached to the glass wall. Our calculations using models that combine both the dynamics of bubble ascent and mass transfer equations found that if the champagne is poured straight down the middle of a vertically oriented flute, then, depending on various perameters such as temperature, glass shape and ambient pressure, about one million bubbles are likely to nucleate. Otherwise, champagne served more gently in a tilted flute – the technique that better preserves the dissolved carbon dioxide – will yield 10s of thousands more.

Flute Versus Coupe: And the Winner Is...

The advantages and disadvantages of both shapes – the flute vs the coupe – have long been debated in bars, clubs, restaurants and popular wine magazines. But to date little to no analytical data has ever been brought to bear on the age-old dilemma of how these shapes affect the champagne inside them.

Let's bypass the Freudian connotations of the coupe and consider some science. When one sips champagne from a glass, gaseous CO_2 and volatile aromatic compounds progressively invade the 'headspace' above the glass, thus modifying the taster's global perception of aromas. We were very curious to discover how the flute and the coupe differ in their effects on tasters' perceptions of gaseous CO_2 and aromas...

To answer this question, we measured the levels of gaseous CO_2 and ethanol via gas chromatography (a technique that allows us accurately to measure the various chemical components in a mixture). Our results suggest that the narrow flute funnels the gases upwards efficiently, whereas the broader coupe dilutes them. Gaseous CO_2, which may irritate the nose if too concentrated, was found above the flute in nearly twice the concentrations found above the coupe. These results are consistent with sensory analyses of champagne and sparkling wines conducted by human tasters; it is generally accepted that the smell of champagne, and especially its first 'nose', is more irritating when champagne is served in a flute than when it is served in a coupe, and this is because there is a greater concentration of gaseous CO_2 funnelled directly up to the nose. Infrared imaging also made it possible for us to see the gaseous CO_2 escaping from both glass types (as seen in the photograph, *left*), and this confirmed the tendency of flutes to hang on to concentrated quantities of CO_2.

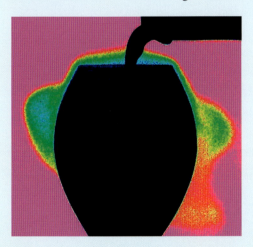

From a flute, CO_2 sent directly up to the nose, can irritate. A tulip glass takes a softer approach...

There is another small problem with tall flutes. Bubbles at the champagne surface are much larger than those above a coupe, simply because they have to travel a longer distance to the top of the glass and thus have more time to grow in size than they do in a shallow coupe. The coupe therefore has the advantage that it keeps those bubbles tiny. In my own opinion, a tulip-shaped wine glass (a bit shorter than a traditional flute and curved slightly inwards at the top, just like the glass shown on the previous page) would yield the best compromise between bubble size and the release of aromas, and would provide a better overall sensory experience than either the tall flute or the shallow coupe.

Jet Drops, Sensation and Flavour Release

The characteristic 'mouthfeel' of champagne is an important part of drinking it and contributes to the pleasure of tasting. During the first few minutes following the pouring of a flute of champagne, the liquid surface is literally spiked with conical structures we call jet drops. Jet drops are ejected up to several centimetres above the surface with a powerful velocity of several metres per second. In the very first few seconds after pouring, hundreds of bubbles are bursting every second at the liquid surface, and hundreds of tiny jet drops about 100 micrometres in size are launched – in the form of a refreshing spray that pleasantly tickles the taster's face. Indeed, if you wear glasses and take a sip from a freshly poured flute of champagne, you surely have noticed the light spray that forms instantaneously before your eyes. The few centimetres the liquid jets reach in height are just enough to reach our nociceptors (the scientific term for very sensitive nerves that act as pain receptors) in the nose; these are thus highly stimulated during champagne tasting, as are receptors in the mouth when bubbles burst over the tongue.

In addition to these mechanical stimulations (and, occasionally, irritations), bubbles bursting at the surface play a major role in flavour release. Many aromatic compounds in carbonated beverages show surface activity, including alcohols (such as ethanol, butanol, pentanol, and phenyl-2-ethanol), some aldehydes (such as butanol, hexanal and hexenals), and organic acids (such as propionic and butyric acids). Bubbles rising and expanding in the liquid act like tiny elevators for surface-active and potentially aromatic molecules, carrying them along as they make their way up.

A technique called laser tomography was used to reveal what the naked eye could not. The photographs on the facing page show the beauty of the flow patterns found in champagne glasses. By increasing the diffusion of aromas above the champagne surface, the flow patterns driven by ascending bubbles are indeed a wonderful gift to the champagne taster. They continuously renew the air/wine interface, thus allowing volatile aromas to escape from the wine surface much more efficiently over a longer period of time, whereas the surface of a wine at rest progressively becomes odourless.

Because of the flavour- and scent-carrying bubbles, there is no need to swirl champagne as you would still wines. Rising and bursting bubbles do the work for you, bringing flavours and aromas above the liquid surface directly to your senses.

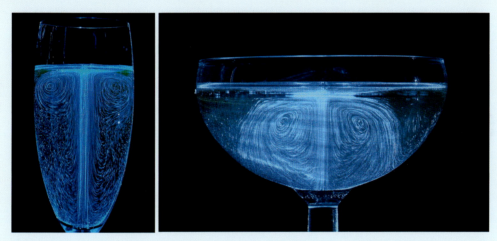

Left and *right* These classic bubble flow patterns only develop where there are 'nucleation sites' encouraging bubbles to form. As they ascend through a glass of champagne, bubbles allow volatile aromas to escape from the wine's surface – still wine, at rest, would become progressively odourless.

Comparing Champagne and Sea-Spray...

A nice parallel can also be drawn between the fizz in a glass of champagne and the 'fizz' of the ocean. The major sources of bubbles in the upper ocean are the breaking action of waves and rain impacting on the sea surface, both of which trap air within the seawater. When bubbles created by waves and rain burst at the surface of the sea, they form jet drops just like those in champagne. In the early 1970s, oceanographers found that droplets ejected into the air at the ocean surface contained much higher numbers of particles and greater amounts of surface-active materials than those found in the bulk of the water directly below; essentially, the jet drops were skimming off the surface layer of the ocean to eject it into the atmosphere.

It's just the same with champagne: the jet drops skim off the aromatic particles from the surface of the wine. While bursting bubbles in champagne act to create a sensual effect, bubbles bursting at the sea surface are actually the most significant source of sea salt particles – and these particles act as condensation nuclei to create clouds.

The Fizzing Sound of Champagne

As suggested by our high-speed photographs of bursting bubbles, a lot of energy is released during the collapse of a champagne bubble. Some of this energy is used to create the upward liquid jet; some, however, is also released into the atmosphere in the form of a tiny auditory shock wave. The fizzing sound of champagne is therefore the sum of thousands of individual audible 'pops' at the surface of the foam… bubbles do not pop independently of one another. The collapse of a bubble strongly affects its surrounding neighbours – which may then collapse in turn, causing a chain reaction throughout the liquid. Scientists call this chain reaction 'avalanche behaviour', comparing it to snow avalanches in which a falling pocket of snow can destabilize other pockets of snow and cause a whole mountainside to slide away.

…If the bursting events happened at a constant rate while foam collapses, we would expect to hear a constant and uniform noise similar to white noise, like radio static. Instead, champagne seems to crackle and is not at all monotonous. The acoustic signal is 'spiky', and it changes unpredictably in volume as time passes, depending on the amplitude of the chain reactions induced by bursting events. The result? A characteristically capricious fizzing sound that further enriches the sensual experience of champagne, sparkling wines and beers for the taster.

Since I became a scientist, many people have remarked that I seem to have landed the best job in all of physics, as my research into bubbles requires that I work in a lab stocked with top-notch champagne – and I'd be inclined to agree! However, my pleasure comes from the fact that I still have the same child-like fascination that I first felt as a boy when I was entranced by blowing and watching soap bubbles. May you also be enchanted afresh by the beauty hidden deep inside your next glass of champagne.

Excerpt from *Uncorked, the Science of Champagne* by Gérard Liger-Belair, Princeton University Press (New Jersey) 2004. Reproduced here with kind permission of the author and publishers.

BETTER, BRIGHTER, BUBBLIER...

7

How to improve on perfection? The constant incremental changes required for champagne to 'stay the same' in this wild northern corner of France with its incalculable climate, are many. But there's always scope – in using oak casks, adding reserve wines, changing cellar conditions, taking time – for its blends to become better...

THE 'O' WORD
Margaret Rand (2018)

MARRIAGE OF AGE AND YOUTH
Anne Krebiehl MW (2017, 2018, 2022)

QUALITY TIME
Tom Stevenson (2014)

THE UNDERCOVER MAVERICKS
Margaret Rand (2011)

CELLAR IN THE SEA
Essi Avellan MW (2022)

Margaret Rand (2018)
THE 'O' WORD

Oak in champagne is a complex, contradictory business, with producers variously using it to add weight, to deliver extra briskness, to underpin or reveal the fruit, or simply to stand out from the crowd. Margaret Rand sifts the competing approaches.

There's oak, and there's how you use it.

Sorry if that sounds obvious, but to venture into Champagne to look at how growers and houses are using oak these days is to risk getting submerged in detail. One has periodically to stand back and refocus in order to tell the wood from the trees. That, up there on top of the Montagne, is forest; down here among the vines is wine. Where and how they meet is not clear-cut. If oak trees had tendrils they'd be the perfect metaphor for something curling its way into cellars and getting a grip on the wine without drawing too much attention to itself.

So, first focus: what is oak for?

Creaminess, complexity and weight, is the short answer. Not tannins: tannins in champagne are uncomfortable. Sometimes, yes, you can trace the oak even if you can't precisely taste it – in the muscularity of Henri Giraud, for example. Billecart-Salmon's Cuvée Sous Bois doesn't taste oaky, although there's a firm edge to its lovely toasted almonds and Bakewell-tart richness. (Its Cuvée Nicolas François 2006, with just 20 percent fermented in barrels and given partial malo, is much more dominated by the flavours of age, so it's not a like-for-like comparison, and the oak gives just a subtle underlining of the confit fruit and fresh plum flavours.) At the other end of the scale, Veuve Clicquot ferments some wines in big François Frères *foudres* for a seasoning of about one to two percent for Yellow Label and five to 10 percent for vintage; the structure still comes from Pinot Noir. *Chef de cave* Dominique Demarville is working towards using each *foudre* for the same *cru*, year after year, to amplify the individuality of each vat. Roederer gives some of the Cristal juice, particularly that from tighter *crus* like Verzenay, some oak treatment to round it out, though the fatter *crus* like Aÿ and Bouzy are still restrained in steel.

Oak can be a point of difference in a crowded market, or it can be what Gilles Descôtes, *chef de cave* of Bollinger, describes as 'a tool, not a project in itself'. It can be used for slow micro-oxygenation. It can be used, counter-intuitively, for extra briskness. It can be a revealer: of differences between terroirs, of fruit richness. But not all richness comes from oak.

That toastiness you'll find in Krug, for example, doesn't come from oak. In fact, mention oak to Olivier Krug and he says: 'We don't talk about oak. I've forbidden the team to talk about it. It's "the O word".'

This is, you will admit, not a very encouraging start. Krug's toastiness, he insists, comes from oxidative racking: the wine is fermented in 205-litre *pièces Champenois* made to Krug's guidelines at Taransaud and Seguin-Moreau (both known as makers of powerful barrels) from wood that has been dried for two to three years and given a light toast before being washed with hot water in the cellars to get rid of the tannins. For two years a new barrel is used for fermenting second pressings, which are not kept. The average age of the barrels is 20–25 years, and they buy a few new ones each year.

At Krug, barrels are used not for the toastiness they give a wine but for the oxidative benefits they bring during fermentation.

After fermentation the wine is racked into open troughs and then run into steel; it never sees oak again. So one can see his point. 'Krug became the oak house because we were the only house to ferment everything in oak,' he says. But oak is not actually what Krug is about, and it doesn't want to be defined by it. That brief exposure to the open air during racking is enough, apparently, to give that trademark richness; that, and the micro-oxygenation during fermentation. 'We explored other ways of racking, and it didn't taste the same,' says Olivier. 'We tried extra oxygenation, and that didn't work either. [Oxygenation during racking] is a vaccination against oxidation.'

In which case, what is the point of all those barrels? 'Individuality' is the answer. 'Oak contributes nothing; individuality contributes everything.' (They're good at soundbites at Krug.) Lots of different barrels equals lots of different wines for blending. And 'big casks would have a different effect'.

The 'O' Word

Age, size and provenance…

Oak that is *not* for oak flavour has to be chosen differently from oak intended to influence flavour. Alfred Gratien gets its barrels from La Chablisienne (Chablis' highly reputable wine co-operative), where they will have been used for four or five wines before being despatched to Champagne. And here they celebrate oak: glasses are brought on trays made from barrel heads, and staves painted red, green and purple to match the neck labels decorate the new shop. Secondhand barrels are a relatively new idea at Gratien: in 1991 they started buying new barrels from M Santot, who was the last cooper in Aÿ; then they bought new from Seguin-Moreau, and they've tried François Frères, St-Romain and others. But *chef de cave* Nicholas Jaeger likes what he gets from La Chablisienne, and thinks their previous life doesn't affect his wine. 'But I don't know. Chablis feels more woody, and here we want something more neutral.' But an ex-Grenouilles barrel from the famous Chablis Grand Cru can be no bad thing, he agrees.

La Chablisienne is supplied by half-a-dozen or so different coopers, and 'they still show a difference even after four or five years,' says Jaeger. 'The AquaFlex barrel from Seguin-Moreau is very good – they don't burn the wood, and it's very delicate, even when new. Taransaud can be more drying, and it stays on the finish longer.'

At AR Lenoble, Antoine Malassagne favours a mix of fine-grained Taransaud and François Frères barrels, with different toasts (though all medium, and not too pale), but not everything gets the oak fermentation treatment: that decision is made year by year. 'Very dilute juice is not good for fermenting in barrel. In 2017 I used a big 50-hectolitre barrel, and *barriques*, and the Pinots were nearly all in steel.' New barrels are used for fermentation, never ageing, and barrels are only used for fermentation for three years; after that, it's ageing only. It's the cream and butter flavours from oak fermentation that are the attraction for him, but also the muscle and structure, and the spice that Chardonnay gets from ageing in *barrique*. 'I want vinous wines, complex and rich,' he says, 'and I want a balance between richness and elegance and freshness. It's a challenge to find this balance.'

Anselme Selosse finds that balance by varying barrel sizes and shapes and types of wood: for him, acacia keeps the freshness better, whereas oak gives roundness and fat. The big wines of 2009 would have been too heavy if he'd used only oak, but the 2008s in acacia would have been too tight and narrow. A compromise is acacia heads on oak barrels. The toast he leaves to the *tonnelier*:

'They come here and taste.' He doesn't wash them out with hot water, either. 'The oakiness [in the wine] peaks in November/December, then declines.'

(Sebastien le Golvet at Henri Giraud gives it a bit longer: 'After fermentation, you get wood on the wine. From six months you get balance, and if you work well you get other aromas, and wine on the wood.')

In July, Selosse counts the pips in the grapes, which gives him a measure of the capacity of the wine to resist oak: if there are two or fewer, it's a year for 400-litre casks. Otherwise it's 228-litre barrels; all wines are fermented in wood, and 20–25 percernt of the wood is new every year ('new oak breathes better'), from Radoux, Taransaud, Mercurey and Cavin.

Terroir for the trees

How late you can leave your annual oak decisions depends presumably on how much new oak you use – and on your relationship with your coopers. Henri Giraud has a love affair with the Argonne forest and is clearly very good friends with his *tonnelier*, because he confirms his annual order just one week before harvest. The *tonnelier* already has the oak, of course, but even so…

One month before vintage, Giraud and *chef de cave* Sebastien le Golvet look at the maturity of the grapes, and one week before, when they are sure of what they are dealing with, they pick up the telephone. But before that – some three years before, since that's the length of drying he favours – they have chosen the trees. And before that, they have chosen the plots, and the stations, which are even more precise than plots, in the forest. A station will have homogeneous soil, sub-soil, exposition, climate and flora, and they will study every tree in a station to understand them. How big is a station? Clearly, I might as well have asked about the length of a piece of string. 'Usually smaller than a plot of vines,' is Golvet's answer: shorter than another piece of string, in other words. To give some idea, one hectare of forest will probably have just four to five suitable trees.

The Argonne forest, Golvet explains, consists of lots of little hills, formed as the Paris Basin drained against the Vosges mountains. All those different expositions give different aromas, and Golvet runs through a few: 'Minerality, and length and vivacity from Châtrices, apricots from Lachalade, undergrowth and *crème de marrons* from Valmy'. Beaulieu, on the plateau of the forest, is faster growing and gives more tannins. They have a soil map of the forest and choose the exact exposition they want.

Not everything at Henri Giraud is fermented in oak, however. Steel no longer features, but there are clay amphorae and sandstone eggs, the former very porous, the latter not at all. The sandstone is covered in clay from – you guessed it – the Argonne forest, and is used for juice that doesn't have the right structure for oak.

Their choice of toasts is equally precise. The toast might be *pain de campagne*, or brioche, or *pain d'epices* or even fruit pie – 'We look for a black-cherries aroma when toasting,' says Golvet – but it has to be long and slow. The toast is different for every plot in the forest; and each batch of juice will suit a particular part of the forest.

Revealing, not swamping, the fruit

The sourcing of oak leads naturally to a discussion of sessile versus pedunculate oak (stalked vs unstalked); and, for Bollinger, at least, it's too early to say which is better. 'Maybe sessile for reds [in Burgundy],' muses Gilles Descôtes. 'It has more lactones. For Champagne, maybe pedunculate? Maybe with old oak there is less difference, but we will see.' (Over at Roederer, Jean-Baptiste Lecaillon prefers sessile, for its sweetness, over the bitterness of pedunculate.)

Bollinger's 3,500 barrels have an average age of 20 years, and start at six or seven years; owning Chanson (the burgundy house) means it has a guaranteed source of secondhand wood. Descôtes experiments with different sizes and ways of making to fit the Bollinger style. 'The goal is to get new wood without the taste of new wood.' So a very, very light toast, and in the future, perhaps trees from the Bollinger family's own forests in the Champagne region. 'We've found some [suitable] trees, but there are no barrels yet.' What Descôtes seeks from oak is 'a fruit booster, a fruit revealer'.

This is the difference between those who welcome some oak muscle and those who want just a touch more creaminess and richness from oak – though all want precision and finesse as well. At Bollinger, where 20 percent of the non-vintage and all the vintage is fermented in oak, the move to a fresher, less oxidative, though still vinous style, via better control of oxygen, has included not just an insistence on better selection of grapes (and therefore less botrytis), better pumps in the winery, and jetting[1] at bottling, but also involved replacing a lot

---

1 Jetting takes place immediately after disgorgement and just before a champagne is corked. A micro-stream of water or liquid nitrogen is jetted into the bottle so that a barrier of mousse rises up and pushes out any oxgen caught in the bottleneck. Jetting technology is now incorporated into many champagne disgorging lines.

of barrels and ensuring that the bungs actually fit properly. The easiest place for oxygen to enter a barrel is through the hole. Make sure your cooper is giving you bungs that fit his barrels, and instantly you reduce oxidation.

The good servant…

Laurent Champs of Vilmart, another big, vinous wine which has become more precise, talks of his search for purity, finesse, elegance, structure, delicacy and complexity: 'Structure comes from low yields and from viticulture, and elegance from no malo and from the winemaking.' Where, then, does oak fit into this famously oak-friendly house – so oak-friendly that 15 or 20 years ago it was nicknamed 'dinosaur' for using oak? 'What we've learned is that we can get more complexity and more integration. "Wood is a good servant but a bad master",' he adds, quoting the wine importer Thierry Theise.

Damy and Rousseau are the chosen coopers at Vilmart; 'Damy doesn't shout,' says Champs, and he likes the toast. Rousseau, he says, is a specialist in larger casks (30 hectolitres in Vilmart's case): with these 'you don't feel the wood or the tannins'. Micro-oxygenation with no woody taste is the aim, and those larger casks are used for younger vines, which here means 15 to 35 years old. Older vines, from 45 to 60 years old, get 228-litre Damy barrels. All are fine-grained, medium-toast Alliers oak, and they're kept for six or seven years. After that, says Champs, 'you lose the identity of the wood, but you keep the micro-oxygenation'. So while oak is not just about micro-oxygenation here, it's also not about wood forcing itself into visibility.

'Today, how many young growers want a special cuvée in wood?' asks Champs rhetorically. 'There is an interesting and important future for oak in Champagne. Drinkers want a story, and something different, not something uniform.'

'But you need structure in the wine first,' he adds. 'If it's too light, it won't match with this kind of winemaking. You don't learn in one day or one year; you need a minimum of 10 or 15 years to feel, to see, to taste your wine. You must be very precise from A to Z; you can't miss anything. And you need very long on the lees, so you need to plan ahead.'

Common mistakes? According to Pascal Agrapart of Agrapart: 'Buying new oak, and lack of hygiene'. The second is unarguable; the first, as we've seen, is more contentious.

The right upbringing…

Which brings us to *élevage* and the three kinds of ageing found in Champagne. Oak and its effects need to be balanced. So what about the malo – does oak plus malo equal too much? Is lees ageing crucial for integration and freshness? And reserve wines: both Krug and Bollinger eschew oak for these; Roederer favours big, old oak.

The answers, not surprisingly, show that there are no rules: producers do what works for them, and the permutations are endless. Fermenting in wood obviously integrates the flavours earlier, and is favoured by Taittinger for about five percent of Comtes de Champagne. Champagne Mailly Grand Cru has introduced some two-hectolitre barrels for fermentation. Jacquesson and Jérôme Prévost ferment everything in wood, and a long list of producers, including André Jacquart, Benoît Lahaye, Drappier, Eric Rodez, Philipponat and Tarlant, ferment partly in wood. At Agrapart, Pascal ferments partly in steel and partly in *barriques* or *tonneaux* (from François Fréres and Taransaud), does the malo in *barrique* and keeps the wines on lees until bottling. But at this producer of notably tight, fine-grained wines, the barrels are always bought in Burgundy or the Loire at five years old: 'The effect of the tonnelier is over by then.' He keeps them, he says, for 25 or even 40 years.

Micro-oxygenation, after all that time, is what is left: 'Fermentation opens the pores of the oak through warmth, and then they close afterwards. The grain is less important.' What is important is the lees – 'as important in the barrel as in the bottle'. Providing, of course, that the lees are the right sort of lees. If they're not, then the wine is racked off. 'I don't want to fatigue the wine.'

What Agrapart does want to do is display his terroirs. 'Terroir is more important than you can imagine. Champagne is like Burgundy: there are lots of different terroirs in one village.' His Complantée cuvée is from Pinots Noir and Blanc, Meunier, Arbane and Petit Meslier, co-planted in equal quantities, in Avize. 'The terroir of the Côte de Blancs makes them all taste like Chardonnay.' Rather like Chardonnay from Aÿ tasting like Pinot Noir, one might add – but the particularities of terroir are another subject.

One can play endlessly with the permutations of malo and length of ageing, of lees and the ageing of reserve wines. (Also of dosage: in a zero-dosage wine where there are no extra sugars to produce toastiness from a Maillard Reaction [*see* page 20], the reducing sugars that come from oak ageing can do the job.) At Vilmart, 10 months in *barrique* on the fine lees and no malo is the norm, and reserves are kept in wood and tank. Some wines spend even longer in 30-hectolitre barrels. Agrapart does the malo in *barrique*, with all wines kept on lees until bottling, and wines fermented in steel go into *barrique* until the next harvest, and become reserves.

At Gratien: 'The lees keep the wood flavour. If you put wine in barrel with no lees, you feel the wood more. I've found this for four or five years: without the lees, the wine is too hard.' Once the blend is decided upon the wines are racked into steel, and reserves are kept in steel: 'If you keep reserves in barrel you get too much maturity.' He balances the oak by preventing the malo: 'Otherwise it would be heavy, and you wouldn't want more than a glass… But you have to avoid VA.' Bollinger (Gratien's parent company), he adds hastily, does a great job of doing the malo in oak.

For Anselme Selosse: 'The important thing is that the wine and the oak can have time to get to know each other.' His wines, accordingly, spend a relatively long time in wood; he bottles in July, from wood, and keeps his reserve wines in mostly big wooden vats, though some are in steel. Do the wines age faster that way? 'I'm not trying to give immortality to the wine,' he cautions. 'Inshallah', he might say, and does: 'Whether the malo happens or not is an inshallah matter, possibly influenced by low levels of sulphur dioxide.'

At AR Lenoble: 'When I explain my champagne to clients, I don't mention oak,' says Antoine Malassagne. 'I talk about farming, and ageing, and reserve wines – it's particular to Champagne to use reserve wines.' He wants vinosity, but not heaviness, and maintains that 'you have to block the malo if you vinify in barrel'.

Sebastien le Golvet would not agree: all the Henri Giraud wines do the malo – partly because if they didn't he'd need sulphur to stabilize them, 'which gives me a headache… It's not a matter of barrels, it's a matter of philosophy of winemaking. You have acidic wines. Then what? You need acidity, but if you stay on the lees a long time you get roundness. It's a matter of how you want to work.'

In short, finding the right balance of oak in champagne can be head-spinning stuff. Let's wrap up this exploration with a last comment from Laurent Champs: 'Steel is safer.'

First published in *The World of Fine Wine*, issue 62, in 2018. Reproduced here with kind permission of the editor, Neil Beckett, and the author.

Anne Krebiehl MW (2017, 2018, 2022)

MARRIAGE OF AGE AND YOUTH

Anne Krebiehl explains that rather than regarding champagne's reserve wines, stored from its finest vintages, merely as a blending component to ensure consistency across its range, several leading champagne producers are exploring the ability of *réserves perpétuelles* and 'soleras' to deepen the expression of their signature style – and sense of place.

Champagne, perhaps more than most classic wine regions, has made an absolute virtue of necessity. By perfecting every aspect of production, the region has overcome climatic challenges and dramatic vintage variation. Second fermentation and extended lees ageing add extra body and creaminess to slender, acidic base wines. Careful blending of grape varieties, origins and vintages creates cuvées that far exceed the sum of their parts. The keeping and blending of reserve wines is and has been central to this, evening out vintages as variable in quality as in quantity. But reserves can be a stylistic tool, too. While most houses keep their reserves separate according to vintage, grape variety and site, some producers keep a *réserve perpétuelle* (RP) to create champagnes that taste of both time and timelessness. There is a lot of talk, too, about so-called champagne soleras…

    But, some definitions first: to my mind, the distinction between the ideas is clear: a solera will have equal and exact parts taken away and added each year, always measured, always static, so that the solera itself would always have equal parts of every vintage. A *réserve perpétuelle*, on the other hand, would have added reserves from many different vintages, their proportions varying with their availability. So, where a solera is exact, a *réserve perpétuelle* is flexible and variable, depending on the generosity and character of each added vintage. It turns out, however, that for many producers such clarity in distinction does not really exist.

Some voice their doubts as to whether a solera could be kept in stainless steel, as some cellars clearly do, fixing the use of the term to the vessel rather than the proportional concept; others rejected the term as belonging to Spain – as does the Comité Champagne, which is understandably wary of appropriating it for this region. Yet others even put 'solera' on their front labels. While the terms thus remain officially undefined, for me the distinction between the two is whether the proportions removed and added are exact and constant or fluid. Those winemakers who keep both a solera and an RP largely stick to this distinction.

A more pragmatic approach is that an RP is just a rather practical, old-fashioned, and possibly even home-spun way of keeping reserve wines. Some winemakers even think of their RP as the backbone of their non-vintage blends, and it is easy to see why. Others use it as a stylistic departure from their regular bottlings, which are made with reserves aged in the conventional manner – that is, matured separately according to grape variety and origin. Then there are growers who have a so-called *réserve parcellaire*, a perpetual reserve, fluid or not, made each year from the same vineyard parcel, which, with increasing age, represents that very parcel in ever greater depth. Other *réserves parcellaires* may always be from the same parcel but not have additions in each year. The variations and permutations of these unusual reserves seem endless – their composition and stylistic potential will only be enhanced by the second fermentation in bottle. Which brings this discussion to a point that, for me, is central to the fascination of champagne: the sheer creative latitude that is possible and actively practised even within this most regulated of appellations, where almost every aspect of production is legally prescribed.

I believe that the decision to create such a reserve is more closely linked to the desire to show the true nature of a site or a variety. In any case, reserve wines, whether solera or RP, each contain precious essences of time. With every addition to this kind of evolving reserve, the oldest portion becomes smaller but, essentially, its life is magically extended. The fact that a wine bottled 10 years ago and tasted today contains tiny portions of wines harvested 30 or even 35 years ago is a wonderful contemplation.

While not every producer sees a clear distinction between these techniques of keeping and blending reserve wines, those featured here are careful not to mislabel what they are doing and are also absolutely clear about their technique. What differs is their motives…

Selosse: Reflecting history, revealing personality

'For me, the solera exists to create a climatic average and therefore one constant of a terroir; what is constant is the origin,' says Anselme Selosse of Champagne Jacques Selosse in Avize. 'The *réserve perpétuelle*, on the other hand,' he explains, 'is a reserve that families used to keep in order to reduce the variations between the years.' Depending on how large or small the harvest was, he says, the perpetual reserve was fluid; sometimes there was more, sometimes less. 'The *réserve perpétuelle* is not systematic; it is variable and a function of the volume of the new vintage, whereas the solera always has the same quantity.' He keeps both a solera and a *réserve perpétuelle* and clearly distinguishes between the two. His adoption of these practices is linked to different ideas, memories and experiences.

Selosse started his solera many years before he started the perpetual reserve and delves far into the past to explain. He studied viticulture in Beaune from 1969 to 1973, and it was during these student days in Burgundy that sporting excursions took him to the Bresse countryside (the Rhône-Alpes, Bourgogne and Franche-Comté), where he got to taste very simple local wines, often made using *réserve perpétuelle*. 'They were family wines, not about vintages at all: reds were made from Pinot Noir and Gamay, not for the market but for home consumption. Just because they were simple does not mean they were not good,' he emphasizes. He likens the perpetual reserve to the stockpots of the past that were kept on the stove continuously, serving as the base for soups and sauces and constantly having quantities taken out while being replenished with more water and ingredients.

'In 1972,' he says, 'I went to Spain to visit Penedès, Rioja and Andalucía, and I saw the *gran reservas* there. I saw cathedrals of barrels, which had almost completely disappeared from Champagne and were in the process of disappearing from Burgundy. In Andalucía, I saw the practice of the solera and its usage. I saw it, but I still had no idea.' In 1974, once he had returned home after his studies, Selosse's parents handed him the keys to the cellar. They were keen to retire and told young Anselme to get to work. 'At first I just continued what they had started. But I soon realized that I had to offer something different.'

It also occurred to him that the most expensive wines in Champagne at that time were vintages. In Burgundy, however, the most expensive wines were those from specific parcels. These wines were not about the year but about the place. 'I wanted to give more "place" to the wine, but it was difficult. The only way to put more of the "where" into it was to have less of the "when".' This is why he started to keep back the reserve wines that would eventually form a solera. The solera focuses only on the 'where' and has the average of the 'when'. 'I did not have the money to buy a small, stainless-steel tank; I only had big tanks.' So, the reserves from 1986, '87, '88 and '89 were kept separately in 600-litre *demi-muids* until, together with the 1990 base, he had enough to put these five vintage reserves together to start his first solera. From 1991 onwards, he has always taken 22 percent of the volume from the solera and replenished it with the same amount of new base wine from the most recent harvest.

It is now over 30 years since Selosse created that first solera. Is it difficult to keep it alive? 'No,' he says. He does not add sulphur dioxide to the solera. He instead relies on the protective properties of lees. Occasionally, too, some of the barrels in which the base wines are fermented and matured have a film of flor. 'Flor, for me, is no accident; it is a protection,' Selosse says. He likens the difference between the wines in his solera to the variation between phenotypes of the same genotype: from one tank they taste completely rounded, like a full-bodied Chardonnay, fresh and complex. From another, more slender, taut and austere. These will be bottled and fermented as his famous cuvée Substance. We taste it later: it is salty, individual, fresh but full-bodied, and so good that it is impossible to spit.

Devaux: Increasing the aromatic range

Another keeper of true soleras is Michel Parisot, *chef de cave* at Champagne Devaux in Neuville-sur-Seine, further south in the Aube district. Parisot, who joined Devaux in 1991, is an olfactory obsessive. The creation of the solera in 1995 was driven by the desire to create more complex aromas. 'I work like a perfumer,' Parisot says: 'A perfumer has many scents; the winemaker has Pinot Noir and Chardonnay. So, in order to increase the aromatic range, I decided to have different vinification and ageing techniques. The solera is just one of these possibilities, because you have the aromas of very old wines and the aromas of the new wines, so a balance between age and youth.'

Strangely enough, this Aube winemaker started the solera with a Chardonnay from Chouilly in the Côte des Blancs. 'In 1997, part of the 1995 reserve was used and topped up with the 1996 reserve. Since then, one-third has always been removed and replenished with the same *cru*. I knew that every year I would have Chouilly; it is a part of the Côte des Blancs that is very elegant – it's like lace. For me, this finesse and elegance are important.' In order to preserve this, Parisot has always kept the Chouilly solera in stainless steel, on its fine lees. The brilliance of the 2002 vintage, however, sparked another solera that is a blend of Pinot Noir and Chardonnay, kept in a 14,000-litre *foudre*. 'We had the experience of Chouilly, and every year we saw it getting more and more interesting, so we wondered whether we should have another solera from another *cru* – but which one? We always had reserves in *foudre* and 2002 was a marvellous year; we thought it would be beautiful to start with such a great vintage.' Both the Chouilly solera and the Pinot-Chardonnay solera make up some of the NV Cuvée D. But Parisot also has other reserves separated traditionally by year and site. All of these serve to increase the blending elements and, therefore, the complexity of the wine.

Michel Parisot, a keeper of true champagne soleras at the house of Devaux.

Bruno Paillard: Stylistic continuity born of necessity

Bruno Paillard in Reims, of the eponymous house, was an early adopter of the *réserve perpétuelle*. He explains: 'In 1984, we had an absolutely disastrous vintage. As I had started my *maison* in 1981, I was not very rich in reserve wines. At that time, I kept my reserve wines just like my colleagues did, variety by variety, *cru* by *cru*.' When it came to making the blends for bottling in the spring of 1985, 'it was just impossible to do anything, and we sold all of our 1984s. We were left only with what we had as reserves. So, we started to acquire reserve wines on the market, making sure they were not from 1984. We ended up with much less but much better wine – an excellent wine, in fact. This was the period when we built our reputation. And this is the reason for which we decided to keep our reserve wines in a perpetual reserve.'

Since Paillard makes three multi-vintage cuvées – Première Cuvée, a Rosé and a Grand Cru Blanc de Blancs – he has three different perpetual reserves with the same varietal composition as the finished cuvée. 'The proportions of the grape varieties never vary in the multi-vintage cuvées,' he explains. 'What changes is the origin of the varieties. The vinification does not change; most of our wines do the malolactic; the proportion of barrel fermentation does not vary very much, being always between 20 and 22 percent. The only thing that varies enormously is the proportion of reserve. We use a minimum of 25 percent of the reserve and a maximum of 52. The last time we used 52 percent was in 2004 when we worked with the 2003 vintage, which was beautiful but unbalanced. Roughly, over the past five years, the average of reserve wine has been between 38 and 40 percent.'

Each year, Paillard composes his cuvée in far greater quantity than is needed for bottling. Whatever is not bottled is returned to the *réserve perpétuelle*. The three *réserves perpétuelles* are thus refreshed every year with the new *assemblage*, which already contains a significant proportion – of exactly the same grape composition – of the reserve itself. The use of reserve is less in the Rosé, Paillard explains: 'We want to express the fresh berry aromas, not just floral notes; we want redcurrant, so we insist on fresher wines here.'

The perpetual reserves are kept at a constant temperature of 10.5°C, mostly in stainless-steel tanks but a small part in barrels. Keeping the wines for this length of time is not difficult; the challenge, Paillard says, is more financial and logistical, due to the space required. The perpetual reserve for the Blanc de Blancs was started later, around the turn of the millennium, but those for the Première Cuvée and the Rosé go right back to 1985. Alice Paillard, who works alongside her father, says the perpetual reserve 'is one element that gives a lot of continuity of style. It's the thing that really helps us build consistency. It really is a treasure, because it helps us build the balance we need.' The high proportion of reserve wines in the blend explains the unusual depth of his multi-vintage cuvées. It is especially at the table that their profound nature comes into play. It is a delicious notion that a current, highly affordable, multi-vintage Première Cuvée should still have a tiny portion of 1985 in it.

Drappier: Nature and nurture

Likewise, for Michel Drappier of Champagne Drappier in Urville, again south in the Aube, a perpetual reserve is a way of adding depth to a non-vintage wine. He started his when two factors coincided: the purchase of 'beautiful, new 5,000-litre *foudres* with very tight oak from the Forêt de Tronçais' and a beautiful vintage.

Drappier explains: 'The idea was not to make oaky wines but to be more natural and get away from stainless steel a little. We filled them with Pinot Noir from 2002, and when bottling the 2002 Grande Sendrée [Drappier's top cuvée from a single vineyard in Urville] in the spring of 2003, I thought: 'Why don't we keep a little of this beautiful wine on the side and see what happens?' That has become a sort of *réserve perpétuelle*. What we add is always the best Pinot Noir from Urville with the ability to age. This does not happen every year. We remove what we need, which is 10–20 percent, as a mature, slightly oaked reserve. We then top it up with the most beautiful wine from the most recent vintage. By now we've been using it for many years in our blends to add a little bit of what we think helps produce good NV wines. Because this *réserve perpétuelle* has been enriched by so many different vintages, we have something very nice.'

AR Lenoble: Flexibility and stylistic stability

For Antoine Malassagne, co-owner and winemaker at Champagne AR Lenoble in Damery, which he runs with his sister Anne, the perpetual reserves are a stylistic constant. The trained chemical engineer returned to his family business in 1996 and has continually worked to improve every aspect of the house. Why did he start a perpetual reserve in 2001? Malassagne's answer is prompt: 'More stylistic stability.' There are two perpetual reserves: one is the Chardonnay-based perpetual reserve for the Grand Cru Blanc de Blancs NV from Chouilly; the other, based on Chardonnay, Pinot Noir and Meunier, goes into the Cuvée Intense Brut, Cuvée Dosage Zéro Brut Nature and Cuvée Riche Demi-Sec. Malassagne, however, adds a twist: 'We keep the perpetual reserves in 5,000-litre barrels and in stainless-steel tanks, but we also have some perpetual reserves in magnums. This gives you different characters,' he says, explaining that while he is after a constant house style, his approach is flexible: 'It's not enough to have reserve wine; it also depends on how you age it. Each year, the harvest is different. Each year, I vinify in a different way. I have to adapt my vinification, and sometimes the ageing of my reserve wine. The quantity of reserve wine I have also depends on the last harvest. We do or we don't do malo; I do sometimes, partially or fully – it all depends on the wine. It's like a journey: I know where I want to go, but the ways of getting there are different.'

Ageing some of the perpetual reserve in magnums offers another chance to find the right balance between oxidation and reduction. 'I want something vinous, complex, but not too rich. I want to find a balance between vinosity, femininity and elegance. Just purity and elegance is not enough: I also want to have some richness on the nose and in the mouth – I just want it all,' he laughs. Just enough sugar and yeast is added to the magnums to get 1.5 bars of pressure, 'just to protect the wine with carbon dioxide,' Malassagne says. 'It's not a real second fermentation; we do this to keep the freshness. The thing with the *réserve perpétuelle* is that there is a danger of too much oxidation. I like oxidation, and our style is more marked by that roundness, but not too much. We started the magnums in 2010. Each year we increase the quantity a little.'

The house also keeps other reserves, separated by year, in small, 225-litre barrels, but only from exceptional harvests. 'We do this when we have very interesting vintages, and these are kept for the next one or two years.' The blended reserves make up a substantial part of the non-vintage wines: 'This year, for the Cuvée Intense, we had about 45 percent of the *réserve perpétuelle* in the blend; for the NV Chardonnay it was about 50 percent,' he explains and says that he likes to keep about 50 percent of the perpetual reserve back. Adopting this practice has also changed his approach to making vintage wines, of which Malassagne notes that he releases fewer and fewer…

Bérêche: History, security and the image of a terroir

To Raphaël Bérêche, who, together with his brother Vincent runs the small house of the same name in Ludes (Montagne de Reims), perpetual reserves merely represent good housekeeping. Yet his family was the first to release a wine solely based on such a *réserve perpétuelle*. 'If you are normal and you manage your cellar like a father, you don't take all of the reserve wine to put into your blend. You keep a part to have information on your style, on your ageing, for the new wine. It's just logical,' he says but also notes that the reserve is a kind of essence. For Bérêche, the new wine is 'informed' and 'educated' by the old wines in the reserve. 'It's like ageing on lees – the lees give you the feeling from the vineyard, because the lees are the last solid part from the vineyard.'

It was his grandfather who started the perpetual reserve, but in the 1980s his father Jean-Pierre decided to bottle some of it separately. Jean-Pierre says: 'It was an idea. I had these demi-muids with the *réserve perpétuelle*, and I had more than normal. I decided to make this extra cuvée to extend the range.' At the time, Raphaël explains: 'We just had the Brut Réserve, the Millésime, the Blanc de Blancs and a Demi-Sec, but we wanted to have something extra at the top of the range. My mother thought of the name, and it's been called Reflet d'Antan ever since.' Its first release was in the early 1990s. 'That was very original. At the time it was unique in Champagne. In the beginning it was just for friends and long-standing clients, because in the early '90s, that was still unusual. People liked light champagne with a sweet finish; they did not like the aromas of almonds, old stone, humid chalk, biscuits and torrefaction (roasting) – it was not fashionable at this period. But over the past 10 years it has grown, grown, grown, and people like this kind of champagne on the table with food.' He says it's lovely with '*poulet de Bresse*, morilles, truffles, old Comté, or simply after a big meal' on its own. When asked what his perpetual reserve means to him, Raphaël Bérêche's answer is telling: 'It is my heart and soul, it is very important, it is my history, my security.'

Louis Roederer: Preserving freshness and a paradigm shift

It was in summer 2021 that perpetual reserves moved – if not quite mainstream – into more common parlance with the introduction of Louis Roederer's new Collection cuvée which permanently replaced the house's famous Brut Premier, its *brut sans année*. Cellarmaster and visionary Jean-Baptiste Lécaillon explains the paradigm shift: Roederer's Brut Premier had been created in 1986. Agrochemicals had their heyday; new clonal selections had increased yields and the Champenois struggled to ripen grapes. 'We harvested high-acid grapes in mid-October and Brut Premier was a blending philosophy that would bring ripeness to unripe matter,' Lécaillon says. 'We had to create in the cellar whatever the grapes lacked.'

Climate change and sustainable farming prompted decisive steps. 'They pushed us to rethink,' Lécaillon says. 'Today the fight is not for ripeness but for freshness. We believe in the constant adaptation of winemaking to the raw material we get.' It was the 'fantastic' 2002 vintage that made Lécaillon change course. In 2012 he started a perpetual reserve of half Pinot Noir, half Chardonnay and has added equal amounts of this mix each year since. With the 2017 harvest, the new multi-vintage cuvée that is Collection was born: a revolutionary move for a producer on Roederer's scale: basing a *brut sans année* on a perpetual reserve turns the usual modus operandi on its head. The 'house style' is no longer the result of blending towards a certain goal but based on the ever-increasing complexity of the perpetual reserve.

Rather than choosing wines from the same plot every year to go into the perpetual reserve, which does not undergo malolactic and is kept in stainless steel, 'with very strict oxygen management,' Lécaillon chooses the base wines with the lowest pH level and greatest dry extract. 'Each year Collection will be different, but the core will be the *réserve perpétuelle* and oak reserve wines. Each new vintage will add a twist,' Lécaillon says. 'This is the end of the era of *brut sans année*, this is a new era, the multi-vintage of the 21st century.'

ALL OF THESE WINEMAKERS speak about their motives and their techniques – and it is surprising how much creative potential there is in just one of the myriad, strictly governed aspects that go into making champagne. What the producers deliver with the help of these astonishing, complex blends celebrates the broad stylistic spectrum now available. It highlights the evolution of the entire category and cements its place at the table. Whatever *cru* or variety these blends contain, they all have one eternal, irreplaceable and absolute thing in common: time. The more philosophically inclined among us might concede that wine has a memory, and indeed some of the producers believe that the old wine 'informs' and 'educates' the young wine. The blends themselves are something essential; something true that totally transcends what is in the bottle and touches the soul.

First published as two separate articles in *The World of Fine Wine* in 2017 and 2018. Updated and amalgamated for this book by the author in 2022, and reproduced here with kind permission of Neil Beckett.

Tom Stevenson (2014)

QUALITY TIME

Agreeing to disagree, the winemakers at Dom Pérignon and Roederer clash over the merits of ageing champagne on its yeast lees. Tom Stevenson outlines the debate between the two titans, finding merits – and extraordinary wines – resulting from either argument.

What would be more beneficial: an extra year on lees or an extra year post-disgorgement ageing before a champagne is released?

If I were to put this question to Richard Geoffroy and Jean-Baptiste Lécaillon, two of Champagne's most experienced and naturally gifted *chefs de caves*, I suspect I would receive conflicting answers. Geoffroy was in overall charge of winemaking at Moët & Chandon but had special responsibility for Dom Pérignon from 1990 to 2019, whereas Lécaillon presides over the vineyards and winemaking at Louis Roederer, where he is also joint CEO. I have probably learned more about champagne from these two than from any other individuals in the business.

It is not as if Geoffroy and Lécaillon are of generally opposing philosophies when it comes to the making and appreciation of champagne. They both produce a reductive style of champagne [*see* opposite]; they both avoid oxidative aromas; and they both aim for smooth ageing. Indeed, if they were to sit in each other's tasting room and go through all the vintages to assess how well they had aged, they would come to almost identical conclusions. And yet despite sharing similar reductive philosophies, they make two very different champagnes.

Not that it should be any surprise: they are produced from different varietal proportions, the grapes of which have been grown in different vineyards, and even when the grapes are harvested from the same village, the exposition and harvest dates can differ – in addition to which, the various villages play greater or lesser roles in the final blend. Most importantly, however, one is Dom Pérignon, and the other is Cristal – the difference comes down to that.

> **REDUCTIVE VS OXIDATIVE CHAMPAGNE**
>
> Just as sherry is the world's most famous oxidative wine, so champagne is the world's most famous reductive wine. The second fermentation of champagne takes place in an enclosed environment, where the yeasts suck up all of the oxygen, leaving the wine in a highly reductive state until disgorgement. Such wines are typically well-structured, linear and fruit-focussed. Toasty notes are definitively reductive aromas.
>
> Champagnes produced under an oxidative regime are subjected to a very slow micro-oxygenation and do not necessarily have a noticeably oxidative aroma. Indeed, if produced with skill, they can be as clean as a whistle: think of the most glorious Krug. Truly oxidative champagnes do not have to be produced by an oxidative regime, and are often the result of insufficient sulphur at time of disgorgement (sulphur is used to prevent oxidation and keep unwanted bacteria at bay).
>
> There are extreme cases of deliberate oxidation, of course, but many so-called oxidative champagnes are reductive in style right up to the moment they are disgorged. Add no, or very little, sulphur and the oxidative aroma will develop prematurely. However it is produced, an oxidative champagne is defined by its oxidative aroma, which itself is defined by a preponderance of acetaldehyde, which the Australian Wine Research Institute defines as a fault.
>
> The notion of an oxidative champagne is, for me, as ludicrous as a reductive sherry…

Although Geoffroy and Lécaillon tread a very similar path in their quest to produce an iconic expression of the reductive style, there is one area where they disagree profoundly. Lécaillon believes there is not much to be gained from ageing on lees beyond a certain point (that is, resting the wine in bottle, in contact with its yeast sediment, once it has finished fermentation). Whereas Geoffroy prefers ageing on yeast for as long as possible, even to the point of making this a prerequisite for every vintage of Dom Pérignon. Furthermore, he believes that the longer a champagne remains in contact with its yeast sediment, the more resistant it becomes to oxidation, whereas Lécaillon believes that it becomes more sensitive to the oxidative shock of disgorgement.

I side more with Lécaillon on this particular issue, as does science in general, though I do not dismiss Geoffroy's opinion out of hand. The idea that the longer a champagne has in contact with yeast, the greater its resistance will

The light shining through this champagne bottle shows clearly the sediment of spent yeasts (or lees) remaining after fermentation. Left in contact with the wine, the lees will impart valuable aromas and flavours, but at what stage do the benefits start to dwindle?

be to oxidation might conflict with most experiences I have had, but not all. Pol Roger 1914 was disgorged in 1944 and should have been dead long ago – but it isn't, and that has always niggled me, so maybe there is something to Geoffroy's controversial stance. He has probably tasted more, and seen more analyses of, venerable vintages than anyone else in the world of champagne. Simply to have worked with Dominique Foulon (DP *chef de cave* from 1975 to 1990) on the extraordinary *assemblage* of Esprit du Siècle (one-third 1995 and 1985, plus two-thirds 1983, 1976, 1962, 1952, 1943, 1934, 1921, 1914 and 1911) would give him more intimate experience of these extraordinary vintages than most *chefs de caves* put together. The Esprit du Siècle and some of its constituent vintages rank among the very greatest champagnes I have ever tasted, so while I might still side more with Lécaillon, I have to respect where Geoffroy is coming from. Besides, it is healthy for champagne, and good for its consumers, that two great *chefs de caves* of such similar philosophies should have strongly held opposing views on a subject as basic as ageing.

If nothing else, it emphasizes the differences in their champagnes. Dom Pérignon P2 and P3 (formerly Oenothèque) are the epitome of the multilayered, aromatic and textural complexity achieved through extended yeast contact, their very raison d'être, while the long-awaited, first ever, late release of Cristal will illustrate the virtues of combining 10 years on yeast with 10 years of post-disgorgement ageing. As divulged by Patrick Schmitt, editor of *The Drinks Business*, Lécaillon believes that a decade on yeast is the ideal period. Schmitt quotes Lécaillon's confession that an extra three years' yeast contact for Cristal 'does not make a big difference'.

These are, however, extreme champagnes in every sense of the word – so, what about most others? If I changed the emphasis of my opening question to: 'What would be more beneficial for most champagnes: an extra year on lees or an extra year post-disgorgement ageing?,' would that focus the mind? Notwithstanding that there are windows of opportunity for disgorging that open and shut, and every champagne is different – thus no single answer is applicable to all situations – I would still have to say that there is much less to be gained from an extra year on yeast. If we take a vintage champagne that is released at between five and seven years of age, I would much rather it received an extra year's ageing under the ideal conditions of the producer's own cellars before shipping. This would have a minimal effect on the ageing, in terms of either aroma or flavour, but it would have an immense impact on the mousse, making it softer and silkier, and this would result in more finesse. The higher the quality of the champagne, the slower it ages, thus the longer I would stretch the post-disgorgement ageing. The champagnes sold by most quality-conscious producers would easily benefit from an additional two years, and for vintages released at eight years or older, as much as three years would impart an even more luxurious texture.

First published in *The World of Fine Wine*, issue 45, in 2014. Reproduced here with kind permission of the editor, Neil Beckett, and the author.

> Margaret Rand (2011)
> # THE UNDERCOVER MAVERICKS
> Champagne's most successful *chefs de caves* are those whose wines stay the same. Consistency and reliability are what's wanted from them, even though the vintage, the vineyards and the character of the grapes may change with every season. But Margaret Rand talks to the region's top blenders and discovers a steely rebelliousness and the intent not to alter, but to magnify…

'Wanted: winemaker. Must have the highest possible qualifications, a big personality and the ability to charm journalists in several languages. And must be prepared to spend the next 20 years producing exactly the same wine, year after year after year.'

No, this ad has not, to my knowledge, appeared in any trade publication, and nor have I been eavesdropping on the HR department of any large Champagne house. Because champagne is what we're talking about; and the contradiction between the level of talent required to be a corporate *chef de cave* and the apparent lack of scope for expressing any individuality. If you're that good, why would you want to do a job which offers, as the peak of its achievement, a wine that's precisely the same as it was last year, and the year before that?

And yet they do it; and go on doing it at the same houses, for decade after decade. *Chefs de caves* in Champagne do not flit about between jobs. Dominique Demarville is unusual in having moved from the top job at Mumm to that at Veuve Clicquot. At Mumm he presided over a change in the house style and a big improvement in quality, but he's switched to another house style and doesn't expect to switch again.[1] From now on, the big excitement in his life will be coaxing the dosage of Yellow Label down from 11 grams per litre sugar to about seven or eight, at the rate of half a gram or a gram per year. Comparisons with watching paint dry spring to mind.

1 The world has moved on since this was published in 2011; Dominique Demarville has left Veuve Clicquot and is now at Champagne Lallier; Richard Geoffroy (*see* page 250) is making sake rather than DP.

Yet they don't see it like that. It is the outcome that is the same, they point out, not the job: the job couldn't be more varied. Different weather, different wines, all to be moulded to the same – yes, I'm going to say it – the same straitjacket. Why would such good winemakers want to bow, over and over again, to the great god House Style?

Demarville corrects me: in fact, he says, he's the guardian of Yellow Label. 'The first challenge is to keep it at this level, and that's a big challenge.' The current success of Veuve Clicquot, he says, is down to Jacques Peters, the previous cellarmaster, who headhunted Demarville from Mumm three years ago. 'My objective is to build on that which was transmitted by Jacques, to build on that continuity.' Reducing the dosage is part of that; and it's something that lots of brands are doing at the moment. Moët & Chandon, Ayala, Ruinart: across Champagne, dosage is being or has been slowly, cautiously, drawn back, to reveal greater precision on the palate, derived from better winemaking and greater ripeness.

'Constraints are also opportunities,' says Benoît Gouez, *chef de cave* at Moët. 'It's reassuring to have the house style of non-vintage: you don't have to start from scratch.' And it's not about keeping the house style the same from decade to decade: 'It evolves. Some key elements have to be preserved, but there is an opportunity, even a mission, to keep them relevant.'

That, of course, is brand-speak: one could expect similar statements from car manufacturers, perfume houses, anything. The questions to ask are: how do you keep things the same? And how do you change them? And who decides?

The big decision...

The suspicion of any properly cynical hack, faced with the perfectly oiled machine that is the public face of a Champagne house, is that the marketing department decides and the *chef de cave* obeys. That, too, tends to be the view of small-scale houses and growers who vinify their own wines and answer to nobody. According to this view, *chefs de caves* are there for image, and the decisions are taken by the marketing department, while the real work is done by the *chef de cuvier* or *chef de production*.

With this in mind one thinks back to when quarter bottles of various brands were launched with straws through which to drink them; it was possible to get *chefs de caves* to say that this was a modern way of selling champagne, would appeal to a younger audience, and that one had to innovate, but they would have had to have their fingernails pulled out before they said it was a good expression of the wine. One inferred that it had not been their decision. One also wonders about some de luxe brands, and Dom Pérignon and Cristal are only two examples, where production has increased massively over the years. A series of winemaking decisions or a series of marketing decisions?

But *chefs de caves* can block ideas, too. It is said that someone at Laurent-Perrier proposed selling a cuvée designed to be drunk with ice that was (presumably) made from L-P. The winemaking department, it is also said, stamped on the idea and it died. But at Moët Gouez is thoroughly behind Ice Imperial, the cuvée it is trialling in various markets, and which is designed to be drunk with ice. More Pinot Noir, more dosage and extra emphasis on its thirst-quenching qualities are the key: the wine is designed to find its balance with ice and doesn't work without.

How much autonomy the *chef de cave* has within the organization is clearly important. At Dom Pérignon, which is part of Moët Hennessy Louis Vuitton (LVMH), Richard Geoffroy (who retired in 2019) was *sui generis*; he had the useful knack of appearing outspoken while always being resolutely on-message. 'There is no relationship between the *chef de cave* and house style,' says Geoffroy. 'The *chef de cave* is the style.' That's the case at Moët, too: Gouez says, 'My personal taste is in tune with the Moët style. There is no psychological drama' in maintaining it. This perfect synthesis is achieved in the cellar, very slowly: 'It takes seven to 10 years to understand the style of DP if you're working in the cellars, under me,' says Geoffroy. 'And it takes about 10 years to understand the vineyards.' He worked with more than one potential successor under his eye: 'It's a long process, and I didn't want pressure.' Over at VC, Demarville has 'train a successor to Philippe Thieffry' on his list of Things To Do Soon: Thieffry is his right-hand man, as he was to Jacques Peters, and would have had the *chef de cave* job at VC had he wanted it. Demarville clearly relies on him heavily. Demarville is a team player and says of the long, long tastings of each year's *vins clairs* (600–700 wines over two to three months) that 'the voice of the *chef de cave* is not higher than the voice of any other winemaker'; each *vin clair* tasting panel comprises at least eight of the 10 VC oenologists. But the decision on the blend of Yellow Label is taken by just Demarville and Thieffry. 'To be only one is too dangerous,' says Demarville. In the unlikely event of them disagreeing, Demarville has the last word – but it takes some coaxing to get him to say so.

At DP five people take part in the decision-making: Geoffroy was the one who listened, and then made up his mind. 'I don't believe in committee decisions,' he says. 'It doesn't have to be a unanimous decision. You go for it, and you are responsible. It always comes down to a personal choice.'

Always making, always moving…

Evolving the style of DP was also his decision, Geoffroy says. He calls it 'pushing the envelope of style', and that he had a free hand. 'I was always afraid of keeping things where they are. If you slow down, you are at risk. You have to be active. It's like an aeroplane: you need a minimum speed to remain in the air.

'No one ever mentions it, but at DP it is the *chef de cave* who is in charge. They are technical director in the sense of making it; the public face, they talk to journalists, and they are in charge of management and people… They have the last say on what the vineyard manager does. He's not producing grapes for the sake of it. The *chef de cave* puts a lot of pressure on the vineyard guys, and they accept it.' What Geoffroy tried to do is not so much change the blending – 'there is one principle, of blending to perfect tension' – as focus on 'the vibrancy of flavours, on super intensity without weight, on tactile dimensions'. It's about magnifying DP, not altering it. 'The clue to the whole thing is integration. You can't alter one element without altering the global picture: if you change one thing, you change the equilibrium. You have to be very cautious. Greater integration is the next step in Champagne, and it's happening as we speak. The vineyard people like it: it makes more sense of their work.' Can it only happen if you own your own vineyards? 'Yes.' Well, DP does own a lot of vineyards – or perhaps 'control' would be a better word, since DP is part of LVMH, and Geoffroy has had first pick of everything. But its own vineyards do not supply all its needs, and the Union Champagne at Avize is proud to name DP among its customers, along with others like VC, Taittinger, Laurent-Perrier, Mumm, Bollinger, Pol Roger and Billecart-Salmon.

Vintage opportunity

Gouez appears to have a lot of freedom at Moët, too. It was his decision, he says, to change the style of Moët vintage from 2000 so that it reflects the year much more, takes more risks. 'I've moved from making a Moët vintage to making a vintage by Moët,' he says. 'The house style used to be dominant. Now I say to the team, don't force it to be Moët; it will be Moët naturally, because of the grapes and the winemaking. Choose an emotional basis rather than a rational one, and make a wine with more personality, more uniqueness.

'It was my idea. It was a matter of feeling. A lot of people need to be reassured: occasional drinkers choose a brand they know. But others, more and more, are less interested in always tasting the same wine, and they want to discover something. They want individuality, and they want to be surprised. Non-vintage has to please everybody, but it might not convince those who want character and individuality. Vintage doesn't need to be mainstream.'

To change the nature of Moët vintage is a big decision, even if it is a relatively small volume compared to the non-vintage. But Gouez says he didn't need to persuade many people: just Richard Geoffroy and Frédéric Cumenal. If Geoffroy had said no it would have gone no further. But Geoffroy said yes.

Gouez would like to go further on the dosage, too. 'I have a vision I should go for a lower dosage, but I don't want to move away from the Moët style that customers like. It's a slow evolution. If I want to reduce the dosage I must improve something else: more ripeness and richness, more cellaring to develop texture, more creaminess… Life is about adaptation. I see champagne developing in two directions: lightness and elegance for knowledgeable consumers, but sweeter styles for new consumers. But if you change one thing you must change another thing. Moët with less dosage means other changes, and it's the same with sweet: you can't just increase the dosage. You must prepare the wine for that, through blending or ageing.'

The bold and brave…

Some brands, however, have changed even more radically. Ayala non-vintage, for example, used to be a deep yellow wine, round and rich; now it's paler, lighter and crisper. The changes date from the 2005 Bollinger takeover, when it became clear that there was no point in having Ayala as a 'Bollinger *bis*', as *chef de cave* Nicholas Klym puts it. Klym has been *chef de cave* for over 25 years, and so put the changes into effect; the man pushing them was Hervé Augustin, the PDG who arrived from Bollinger. And they were substantial. The amount of Pinot Noir in the blend was reduced, and it was pressed more gently; they adjusted the type of yeast, for more complexity; and they cut the dosage. 'The changes were agreed with the group when Ayala was bought,' says Augustin. The dosage is now down to eight grams per litre. The idea had been to bring it down even more, and show Ayala with six or four grams at Vinexpo one June; but the decision was made in May and Klym said June was too soon: the wine would need to rest for three or four months after disgorging. Okay, said Augustin: try zero dosage. Then it won't need to rest. It was well received at Vinexpo, and launched in October. Purity is what Augustin wants, and he has, he says, 'pushed Nicholas more and more in this direction'. Zero-dosage Ayala now sits alongside standard Ayala in the range, and Augustin would like Ayala to be 'the king of zero dosage'; but sommeliers and consumers, he says, are cautious.

Get it right, and no one will notice…

Changing styles is one thing, however. Most of a *chef de cave*'s work is aimed at keeping the non-vintage the same. 'When you join a house like Ruinart you know that it is a standard, a reference,' says Frédéric Panaïotis, *chef de cave* at Ruinart. 'You can't change a reference. Grapes are the most important thing, and they don't change radically from one year to another. If you want to adapt the viticulture to emphasize a point, you have a discussion with the *chef de culture*, you inform your boss, and it's done. But our vineyards are only 10 percent of our supply, and the rest comes from growers. You can experiment with harvest dates and yields, but this takes many years to show any effect.'

So the style of your base wines will be broadly in line with your house style, because of their origins and the way they've been made. But they will vary from year to year according to the generosity of the year, and the style of each *cépage*. Pinot Noir may be powerful and structured one year, light and delicate the next. But if your non-vintage is always about 40 percent Pinot Noir you can't diverge too much from that. In a difficult year you will have to fall back on your reserve wines. But not only must your blend taste the same as last year's, it must also age at the same rate: it can't be too tight for pleasure once it's on the shelf, and nor must it fall apart before it's been drunk. Says Demarville: 'It's a thankless task: it's why my shoulders are heavy.' Get it right and nobody will even notice, far less applaud you, but get it wrong and within months you'll be pilloried for ruining a great wine. Demarville names his first blend of VC non-vintage as one of the wines he's most proud of, but only real VC insiders would have known to congratulate him.

Adds Panaïotis: 'Vintage and non-vintage are not fun in the same way. Vintage is more fun, non-vintage is more demanding. If that's your fun, then non-vintage is more fun. But you have less latitude. Some years non-vintage can be more fun. If the year is easy, vintage is more fun. But in a more difficult year, non-vintage takes reflection, a lot of thought and a lot of tasting.' Dosage helps to smooth out the differences between harvests, so by reducing dosage *chefs de caves* are making their lives more complicated.[2]

But that, clearly, is what they like. Panaïotis agrees that yes, perhaps it does take a particular personality to be a *chef de cave* in a big Champagne house. It is, after all, a corporate role, and if you don't identify with the house style then you'd probably be better off doing something else. Clever corporations know where to allow latitude to mavericks, but clever mavericks know how to survive in corporations.

There's a telling question to ask *chefs de caves*: suppose you were told that for the rest of your life you could either make non-vintage or vintage, but not both. Which would you choose? Their answer, nearly always, is non-vintage. It's the challenge: if you're that good a winemaker, vintage is just too easy. But non-vintage, now: that's a winemaker's win.

[2] Today, the pressure of climate change is making life even more complicated. Many Champagne houses are rethinking the sanctity of perfect consistency in non-vintage, calling their blended wines 'multi-vintage' instead. This new term was first used by Krug but is now used by others, for example Roederer. Each release of such wines can be announced separately, its differences celebrated rather than disguised.

First published in 2011 in *The World of Fine Wine*, and reproduced here with kind permission of the editor, Neil Beckett, and the author.

Essi Avellan MW (2022)

CELLAR IN THE SEA

In July 2010 a dive-team discovered 168 bottles of Veuve Clicquot champagne in a wreck at the bottom of the Baltic Sea, near Finland's Åland Islands, believed to have sunk in the 1840s. There then started a momentous chain of events that culminated in an ambitious 40-year underwater ageing experiment, the first bottles from which were retrieved in 2017 and tasted against duplicates aged in Reims. Essi Avellan asks, are sub-oceanic vaults the storage space of the future?

'I will not forget the Saturday evening text message by which I received the news about the Baltic discovery,' recalls Dominique Demarville, then Clicquot's *chef de cave*. 'It changed a lot of things at Veuve Clicquot – and for me as well.' After the news broke, speculation over the age and producer of the shipwreck bottles increased as the weeks went by, until the Åland government held a press conference on November 17th, letting international journalists see and taste the treasure. Upon opening and recorking the 168 bottles, 79 bottles were rated 'drinkable', and three brands of champagne were identified: Juglar, Veuve Clicquot and Heidsieck & Co. The champagnes were believed to date from the late 1820s to 1840, which would make them some of the oldest in the world after Perrier-Jouët's 1825. 'This discovery stirred in me a great deal of emotion,' Demarville recollected, 'because these bottles were made by Madame Clicquot herself. They date from 1839, when she was still alive and active in the business.'

Going, going, gone

The specimens of liquid history from Madame Clicquot's era spurred two high-profile auctions in 2011 and 2012, with bottles reaching sky-high prices of between €12,000 and €30,000, the interest being boosted by the tasting notes from champagne expert Richard Juhlin and Veuve Clicquot oenologist François Hautekeur, responsible for tasting and recorking. But as time went on and the wine reached the palates of international champagne experts, the verdicts became far more severe. Tom Stevenson, who tasted a bottle at Clicquot in May 2012, did not pull any punches when he wrote in *The World of Fine Wine* magazine about the 'stench of horse shit' in the wine. Demarville, who has tasted four bottles from the shipwreck, characterized them: 'Initially the wine has a strong nose of reduction, with a lot of egg and wild animaly aromas. After oxidation, it becomes more approachable, with candied fruits, leather, dried flowers and fresh mushrooms. The most interesting dimension is the palate, where sweetness and freshness are well balanced, even if the sugar level is 149g/l.'

Having personally tasted the shipwrecked Clicquot twice – first at the initial 2010 press conference and again in 2015 at the French collector François Audouze's Veuve Clicquot tasting – I must admit that, unfortunately, the horse manure has now stolen the show. What was originally an 84-point wine for me, but even then 'overwhelmingly pungent and smoky', was now unbearably pungent – animally (yes, manure) and rubbery. The disappointment was great, especially since that second bottle (numbered A53) had received the highest score (93 from Juhlin) of all those sold at the 2012 auction. Perhaps it is therefore welcome news that the bottles have now been declared cultural artefacts and further sales banned.

But for Dominique Demarville, the sensory pleasure of these bottles is second in importance to the information they can give. The wine was sent for archaeochemical analysis, of which a detailed report by Jeandet *et al* was published in *Proceedings of the National Academy of Sciences* in 2015.

Cellar in the sea

The shipwreck bottles inspired Veuve Clicquot to create the Cellar in the Sea programme with its Åland Vault, a shark cage customized to cellar champagne bottles underwater. For Demarville, the program had two objectives: 'First, to know more about the ageing of our wines after disgorgement by comparing two different ageing atmospheres – one with oxygen, one without. There is also the pressure effect to take into account: five atmospheres in the sea compared to one in the cellars. Second, with the help of the journalists participating in the experiment, it will provide a good opportunity to communicate about champagne's ageing to champagne lovers.'

On June 18th 2014, Veuve Clicquot submerged 300 bottles and 50 magnums of four different champagnes, with duplicates kept in its Reims cellars

Ready to face the world again: after 170 years on the seabed, a diver carefully stores precious bottles of the Åland champagne so that it can be lifted 55 metres (180 feet) to the surface.

for comparison. The perfect setting was found at Silverskär on the northern side of the Åland islands archipelago, not too far from the original shipwreck. I was regretfully unable to witness the submergence of the bottles in person in 2014 but made sure that my calendar was clear for the first taste of the wines three years later. After all, the experiment is taking place in the waters of my native Finland, and we are proud to be hosting this intriguing ageing experiment over the next decades.

In 2017, a small group of Clicquot team members and international journalists embarked to Åland's Silverskär on a perfect midsummer morning from Stockholm. After a short flight and bus and boat rides, we reached our goal, the secluded resort of three islands, Silverskär, Sviskär and Klobben. On our way to Klobben, we were driven past a skerry, a Clicquot-flagged Champagne island, whose 'hermit' supposedly guards the champagnes. But the treasure cage itself is a little further on, marked by a flag for the occasion of our visit. The discoverer of the 1840s shipwreck, Christian Ekström, had already performed his duty by diving to retrieve sample bottles for us from the vault resting at a depth of 43 metres (141 feet).

When the bottles made their entry to the Klobben island's tasting room, the ambience was charged with expectation. A glance at Dominique Demarville sniffing the first samples revealed a lot. The Cellar in the Sea has been a big investment for Veuve Clicquot, but the relaxed cellarmaster was seemingly pleased with what his senses were telling him.

I eagerly delved into the tasting, and the first pair of wines revealed notable differences. The Yellow Label Baltic bottle came across as distinctly more youthful, with a feeling of fruit-forwardness in the absence of any oxidative tones. The mousse was finer and better integrated. The differences became even more accentuated in the magnum version of Yellow Label, with the Reims bottle shining bright but the Baltic bottle showing tight and reserved, almost 'undrinkably' youthful. The differences were at least as great between the 2004 vintage rosés, the Reims bottle showing plenty of aromatic evolution and oxidation, whereas the tannins came across as stronger in the Baltic wine. The last sample pair, the Demi-secs, showed slightly less marked differences, since the oxidative character was not so obvious in the Reims bottle. Still superior, the Baltic bottle showcased a more harmonious character and greater finesse. In conclusion, at this point, the underwater bottles were consistently more youthful, with notably fewer oxidative characters, generally more elegant and more vivacious. The Baltic Yellow Label magnum seemed so youthful that it felt as though it had enjoyed 'reverse ageing'!

The ideal cellar?

This result was not surprising; the seabed is an environment where, due to the greater pressure and lower temperature, time almost comes to a halt for certain processes. Where the Clicquot vault is, at a depth of 43 metres (141 feet), the temperature remains constantly cold at around 4°C (39°F) with a variation of no more than 1.5°C (2.7°F). The static pressure is close to the pressure inside the bottle, at 5.3 atmospheres, the ambient light level and salinity are low, and the tidal effect is minimal. Thus, the Baltic Sea may just be the ideal place to store wine, even if commercial realities might render it uneconomic on a large scale. But for how long might such advantages be clear? Time will tell. And the experiment still has over 30 years to run. 'The differences were in line with what we were expecting, but I am surprised by how great they were after only three years. This tasting has convinced us to go on with the experiment,' concluded Demarville.

Dominique Demarville has since then moved on from Veuve Clicquot, but the new *chef de cave*, Didier Mariotti, is eagerly continuing the experiment. 'This is the beauty of our job, we are still learning and discovering every day. We will probably organize a new tasting in the next couple of years to follow up on the experiment,' Mariotti promises.

The abyss

Veuve Clicquot is not the only house intrigued by underwater ageing, as the likes of Louis Roederer and Drappier have done their own experiments. But the first Champagne house to commercialize the concept and to bring the special bottles within reach of the consumer is Leclerc Briant.

Having long been a pioneer of biodynamic cultivation in Champagne, a new era for Leclerc Briant commenced in 2012. Following Pascal Leclerc's untimely death, the American couple, Mark Nunelly and Denise Dupré, acquired the house from his descendants. Experienced champagne executive Frédéric Zeimett was put in charge of creating a 'bio-chic' house, and the already existing cooperation with Champagne's leading biodynamics consultant, Hervé Jestin, was immediately accelerated. Under Jestin's guidance the house started to apply the principles of bioenergetics (the study of flow of energy through living systems) in the winemaking. Among many insightful experiments, Jestin wanted to test how the dynamic energy of the sea could contribute to the ageing of champagne, and an underwater ageing programme was initiated in 2012.

The resulting wine, enticingly named Abyss, enjoys 12 months of post-disgorgement ageing at 60 metres (200 feet) in the rough waters near Ile d'Ouessant in Brittany, France. Every summer, several thousand bottles are submerged and the previous year's batch retrieved. The mythical maritime qualities of Abyss speak strongly to the house's fans and the project is growing, with extension of the Abyss product family in sight.

Chalky depths

The Roman chalk pits of Reims have long proven to provide ideal conditions for the ageing of champagne. But what if one could combine chalk and the benefits of great depths? Cyril Brun worked at Veuve Clicquot when the Baltic

Sea discovery was made and became greatly involved with the Cellar in the Sea project. Having subsequently exchanged Veuve Clicquot for Charles Heidsieck, taking on the cellarmaster's big boots, he decided to initiate another ageing experiment in Finland. In 2018, the Tytyri chalk mine in Lohja was the scene. Every year, 30 bottles of the house's Brut Réserve are taken to the Charles Heidsieck vault there and located at a depth of 170 metres, where the ambient temperature all year round is around 4.5°C (40°F) and humidity 98%.

The first comparative tasting was held at Cyril's instigation in 2019 when the bottles had spent one year in the chalky depths. I found the difference to be notable, even surprisingly clear. The bottles from Tytyri came across more youthful, even tight, and with distinct chalky whiffs. 'We are fully convinced that the significant temperature difference does contribute to a longer ageing: in the Tytyri mine, thanks to the depth, humidity and surrounding temperature, the wines seem to age much slower than the same batch in regular ageing conditions at ground level,' Cyril Brun confirms.

But he considers that most of the effect is quickly achieved with more marginal gains yet to become apparent in the years to come. 'My guess is that the peak will be reached in the next couple of years when we will enter a plateau of marginal ageing improvements. But let's save some samples for the distant future, when we will all be old and wise…'

CHAMPAGNE ON THE MOVE...

8

Since its earliest days, champagne has been required to travel. Indeed, it was appreciated more abroad than at home until the late 19th century. But this wine can take the perils of transit in its stride and wherever it arrives, it is greeted with joy.

CHAMPAGNE'S BENEFICIAL PILGRIMAGE
Henry Vizetelly (1882)

BETTER THAN ARMY TEA
Peter Carrington (1989)

CHAMPAGNE AT 30,000 FEET
Hugh Johnson (2022)
Oz Clarke (2022)

JOURNEY INTO SPACE
Giles Fallowfield (2022)

Henry Vizetelly (1882)

CHAMPAGNE'S BENEFICIAL PILGRIMAGE

The journalist and publisher Henry Vizetelly (1820–94) was passionate about champagne and wrote a 300-page history of the wine for which he travelled, interviewed, scribbled and sipped extensively. This gold-embossed, meticulously illustrated volume was published in 1882 and became the champagne bible of the late 19th century. Reading it now, much of the language is outdated – its vantage-points jar with our own – but Vizetelly's portrayal of champagne's Grand Tour reveals an enthusiastic welcome that hasn't dimmed in 140 years…

Champagne sets out on its beneficial pilgrimage to promote the spread of mirth and lightheartedness, to drive away dull care and foment good fellowship, to comfort the sick and cheer the sound. Wherever civilization penetrates, champagne sooner or later is sure to follow; and if Queen Victoria's morning drum beats round the world, its beat is certain to be echoed before the day is over by the popping of champagne-corks.

Now-a-days, the exhilarating wine graces not merely princely but middle-class dinner-tables, and is the needful adjunct at every *petit souper* in all the gayer capitals of the world. It gives a flush to beauty at garden parties and picnics, sustains the energies of the votaries of Terpsichore until the hour of dawn, and imparts to many a young gallant the necessary courage to declare his passion. It enlivens the dullest of réunions, brings smiles to the lips of the sternest cynics, softens the most irascible tempers, and loosens the most taciturn tongues.

The grim Berliner and the gay Viennese both acknowledge its enlivening influence. It sparkles in crystal goblets in the great capitals of the North, and the Moslem wipes its creamy foam from his beard beneath the very shadow of the mosque of St Sophia; for the Prophet has only forbidden the use of wine, and of a surety – Allah be praised! – this stangely-sparkling delicious liquor, which gives to the true believer a foretaste of the joys of Paradise, cannot be wine.

At the diamond-fields of South Africa and the diggings of Australia the brawny miner who has hit upon a big bit of crystallized carbon, or a nugget of virgin ore, strolls to the 'saloon' and shouts for champagne. The mild Hindoo imbibes it quietly, but approvingly, and his partiality for it has already enriched the Anglo-Bengalee vocabulary and London slang with the word 'simkin'. It is transported on camel-backs across the deserts of Central Asia, and in frail canoes up the mighty Amazon. The two-sworded Daimio calls for it in the tea-gardens of Yokohama, and the New Yorker, when not rinsing his stomach by libations of iced-water, imbibes it freely at Delmonico's.

Wherever civilized man has set his foot – at the base of the Pyramids and at the summit of the Cordilleras, in the mangrove swamps of Ashantee and the gulches of the Great Lone Land, in the wilds of Amoor and on the desert isles of the Pacific – he has left traces of his presence in the shape of the empty.

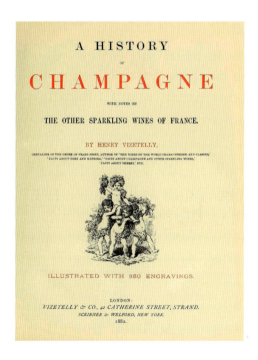

Extract from *A History of Champagne with notes on the other sparkling wines of France* by Henry Vizetelly, Vizetelly & Co (London) and Scribner & Welford (New York) 1882.

Peter Carrington (1989)
BETTER THAN ARMY TEA

World War II veteran, hereditary baronet and long-serving politician, Peter Carrington recalls the benefits (and otherwise) of transporting 20 cases of champagne in a Sherman tank…

In war time, one of the more convenient aspects of serving in a tank battalion rather than an infantry battalion is the ability to carry more of your personal possessions with you. There is a limit to what can be carried on one's back, and uncertainty as to if and when and how the wheeled transport will catch up with you. This was very forcibly brought home to me in 1944 when I used to see my colleagues in the infantry, cold, wet and tired, digging a hole for themselves in which to spend the night while we dug a shallow trench, ran the tank over it and spent a warm, comfortable and safe night surrounded, if not by the creature comforts to which we have all become accustomed in later years, at any rate by much less discomfort than my foot-slogging friends. In September 1944 I discovered another and yet more important advantage.

The Guards Armoured Division entered Brussels on September 3rd to much rejoicing by the population, a welcome which was certainly not matched anywhere else we went. The people of Brussels stormed our tanks, 50 or 60 standing or sitting on each vehicle. Flags, champagne, the lot – it was a riot. Eventually we moved on to spend the night outside the gates of the Royal Palace at Laeken. Providentially (and genuinely) on that very night my tank broke down and, while my squadron moved on, for the next 48 hours I remained behind in Brussels. The following day, accompanied by a brother officer, I was told by a friendly and far-seeing Belgian that not far away, in a railway goods yard just outside Brussels, was a large warehouse used to store the wine of the entire German army on the Western Front. On arrival, we discovered a shed of vast proportions filled to the roof with brandy, champagne, claret and burgundy. Not wishing to appear too selfish we felt it right to inform not only our battalion but also divisional headquarters of this agreeable discovery.

Within the space of a few hours all unwarlike stores had been unloaded from every three-ton lorry and a queue of trucks were loading champagne and brandy for the various regiments and battalions of the division. For myself I decided that probably the claret and the burgundy would not travel very well. I therefore appropriated 20 cases of champagne and loading them with considerable difficulty into my jeep, then set off back to my tank. Those of you who are familiar with a Sherman tank, and I hope for your sake that that is a very small number, will know that the five large Chrysler engines which powered it were to be found under the flat space at the back. My champagne was firmly strapped down and off we went back to the war, opening a bottle now and again as we lay in comfort and security in our shallow trench under the tank of an evening, entertaining occasionally a passing infantryman who eyed my cellar with understandable envy. It must be admitted that it was not very good champagne. It must equally be acknowledged that having been shaken up all day (a Sherman is no limousine) and lying on the equivalent of a red hot Aga did not do too much to improve it. But we were not so sophisticated in those days and it was better than army tea.

Lord Carrington (*centre*) was awarded the Military Cross for his bravery as a tank commander in 1944.

The 20 cases did not last all that long. I drank the last bottle with Chester Wilmot (the war correspondent) at Nijmegen a month or so later. He didn't seem to me to appreciate either the quality of what he was offered or the fact that it was my last bottle*. What happened to the rest of that wine in the goods yard in Brussels? It was taken over by the NAAFI and sold back to us at what in 1944 seemed to us the vast sum of a pound a bottle…

* Note from the editor, Cyril Ray: 'I was waiting at Nijmegen with the US 82nd Airbourne Division for Captain Lord Carrington to arrive with the Guards Armoured. My old colleague Chester might have had the decency to leave me that bottle…'

First published as 'Beaded Bubbles at the Cannon's Mouth' in *Cyril Ray's Compleat Imbiber No 14*, Beaumont Books (London) 1989. Reproduced here with kind permission of Lord Carrington DL.

Hugh Johnson (2022)

Oz Clarke (2022)

CHAMPAGNE AT 30,000 FEET

Being served a glass of champagne on a boat or train is as unusual, yet delightful, a prospect today as it would have in Henry Vizetelly's time. Encountering a glass of bubbly on a trans-Atlantic flight, while perhaps more likely now, is an altogether more worrying matter. Will it taste as it should? Will the pressure and/or the humidity in the cabin damage its flavour? Two well-informed (and much-loved) commentators on wine air their views…

Hugh Johnson

There is sometimes discussion about champagne on planes up at 30,000 feet (10,000 metres for those metrically inclined). Can it be unaffected by the lower cabin pressure – half that at ground level? Learned voices say it changes character. My evidence says that it can taste its most delicious with the prospect of a long flight ahead. But then while I was a British Airways consultant I was not cooped up at the back of the plane. First Class passengers, of course, had to be given labels they recognized as very expensive, and travellers on Concorde used to make specific demands ('I'm terribly sorry, Sir, but I'll make sure it's on board this evening'). Conversely, producers of very expensive champagne want to be seen by First Class passengers. British Airways' orders for Krug and Dom Pérignon were alarming, and the hospitality of aspiring *marques* (not to me, I hasten to say) correspondingly warm. Passengers behave in peculiar ways in the air, and champagne is no discouragement. The Steward's Tale, I often think, would make a rip-roaring addendum to *The Canterbury Tales*.

Excerpt from *The Life and Wines of Hugh Johnson* published by Académie du Vin Library (London) 2022.

Oz Clarke

Sorry. Have I got the question wrong here? How does flying at 30,000 feet affect the taste of champagne? Are you kidding? Champagne at 30,000 feet tastes absolutely fantastic!

There are two tests that evaluate how champagne tastes at 30,000 feet. And I've taken both of them.

One involves you glumly trying to record your every response to every mouthful of wine you take as your plane ascends to cruising height. Bleak-eyed helpers in white coats keep offering you tiny samples and give you sheets of paper on which to record your thoughts. I've done this from London to New York. I've done this from New York to Los Angeles and back again. Frankly, I was too clattered at the end to know what on earth I thought. But I can tell you this. I didn't have any fun.

And there's the other way to evaluate how champagne tastes at 30,000 feet. Turn left when you enter the plane. And walk as far as you can towards the captain's cockpit. I absolutely guarantee the champagne is going to taste amazing. And there's going to be lots of it. As I sink back into my leather seat half the size of my house, and barely have to cock an eyebrow for my crystal glass to be re-filled with foaming nectar, a smile of utter contentment plays across my lips.

Dom P or Dom R... Veuve this or Comtes de that... Rare? Ultra Rare? Exquisite? They all taste wonderful. Are the bubbles different at 30,000 feet? Yes. Better! Is the flavour different at 30,000 feet? Yes. Better! Are you happier with a glass of bubbles in your hand at 30,000 feet? Yes. And isn't that basically the whole point of champagne?

Giles Fallowfield (2022)

JOURNEY INTO SPACE

If champagne can survive air travel, why not space? Mumm has developed a gravity-defying champagne bottle adapted for just this purpose, to equip the more intrepid of us for celebrations through the stratosphere… Whatever next? asks Giles Fallowfield.

For luxury space tourism of the not-too-distant future, sipping a glass of champagne while gazing down on our planet, sounds like the ultimate travel experience. But how do you pop the cork, given the fizz inside is under six atmospheres of pressure (similar to the tyre pressure of a double-decker bus) without the precious liquid within erupting?

Impractical or not, it was perhaps inevitable that someone in Champagne would start looking for a solution. After all, the Champenois pride themselves on their innovative and forward-looking approach to building business in new markets. And that's just what space is, as the likes of Virgin Galactic and SpaceX have already shown. What's more, it's a new market where only the seriously wealthy, Champagne's prime customers, are likely to be involved.

Step forward the Reims-based house of G H Mumm, working hand in hand with French space design agency Spade. After three years of experimentation with thousands of Euros invested, they came up with Grand Cordon Stellar. This specially engineered bottle, that retails for around €25,000, contains a small internal piston controlled by a hand valve which, when you trigger it, sends out the champagne in small, controlled bursts. These are shaped into mini clouds of floating, foaming bubbly by a metal ring attached to the rim of the bottle. Spheres of fizz you attempt to capture in tiny, specially designed, tapered stem glasses, bringing the wine to your lips before it floats off.

Mumm's newest bottle prototype to date has a kind of shield around the glass to further resist the pressure in space. This is being trialled on an aircraft that climbs high in the sky, then makes a vertical dive downwards. Head winemaker, Laurent Fresnet, has experienced this plummet and reports that the 30 seconds of zero gravity this gives, while terrifying, is enough to open the bottle and see that it works.

Champagne not only behaves differently in space, it tastes different too. Champagne is full of dissolved bubbles of carbon dioxide which when poured into glasses in our earthly atmosphere expand, float upwards and burst as they hit the surface of the liquid. But as bubbles expert based at Reims University, Gérard Liger-Belair, a chemical physicist, explains: 'At zero gravity, the bubbles don't rise in the glass in the same way that they do on earth; instead, they burst in your mouth on your tongue. This makes the champagne softer, more creamy,' he says, 'and also more intense.'

Apart from bottles designed for space tourists, what else does the future hold for the Champagne region and the world's most famous sparkling wine? The biggest changes in the next couple of decades are likely to come from adapting to climate change. New grape varieties that will help preserve the freshness – a key distinguishing feature in champagne's unique taste profile – are already being tested and likely to be used in future blends. Robots, not men and women, will take on the traditional back-breaking tasks of pruning the vines and picking the grapes. And the heavy, glass bottle will surely be replaced by something lighter, more eco-friendly, whether the fizz is being served on earth or in space…

Retired sprinter Usain Bolt and French interior designer Octave de Gaulle, who designed a bottle of Mumm Grand Cordon Stellar champagne to enjoy in zero-gravity conditions, during a flight in a specially modified Airbus Zero-G plane above Reims, France, September 12th 2018.

ON CHAMPAGNE, THE AUTHORS & EXPERTS

ESSI AVELLAN MW is Finland's first Master of Wine and an esteemed judge, journalist, author and educator specializing in champagne. According to Tom Stevenson (its most powerful voice) she '... knows champagne like the back of her hand'. Essi returns to the region again and again, drawn in by the 'invigorating energy' of its wines.

PETER CARRINGTON's housemaster said of him, on leaving school: 'For a really stupid boy, there are three possible professions: farming, soldiering and stockbroking.' Lord Carrington went on to become a junior minister under Winston Churchill and thereafter defence secretary, foreign secretary and secretary general of NATO. He served with the Grenadier Guards during World War II (receiving the military cross in 1945) and found his thirst for champagne rewarded during its closing stages…

OZ CLARKE OBE has championed fizz ever since he was an impoverished young actor with the Royal Shakespeare Company discovering (quite by accident) the joys of Schramsberg sparkling wine in California. But it's dawned on him since then that behind the razzmatazz, champagne can be a really serious wine, made from really serious grapes… 'We should be prepared to treat champagne like any other fine wine. Serious wine with bubbles? Yes.'

GILES FALLOWFIELD There's not much Giles doesn't know about champagne. Having visited the region regularly for the last 30 years, he is the 'go-to' journalist when it comes to revealing new wines, new vintages and new technology there. Here, he investigates champagne in space…

JOE FATTORINI If you've enjoyed wine anywhere between Wick and Whitstable in the UK, Joe has probably been involved – selling, serving, teaching and broadcasting, the last 20 years have seen him getting in touch with almost every bottle reaching these shores. He has an opinion on all of them. Here, he shares his views on champagne's effectiveness as a social barometer.

NATASHA HUGHES MW, wine consultant, judge and writer, became a Master of Wine in 2014. She has long been involved in the food and wine scene, initially as a professional cook, and offers insights and sound counsel to those in need of advice on menus, wine lists and the interaction between the two. Natasha's great skill is food and wine pairing; she can always be relied upon to team her favourite champagnes, Australian or California wines with pinpoint gastronomic accuracy.

ANDREW JEFFORD discovered the pleasures of wine in his early teens, learning about it by making it – from carrots, apples, nettles and elderflowers. The finished wine (swallowed with a grimace) contributed to mealtime merriment and led him, eventually, to find work as a wine writer, educator, taster, tour guide and occasional radio presenter. Andrew has written for many British newspapers and magazines; his latest book, *Drinking with the Valkyries*, was published by Académie du Vin Library in summer 2022.

HUGH JOHNSON OBE needs very little introduction, except to say that he is the world's best-selling wine writer. His easy, eloquent prose is as distinctive as it is spellbinding – there is truly no other writer like him for gently enticing a reader to his subject – and we are lucky to have his words grace these pages.

DR WILLIAM KELLEY has reviewed the wines of champagne for *Decanter* magazine and *The Wine Advocate*. As well as writing about wine, he produces some of his own, in Clarksburg, California, and Chambolle-Musigny, Burgundy. Making wine informs the way he writes about it.

DON & PETIE KLADSTRUP are American journalists settled in France. Their writings, steeped in the language and history of wine, here vividly portray the conflict between wartime winemakers and the 'Weinführers' during the WW2 occupation.

ANNE KREBIEHL MW German-born and London-based, Anne is a wine judge, author and editor with a passion for high-acid wines – her work often focuses on Pinot Noir, Riesling and traditional-method sparkling wines.

ADAM LECHMERE is a wine journalist and consultant editor for *Club Oenologique*, which he launched in 2018. He was launch editor for *Decanter.com* in 2000, editing the site for 11 years. He has written for *The World of Fine Wine*, *Meininger's*, *The Guardian, The Observer* and many others. Before joining the wine world he worked for the BBC, and as a music and film journalist.

PETER LIEM is an American wine writer living in Epernay. His book *Champagne* was the recipient of a James Beard award and an André Simon book award, and he is the co-creator of *La Fête du Champagne*, one of the world's largest champagne events. He also serves as the Regional Chair for champagne at the Decanter World Wine Awards, and as an instructor for the Wine Scholar Guild.

GERARD LIGER-BELAIR is a professor of physics at the University of Reims; he is the only researcher in the world to specialize in the mechanics of the champagne bubble – the way it forms, the way it moves, and the way it distributes flavour. His detailed photography and easy explanations reveal how this wine brings magic to our glass.

JANE MacQUITTY MBE has been writing about wine for *The Times* since 1982 and is revered for her honesty and forthright opinions. Jane has reviewed everything from the humblest cava to the loftiest *grande marque* magnums in her pursuit of the best, and leapt at the chance to write for this book as fizz is her desert island wine..

ELIN McCOY is an award-winning journalist and wine author. A skilled communicator, she also serves as a wine judge for American and international competitions, and appears on radio and at festivals and industry events.

JAY McINERNEY found fame as a novelist in 1984 with the novel *Bright Lights, Big City*; his subsequent literary success is testament to the fact that (he says) writing mostly comes easily. For Jay, his books about wine are 'a nice way of legitimizing a somewhat obsessive hobby'. And champagne? 'The most versatile food wine in the world… It's foolish to save it for special occasions!'

VICTORIA MOORE is a best-selling author and wine columnist for *The Daily Telegraph*. Her journalism has taken her from Chile's Atacama Desert to the labyrinthine chalk cellars of Champagne, from which she reports on the changing fortunes of its rosé wines for these pages. Victoria's special interest is flavour and smell; here, she finds particular joy in the special spiciness of champagne's Meunier grape.

FIONA MORRISON MW is an acclaimed writer, author, merchant and négociant with a 30-year wine career spanning both sides of the Atlantic. She is managing director of Thienpont Wine and with her husband, Jacques Thienpont, runs their three Bordeaux estates, Le Pin in Pomerol, L'If in St-Emilion and L'Hêtre in Castillon. Fiona's long love affair with champagne began in 1982 when she visited the region as a student and was invited to lunch by Christian Pol Roger and Winston Churchill (grandson of Winston Churchill, the first!).

MARGARET RAND is an award-winning author, wine writer and journalist. Her whip-smart interviewing skills ensure that her copy always delivers the most informative quotes and insightful character portrayals. Margaret is general editor of *Hugh Johnson's Pocket Wine Book*.

STEPHEN SKELTON MW is a viticultural consultant and champion of English wines; he has been involved with establishing many of the vineyards now in direct competition with the chalky slopes of Champagne in producing fine sparkling wine. Stephen has great admiration for fizz from either side of the English Channel, but is very keen to set the story straight regarding who first invented it…

TYSON STELZER's passion for champagne knows no boundaries. As an Australian, the 16,000-kilometre hop from home to Epernay has been no hindrance in the production of six editions of his bi-annual 500-page *Champagne Guide* – from which he entertains with wit and wisdom on these pages. Tyson is a wine communicator par excellence: his writing, judging, keynote speaking and television hosting have rightly won him many awards.

TOM STEVENSON is regarded as the world's leading authority on sparkling wine; he has judged at wine competitions in Australia, France, Germany, Greece, Italy, South Africa and the USA; in 2014, he launched his own, the Champagne & Sparkling Wine World Championships. No one writes so compellingly, so provocatively or so authoritatively on champagne. Here, we have excerpts selected from his first book (published 1986) to his latest research for *The World of Fine Wine*.

SERENA SUTCLIFFE MW is a highly respected writer and commentator whose passion for champagne – her 'constant companion and permanent delight' – sees her words almost fizz from the page. Serena headed up the international wine department at Sotheby's for 24 years, and is now its honorary chairman. She was the second woman to pass the Master of Wine examination, and was awarded the *Légion d'Honneur* in 2006.

TIM TRIPTREE MW is international director of Christie's Wine & Spirits department; his role involves curating, planning and executing its international fine wine and spirits sales and auctions, as well as sourcing business in London, Geneva, Hong Kong, Shanghai and Los Angeles. Unsurprisingly, it is champagne – particularly in its finest prestige cuvées and vintages – that receives some of his highest bids…

HENRY VIZETELLY (1820–94) was a London printer's son, whose tumultuous career spanned apprenticeship as a wood-engraver, a stint as Paris correspondent for the *Illustrated London News* and a three-month spell in prison for his translation of Zola's *La Terre* (banned for its 'obscenity'). In 1886 he founded the publishing house Vizetelly & Co. Wine, particularly that of Champagne, was a great fascination for him, and he wrote about it in captivating detail.

ROBERT WALTERS is an Australian wine merchant, vineyard owner and author, whose writing on champagne is both passionate and provocative. He is a regular visitor to the region and is obsessive in his search to single out its finest growers. His book on the subject, *Bursting Bubbles* (2017), lifts the lid on the many champagne myths.

EVELYN WAUGH was widely acknowledged to be England's leading satirical novelist of the 1930s; his brilliant and prolific writing career leading him to travel widely and pen news of his journeys from as far afield as Mexico, Abyssinia, British Guiana and Brazil. Hugh Johnson (in his magazine *Wine & Food*) persuaded him to report back from an eventful foray to Champagne in 1964…

KELLI WHITE is director of education for Napa Valley's Wine Centre at Meadowood. Prior to this, she worked as a sommelier in New York City and in Napa. She published *Napa Valley, Then & Now* in 2015 and has won two Roederer Awards for her articles. She is a celebrated speaker and educator, and has contributed to several books, including the eighth edition of *The World Atlas of Wine* (2019) and the forthcoming *Oxford Companion to Wine*.

INDEX

Page numbers in *italic* refer to the illustrations

Acheson, Lauren 97–8, *98*
ageing 20, 232–3, 244–7, *246*
  underwater ageing 255–60, *257*
Agrapart, Pascal 71, 168, 170, 185, 231, 232, 233
air travel 266–7
Åland Islands 255, 256–8
alcohol levels 15, 62, 100, 222
Alexander II, Tsar 50–1, 61
Allen, Lily 165
Allison, Rachel 96
Ambonnay 16, 170, 174, 186
amphorae, clay 230
Apollonis 189
Appellation d'Origine Contrôlée (AOC) 141, 173
Arbane grape 15, 66, 71, 210
Archer, Jeffrey 91–2
Argonne forest 229–30
assemblage see blending
Association des Champagnes Biologiques 200
Association Viticole Champenoise 34
Aube 16, 69, 141, 193–8
Aubrey, L Fils 71
Audouze, François 256
Augustin, Hervé 252–3
autolysis 19, 61, 79, 90
Avellan, Essi 66–71, 253–60, 270
Avenay 108
Avize 16, 43, 114, 170, 174, 181, 185, 232
Aÿ 16, 27–9, 48, 107, 108–9, 112, 126, 188, 227
Ayala 37, 61–2, 249, 252–3

Baddiel, David 165
Baltic Sea 255–9
Bar-sur-Aube 192
Bar-sur-Seine 192
Baron, Christophe 189
Barrat-Masson 191
barrels 19, 44, 103–4, 226–33
Beckwith, David 96
Bedel, Françoise 189
Bedford, Earl of 112
Belenet, Charles-Armand de 29

Belle Epoque 134–8, *135*
Bénard, Laurent 205
Bénard Pitois 205
Bérêche 168, 187, 241–2
Bergères-les-Vertus 185
Bernhardt, Sarah 137
Berry, Duchesse de 116
Bettane, Michel 168, 174
Billecart-Salmon 56, 59, 71, 74, 204, 209, 226
Billy, Christian de 47, 146
Billy, Hubert de 47–8
biodiversity 29, 42
biodynamism 15, 17, 178, 204–6
Bisseuil 188
Bizot, Christian 60
blancs de blancs 16, 66–8, 89, 92, 158
blancs de noirs 16, 70–1, 88, 89–90
Blankpain, George 103–4
blending 19
  in 19th century 172–3
  consistency 14–15
  Dom Pérignon and 110
  Moët & Chandon 126–7
  reserve wines 234–43
Bligny, Château de 71
Boizel, Evelyne 34, *35*
Bollinger 46, 48–9, 65, 164
  barrels 230–1, 232, 233
  Charter of Quality 60
  grapes 68, 210
  rosé champagne 57
  sustainability 204
  Vieilles Vignes Françaises 27–9, 29, 49, 53, 71, 188
  vintage champagne 74, 76
Bollinger, Jacques 32–3, 49
Bollinger, Joseph 49
Bollinger, Lily 28, *31*, 32–3, 49, 60
Bollinger, Maurice 48, 49
Bolt, Usain *269*
Bomers, Heinz 144, 146
Bonnet, Alexandre 71
botrytis 202, 206
bottles
  bottling 19
  Cristal 50–1, *51*
  exploding 101, 114, 115, 128
  history 103, 113, 115
  magnums 84–7, *85*, *87*
  Moët & Chandon 128
  opening 94–8, 97, 118, *119*
  remuage 19–20, 115–16, 130, 137

  sabering 97–8, 97
  sizes *87*
  for space travel 268–9
  verre Anglais 102
  washing 125
Bouchard, Cédric 71, 168, 175–7, *175*
Boulard, Francis 187
Bourgeois-Diaz 189
Bouzy 16, 43, 126, 186, 227
Bray, Sarah 95
British Airways 266
Brochet, Emmanuel 187
Brulart family 108, 109
Brun, Cyril 207, 208, 210–13, 259–60
Brussels 264–5
Brut 32, 62, 64–5
bubbles 216–24, *217*, 268–9
Burgundy 15, 17, 108, 172, 173, 179, 213, 236
Butler, Samuel 112

Camus, Régis 37
Cappiello, Patrick 98
carbon dioxide 18, 19, 100–1, 218–21, *219*, *221*, 269
Carbonnell and Co 123
Carrington, Peter 264–5, *265*, 270
Cavil, Julie 30, 39, *40*, 42, 44, 203
Cazals, Delphine 35, *35*
Cazé-Thibaut 189
Ceaușescu, Nicolae 164
Cellar in the Sea 256–9
cellars 16, 22, 114–15
  Moët & Chandon 125–33, *125*, *127*
Celles-lès-Condé 189
La Chablisienne 228
chalk 15, *15*, 16–17, 114–15
Champagne Mercier 22
champagne nature 158
Champagne Socialism 160–6
Champs, Laurent 231, 233
Chandon de Briailles, Pierre-Gabriel *122*, 123
Chanoine Frères 118
Chanson 230
Chantilly, Château de 117
Chaperon, Vincent 209, 212, 214
chaptalization 15
Chardonnay grape 15–16, 18, 66–8, *67*, 184, *202*, 211
Charlemagne, Guy 191
Charles VII, King of France 121

Index 273

Charles X, King of France 124
Charleton, Dr Walter 105
Chartogne-Taillet 71, 168, 187
Château-Thierry 189
Chavot-Courcourt 190
chefs de cave 14–15, 36–7, 248–54
chilling grapes 209
Chiquet, Gaston 188
Chiquet, Jean-Hervé 201, 206, 214
Chouilly 126, 185, 237–8
Christie's 50
Church, Charlotte 165
Churchill, Winston 46, *54*, 146, 165
cider 17, 103, 104
CIVC *see* Comité Champagne
Clandestin 71
Clarke, Oz 267, 270
Clicquot, François 31–2
climate change 15, 23, 73, 202, 207–14, 269
Cliquot, Widow 157, 255
clones 211
Clos d'Ambonnay 41, 44, 53, 54, 71
Clos des Goisses 53, 68, 173, 188, 214
Clos du Mesnil 42, 44, *44*, 53, 54, 185
Clos Saint-Hilaire 71
La Closerie Les Béguines 71, 168
Clouet, André 213
Colebrook, Chevalier 123
Collin, Olivier 175, 177–8, *177*
Collin, Ulysse 71, 168, 190
Comité Champagne (CIVC) 50, 58, 69, 146–7, 149, 153, 154, 184, 204–5, 210, 235
Congy 170
Copinet, Marie 67, 191
copper sulphate 178, 205–6
corks 20, 95–7, 115, 118, 119, 129, 218, *218*
Côte des Bar 16, 36, 40, 69, 71, 177, 184, 191–2
Côte des Blancs 16, 45, 53, 67, 184–5, 193–4
Côte de Sézanne 67
Coteaux Champenois 78, 213–14
Coteaux de Cumières 64
Coteaux du Petit Morin 190–1
Coteaux Sud d'Epernay 190
Coulon, Roger 187
coupes 80–1, *81*, 221–2, *223*
Cramant 114, 126, 185

Cristal 50–2, 51, 68, 75, 188, 227, 244, 246, *247*, 250
Croser, Brian 84, 85
crown caps 19
Cuis 185
Cuisles 189
Cumenal, Frédéric 252
Cumières 182, 187, 188–9
Cunard, Nancy 142

Danton, Herve 202–3
débourbage 18
Decanter magazine 179
dégorgement see disgorgement
Dehours 189
delimitation 140–1
Demarville, Dominique 200, 202–3, 206, 208–10, 226–7, 248–9, 250, 253, 255–8
Demi-Sec 45, 92
Dervin, L'Abbé 138
Descôtes, Gilles 210, 227, 230
Déthune, Sophie 208–9
Devaux 237–8
Dhondt, Adrien 181
Digby, Sir Kenelm 102, 103, 112
disgorgement (*dégorgement*) 20, 85, 131, 137, 245–6, *247*
Dizy 188
Dom Pérignon 17, 22, 52, 96
 ageing 244–6
 chef de cave 250, 251
 and climate change 212
 dosage 64
 labels *247*
 rosé champagne *58*
 vintage champagne 74, 75
Doquet, Pascal 191, 200, 205
dosage 20, 23, 61–5, 73, 131–2, 248–9, 254
 zero-dosage champagne 15, 32, 62–3, 64, 232
Drappier 36, 71, 192, 232, 240, 259
Drappier, Charline 34, *35*, 36, 38
Drappier, Michel 240
Dupré, Denise 259
Duteutre, Bruno 217
Dutournier, Alain 74
Duval-Leroy 34, 212–13

Edward, Prince of Wales (Edward VII) 61, 137, 141
Egly, Francis 168, 170, 174, 214

Egly-Ouriet 71, 186
Ekström, Christian 257
Engels, Friedrich 164–5
English sparkling wines 16
Epernay 47–8, 121, 124, 125–33, 139, 141, 158, 172
Eschenauer, Louis 144
Escoffier, Auguste 137
Esprit du Siècle 246
European Commission 205
European Union 206
Eznack, Floriane 37

Les Fa'bulleuses 36, 38
Fallowfield, Giles 268–9, 270
Famille Moutard 71
Farquhar, George 114
Fattorini, Joe 160–6, 270
fermentation 100–1
 first fermentation 18–19
 malolactic fermentation 19, 211, 232–3, 245
 second fermentation 18, 85–6, 101, 245
 tank fermentation 73
 wild-yeast fermentation 15
fertilizers 168, 201, 205
Festigny 189
Feuillatte, Nicolas 204
films 163
Finland 255–60
fizzing sound 224
Flanner, Janet 153
Fleur de Miraval 58–9
Fleury 71, 192
flor 237
flutes 80, *81*, 83, 88, 115, 219–22, *219*, *221*, *223*
foil 132–3
food and wine 88–92, *91*
Forest Fourneaux 118
Formula One racing 163
Foulon, Dominique 246
Fourmon, Claude 146, 151, 152, 155
Fourny, Charles-Henry and Emmanuel 208
François I, King of France 107
François Frères 228, 232
Freeman, Martin 165
Frerson, Severine 37
Fresnet, Laurent 268–9
fungicides 201, 204, 205–6

Gaddafi, Muammar 164

Gaulle, Octave de *269*
Geoffroy, René 188
Geoffroy, Richard 26, 244–6, 250, 251, 252
Gerbais, Pierre 192
Germany 32, 48, 56, 139, 140, 143–55, 264–5
Gestapo 151
Gimmonet, Pierre 67
Giraud, Henri 226, 229–30, 233
glassmaking 102, 103, 113
  see also bottles
glassware 80–3, *81*, 88, 115, 118–19, *119*, 219–22, *219*, *221*, *223*
Gleave, David 64
global warming *see* climate change
Godinot, Canon 109–10, 113–14
Godmé, Hugues 186
Golvet, Sébastien le 229–30, 233
Gonet, Chantal 34, *35*
Göring, Field Marshal 147, 153
Gouez, Benoît 58, 212, 249, 250, 251–2
grafted vines 28
Gramont, Duc de 121–2
Grand Cru 16
Grande Vallée 187–8
grandes marques 14, 167–8, 169, 174–5, 198
grapes 15–16, 18, 66–71
  chilling 209
  and climate change 210
  clones 211
  harvesting 18, 109–10, 208–9
  see also individual types of grape
Gratien 228, 233
Grauves 126
Grossard, Dom 106
grower movement 168–70, 173–81
Gueux 170
Guy, Kolleen M 33, 162–3

Harcourt, Laurent de 47
harvesting grapes 18, 109–10, 208–9
Hautekeur, François 255
Hautvillers 17, 70, 126, 188
Hautvillers, Abbey of 106–11
Hébrart, Marc 188
Heidsieck, Charles 54, 142, 196, 207, 213, 259–60
Heidsieck & Co. 255

Henri IV, King of France 108
Henriot 37
Henriot, Apolline *31*, 32, 37
Henríquez, Maggie 34–5, *35*, 45
herbicides 38, 42, 168, 201, 204–5
Heucq, André 189
Himmler, Heinrich 154
Hobsbawm, Eric 162–3
Hodez, Roger 148
Holt, Douglas 163
Horiot, Olivier 71
Hughes, Natasha 88–92, 270
Hundred Years' War (1337–1453) 107
Hunt, Tristram 164
Huré Frères 71, 187

ice 120
INRAE 69
Instagram 98
Izzard, Eddie 165

Jacquart 20, 37, 232
Jacquesson 201, 206, 232
Jaeger, Nicholas 228
James I, King of England 101–2
Jay Z *166*
Jazz Age 142
Jefford, Andrew 78–9
Jerez 180
Jéroboams 84–5, *87*
Jestin, Hervé 259
Joan of Arc 121
Johnson, Hugh 106–16, 266, 270
Josephine, Empress 124
Jouët, Rose-Adélaïde 37
Juhlin, Richard 255, 256

Kelley, Dr William 172–81, 270
Khorsandi, Shappi 165
Kladstrup, Don and Petie 143–55, 271
Klaebisch, Otto 143–55
Klym, Nicholas 252–3
Knowles, Beyonce *166*
Krebiehl, Anne 234–43, 271
Krug 14, 22, 39–45, *41*, *44*, 65, 71, 91–2, 185
  ageing 68,
  barrels 227, *227*, 232
  blends 184
  chefs de cave 30

prestige cuvées 53–4
rosé champagne 57
vintage champagne 74
Krug, Henri 42, 74
Krug, Joseph 39–40
Krug, Olivier 39–43, *40*, 45, 74, 203, 227
Krug, Rémi 74
Kühnemann, Ernst 144

labels 20, 33, 132–3
Labour Party 165
Lagrange, Comte de 137
Lahaye, Benoît 186, 232
Laherte Frères 59, 71, 190
Lanson 61, 68, 143, 202–3
Lanson de Nonancourt, Marie-Louise 32
Larmandier, Pierre 168, 174, 199, 201
Larmandier, Sophie 168, 174
Larmandier-Bernier 168, 199
Lassaigne, Emmanuel 175, 191, 193–8, *195*
Lassaigne, Jacques 67, 191, 193–4
Lassalle, Angeline 33
Lassalle, Olga 33
Latrive, Caroline 37
Laurent-Perrier 36, 53, 62, 63, 66–7, 164, 204, 250
Laval, Georges 188
layering vines 27–8
Le Mesnil-sur-Oger 16, 53, 59, 114, 126, 173, 185, 199–200, 208
Lebel, Eric 30, 40, 45
Lécaillon, Jean-Baptiste 42, 51–2, 201, 204–6, 209–11, 213, 230, 242–3, 244–7
Lechmere, Adam 22–6, 271
Lechner, James 94
Léclapart, David 186
Leclerc Briant 259
Lee, Robin 179
lees (sediment): ageing on 244–7, *246*
  in barrels 232
  remuage 19–20, 115–16, 130, 137
Lelarge-Pugeot 187
Lenoble, AR 34, 212, 228, 233, 240–1
Les Crayères 174
Les Riceys 40
Les Ursules 175–6
Leuvrigny 70, 189

Liberty Wines 64
Liem, Peter 182–92, 271
Liger-Belair, Gérard 216–24, *217*, 269, 271
liqueur de tirage 19
Liv-Ex (London International Vintners Exchange) 59
Logette-Jardin, Sandrine 36, 212
London 17, 112–13, 138
Londonderry, Marchioness 165
Louis XIII, King of France 108
Louis XIV, King of France 107, 113, 116
Louis XV, King of France 33, 117
Louis Roederer *see* Roederer
Ludes 170, 187
LVMH 22, 25, 43, 46

McCoy, Elin 30–8, 271
Macdonald, Ramsay 165
McInerney, Jay 46–9, 271
MacQuitty, Jane 60–5, 271
magnums 84–7, *85*, *87*, 240–1
Maillard Reaction 20, 232
Maillart, Nicolas 71
Mailly 16, 186, 204, 232
Malassagne, Anne 34, *35*
Malassagne, Antoine 212, 228, 233, 240–1
malolactic fermentation 19, 211, 232–3, 245
Mandelson, Peter 165
Mansell, Sir Robert 102, 103
Mareuil-le-Port 189
Mareuil-sur-Aÿ 16, 188, 205
Margaine, Arnaud 67, 186
Marguet 186
Maria Theresa, of Austria 57
Mariotti, Didier 62, 258–9
Marne, Battle of the (1914) 139–40
Marne Valley *see* Vallée de la Marne
Marquetterie, Château de la 190
Massif de St-Thierry 187
Maxim's, Paris 134
Meneux de Nonancourt, Stephanie 36
Merfy 70, 170
Mérode, Cléo de 134
Merret, Dr Christopher *101*, 105
méthode champenoise 18–20, 115–16, *127*
Meunier grape 15–16, 18, 59, 66, *67*, 69–70, 187, 189

Meursault 16
Michael, Madison 96
Michel, Bruno 190
Michel, José 190
micro-oxygenation 227, 231, 232
Mignon, Christophe 189
mildew 71, 178, 202, 205–6
Moët, Claude 115
Moët, Jean-Rémy 57, 122, *122*, 124
Moët & Chandon 14, 22, 52, 68, 164, 216–17
  ageing 60, 244
  blending 65
  cellars 125–33, *125*, *127*
  chef de cave 249, 250, 251–2
  dosage 64, 65, 249
  history 121–4
  rosé champagne 58
  sustainability 200, *203*, 204
  vintage champagne 74
  in World War II 150–4
Moët family 121–2
Moldova 161
Moncuit, Pierre 191
Mont Aigu 185
Mont-Aimé 185, 194
Montagne de Reims 16, 17, 67, 68, 73, 107–8, 139–40, 186–7, 188
Montgueux 67, 170, 190–1, 193–8
Moore, Victoria 56–9, 271
Morrison, Fiona 27–9, 271
Mortimer, John 166
Moss, Kate 63
Moussé Fils 71, 189
Moussy 190
mouthfeel 222–3
Mouzon-Leroux 186
Mugabe, Robert 164
Mumm 136, 137, 142, 144, 248, 268–9

Nantes 122
Napoleon I, Emperor 57, 124, 129, 157
Napoleon III, Emperor 134
Napoleonic Wars 32
Nazis 143–55, *145*
Neville, Gary 160–2
New York 17, 95, 137, 158, 263
Newnham-Davis, Colonel 138
Nonancourt, Bernard de 143–4
Nowack 189
Nunelly, Mark 259
oak barrels 19, 44, 226–33

Oeuilly 189
Oger 16, 185
oïdium 206
Oiry 170, 185
Oliveras, Abby 95
opening bottles 94–8, *97*, 118, *119*
organic viticulture 176, 196–7, 204–6
Orleans 122–3
Orléans, Philippe d' 116
Otéro, La Belle 134
oxidation 85, 231, 245
oxygen 14, 45, 84, 85–6, 230–1, 243, 245, 256
  micro-oxygenation 227, 231, 232
oysters 118, 120

Paillard, Alice 34, *35*, 36, 38, 211, 239
Paillard, Bruno 36, 238–9
Paillard, Pierre 71, 186
Palais Royal, Paris 116
Panaïotis, Frédéric 22–6, *23*, 59, 208, 253–4
Paris 17, 113, 116, 134–6, 139, 142
Paris Exhibition (1900) 134
Paris World Fair (1889) 137
Paris World Fair (1900) 137
Parisot, Michel 237–8, *238*
Patton, General 153
Pearl & Ash, New York 98
Pehu-Simonet 186
Pereyre de Nonancourt, Alexandra 36
Pérignon, Dom 17, 106–11, *109*, 113, 114
  see also Dom Pérignon
Perin family 58–9
permaculture 29
Perrier, Mathile Emilie *31*, 32
Perrier-Jouët 37, 53, 75, 97, 136, 255
Perrin, Marc 59
Perseval, Thomas 187
Perseval-Farge 187
pesticides 196–7, 205
Pétain, Marshal 146, 153
Peters, Jacques 249, 252
Péters, Pierre 67, 185, 208, 213
Péters, Rodolphe 208, 210, 211
Péters family 59
Petit, Dominique 47
Petit Meslier grape 15, 66, 71, 210
phenolics 73, 212

276 INDEX

Philipponnat 53, 68, 71, 173, 188, 232
Philipponnat, Charles 53, 210, 214
phylloxera 28, 66, 71, 138, 190–1
pickers 208–9
Pierry 126, 190
pink champagne *see* rosé champagne
Pinot Blanc grape 66, 71, 210
Pinot Gris grape 66, 71, 210
Pinot Noir grape 15–16, 17, 18, 66, *67*, 68–9
   blancs de noirs 70–1
   in early vineyards 108–9
   and terroir 182, 188
Piper-Heidsieck 37, 61
Pitt, Brad 58–9
Pluche, abbot 111
Pol Roger 14, 46–9, *54*, 65
   cellars 47, *47*
   Churchill and 46, 53
   disgorgement 246
   dosage 61–3
   vintage champagne 75
   winemaking 48–9
   in World War II 146, 147, 149
Pol-Roger, Christian 47
Polidori, Guillaume 217
politics 160–6
Pommery *145*
Pommery, Louise *31*, 32, 33
Pompadour, Madame de 33, 117
Ponsardin, Barbe-Nicole 31–2, *31*
Pougy, Liane de 134
pouring champagne 219–20, *219*
Premier Cru 16
Prévost, Jérôme 71, 168, 175, 187, 232
Le Printemps de Champagne 36
prise de mousse (second fermentation) 19
Prohibition 141
Prosecco 62
pruning 109
Puligny 16

racking 111, 130, 227
Rand, Margaret 14–17, 226–33, 248–54, 271
Ray, Cyril 28, 32, 265
reductive champagnes 245
Reims 16, 115, 121, 139, 141, 158, 172
remuage 19–20, 115–16, 130, 137
Renaudin, Paul 49

Renaudin, Paul Levieux 49
Renoir, Adrien 186
réserve parcellaire 235
réserve perpétuelle (RP) 234–6, 238–43
reserve wines 15, 19, 30, 43, 60, 62, 89, 174, 178, 180, 212, 234–43
Resistance 150–1
Ribbentrop, Joachim von 144, 152
Richelieu, Duc de 116
Rilly-la-Montagne 187
Rioja 180
Robert-Jean de Vogüé Research Centre, Oiry 25
Robinson, Geoffrey 165
robots 208–9, 269
Robuchon, Joël 17
Rocheret, Bertin de 114
Rodez, Eric 186, 232
Roederer 14, 42, 65
   ageing 68, 244, 259
   barrels 227, 230, 232
   biodynamics 17
   Coteaux Champenois 213
   Cristal 50–2, *51*, 68, 75, 188, 227, 244, 246, *247*, 250
   dosage 63–4
   history 140
   labels *63*
   organic vines 174
   reserve wines 242–3
   rosé champagne 59
   sustainability 200, 201, 202, 204
   vintage champagne 73
Roland-Billecart, Antoine 204, 209
Roland-Billecart, Jean 57
Roland-Billecart, Mathieu 56, 57, 59
Romania 150, 164
Romans 14, 16, 115, 259
rootstocks 28
rosé champagne 56–9, *57*, *58*, 90, 92, 158
Roses de Jeanne 176–7
Rouzaud, Jean-Claude 52
Rowling, JK 165
Royal Navy 101–2
Royal Society 105, 112
Ruinart *26*, 118
   blancs de blancs 67
   chef de cave 22–6, *23*, 253–4
   dosage 249
   rosé champagne 56–7, 59
   vineyards 25
Ruinart, Dom 115

Ruinart, Nicolas 22, 115
Russia 32, 61, 133, 140

Sabbe, René 151
sabering bottles 97–8, *97*
St-Evremond, Marquis de 112–13
Sainte-Gemme 70
St-Romain 228
Saint Thierry 170
Salon 66–7, 74, 75, 173, 185
Salon, Eugène-Aimé 173
Salon Le Mesnil 53, 74
sandstone eggs 230
Saran 126
Savart, Frédéric 187
Schmitt, Patrick 246–7
Schuster, Michael 165–6
Sec 65
Second Empire 134
sediment *see* lees
Seguin-Moreau 44, 227, 228
Sélèque, J-M 190
Selosse, Anselme 168, 170, 173–4, 175, 177, 178–81, *178*, 185, 188, 198, 199, 204, 228–9, 233, 236–7
serving temperature 83, 88
Sézannais 190–1
Sherman tanks 264–5, *265*
Shrigley, David 24
Sillery 103, 104, 108–9, 114, 123
Simon, André 136
Simpson, James 62–3
Skelton, Stephen 100–5, 272
Skinner, Frank 165
Smith, Melissa 96–7
socialism 160–6
soil 15, *15*, 16–17, 114–15
solera 234–8
Soviet Union 160, 161–2
space travel 268–9, *269*
Spain 180, 236
sparkling wine, discovery of 103–4
Special Club (Club Trésors du Champagne) 173, 177
Stalin, Joseph 160, 161–2
Starck, Philippe 64
Stelzer, Tyson 39–45, 199–206, 207–14, 272
Stevenson, Tom 84–7, *84*, 117–20, 139–42, 181, 244–7, 256, 272
still wines *see vins clairs*
Stockholm tasting (1999) 74, 75
Sueiro, Susan 95–6

Suenen 67, 168
sugar: chaptalization 15
  dosage 20, 23, 61–5, 73, 131–2, 232, 248–9, 254
sulphur 178, 197, 198, 233, 237
sustainability 15, 199–206
Sutcliffe, Serena 72–6, *76*, 134–8, 272
sweetness 20
Syndicat des Grandes Marques de Champagne 148
Syndicat Général des Vignerons 200

Taissy-en-Champagne 24
Taittinger 53, 190
  barrels 232
  blanc de blancs 66–7
  magnums *85*
  rosé champagne 59
  sustainability 200, *202*
  vintage champagne 75–6
Taittinger, Claude 147
Taittinger, François 148–9
Taittinger, Guy 149
Taittinger, Vitalie 30, 34, *35*
Taransaud 44, 227, 228, 229, 232
Tarlant 35, 71, 189, 232
Tarlant, Benoît 70
Tarlant, Mélanie 34–5, *35*
tasting champagne 78–9, 222–3
television 163
temperature: and gas pressure 94
  and popping corks 218
  pouring champagne 219–20
  serving temperature 83, 88
terroir 15, 168–70, 172, 177–8, 182–92, 232
Tetienne, Alice 37
Theise, Thierry 231
Thibault, Daniel 196
Thieffry, Philippe 250
Thierry, Dom 22
Thirty Years' War (1618–48) 107
Thompson, David 17
Thompson, Emma 165
Tours-sur-Marne 187
La Transmission: Femmes en Champagne 34–5, *35*, 38
Trépail 67, 186
Triolet, Thierry 191
Triptree, Tim 50–4, 272
Troy, Jean François de, *Le Déjeuner d'Huîtres* 117–20, *119*

Turenne, Marshal 107
Tytyri chalk mine, Lohja 260

umami flavours 90–1
underwater ageing 255–60, *257*
United States of America 58, 136–7, 141
University of Reims 217

Vallée de la Marne 16, 69, 188–9, 190
Vandières 189
de Venoge 71
Venteuil 189
Verneuil 189
Versailles 17, 116, 117, 120
Vertus 16, 170, 185, 199, 201, 208
Verzenay 16, 126, 182, 186, 227
Verzy 16, 126, 186
Veuve Clicquot 14, 22, 31–2, 136, 142, 195
  Baltic shipwreck 255–6
  Cellar in the Sea 256–9, *257*
  chef de cave 248–9, 250, 253
  Coteaux Champenois 213
  dosage 62, 65
  oak barrels 226–7
  Pinot Noir grape 68
  rosé champagne 158
  sustainability 200, 202–3
  vats 17
  vintage champagne 75
Veuve Henriot Aîné 32
Veuve Laurent-Perrier 32
Victoria, Queen of England 33, 48, 262
Vieilles Vignes Françaises 27–9, *29*, 49, 53, 71, 188
Villers-Marmery 67, 186
Vilmart 187, 231, 232–3
vin de goutte 110
vin de taille 110
vines, layering 27–8
Vinexpo 253
vineyards *see* viticulture
vins clairs (still wines) 16, 18–19, 78, 79, 207, 213–14
vins de pressoir 110
vintage champagne 72–6, 90–1, 92, 212–13, 254
viticulture 167–70

biodynamism 15, 17, 178, 204–6
  and climate change 207–14
  cover cropping 24
  organic viticulture 176, 196–7, 204–6
  robots 208–9
  soil 15, *15*, 16–17, 114–15
  sustainability 199–206
Vitry-le-François 191
Vitryat 67, 190–1
Vizetelly, Henry 121–33, 262–3, *263*, 272
Vogüé, Bertrand de 144
Vogüé, Ghislain de 151, 152
Vogüé, Robert Jean de 143–8, 150–2, 154–5
Voltis grape 66, 71
Vouette & Sorbée 71, 168

Walters, Robert 80–3, 167–70, 193–8, 272
Wars of Religion 107
Waugh, Evelyn 142, 156–9, *156*, 272
Wechsberg, Joseph 142
White, Kelli 93–8, 272
Wilde, Oscar 166
William, Prince 48
Wilson, Richard 165
women 30–8
World War I 16, 45, 48, 139–40
World War II 32, 143–55, 264–5

yeasts: autolysis 19, 61, 79, 90
  disgorging 20
  in magnums 86
  second fermentation 19
  wild-yeast fermentation 15
  see also lees
yields 201
Yquem, Château d' 158

Zeimett, Frédéric 259
zero-dosage champagne 15, 32, 62–3, 64, 232
Zimbabwe 164
Zola, Emile 137

ACKNOWLEDGEMENTS

Cover © Lucy Pope. Glasses supplied courtesy of Riedl.
p3 Alamy; p8 © Pol Roger/Mika Boudot; p15 Cephas; p18,19 Alamy; p21 Adobe Stock; p23 © Ruinart; p25 © Ruinart/Mathieu Bonnevie; p26 © Ruinart; p29 Alamy; p35 © La Transmission; p40 Alamy (*left*) Club O/Dominique Silberstein (*right*); p41 Cephas; p47 © Pol Roger; p51 Alamy (*left*), Cephas (*right*); p54 Alamy; p57 Adobe Stock; p58 Alamy; p63 Club O; p67 Cephas; p76 Cephas; p81 Adobe Stock; p85 Cephas; p87 Cephas; p91 Cephas (*left*), Adobe Stock (*centre* and *right*); p93 Adobe Stock; p97 Adobe Stock; p98 © Lauren Acheson; p109 Adobe Stock; p122 Alamy; p135 Alamy; p145 Alamy; p156 Alamy; p166 Alamy; p175 Cephas; p178 Cephas; p183 Cosmographics; p195 © Emmanuel Lassaigne; p202 Alamy; p203, 206 © Moët & Chandon; p215 Beaumont/Liger-Belair/Polidori; p217 Hubert Raguet; p218 Equipe Effervescence/URCA; p219, 221 URCA; p223 Beaumont/Liger-Belair/Polidori; p227 Cephas; p246 Dreamtime; p257 © visitaland.com; p267 Alamy; p269 Alamy; Endpapers Adobe Stock.

With many thanks to Paul Beaver, Natasha Hughes, Tyson Stelzer and Caroline West for all their help and backup with this project.

The publishers have made every effort to trace the copyright holders of text and images used in this book. If, however, you believe that any work has been incorrectly credited or used without permission, please contact the publishers, who will endeavour to rectify the situation.

Other books from Académie du Vin Library we think you'll enjoy:

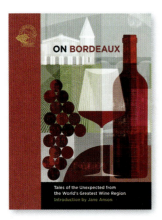

ON BORDEAUX
Tales of the Unexpected from the World's Greatest Wine Region
Susan Keevil
Why these wines are the most talked-about.

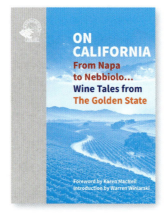

ON CALIFORNIA
From Napa to Nebbiolo… Wine Tales from the Golden State
Susan Keevil
California's great wine adventure as told by our A-list team of experts and enthusiasts.

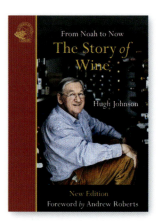

THE STORY OF WINE
From Noah to Now
Hugh Johnson
The new edition of Hugh Johnson's captivating journey through wine history.

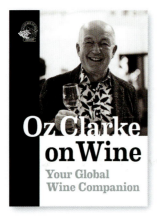

OZ CLARKE ON WINE
Your Global Wine Companion
A fast-paced tour of the world's most delicious wine styles with Oz.

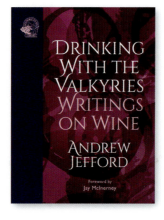

DRINKING WITH THE VALKYRIES
Writings on Wine
Andrew Jefford
Celebrating the limitless beauty of wine difference.

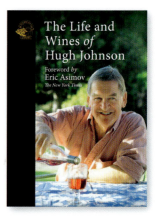

THE LIFE AND WINES OF HUGH JOHNSON
The world's best-loved wine author weaves the story of his own epic wine journey.

www.academieduvinlibrary.com